Praise for *Fluent React*

Carl Sagan once said, "You have to know the past to understand the present." In my humble opinion, this book is nothing but Tejas bringing this mantra into the frontend realm by guiding us through the historical journey of React.

With meticulous detail, he provides an in-depth overview of the key concepts behind reconciliation and Fiber. This is a must-read for anyone seeking a deeper comprehension of React and its ever-evolving ecosystem.

—Matheus Albuquerque Brasil,
Google Developer Expert in Web Technologies

This book made me question everything I thought I knew about React! It is exactly the type of content expected from Tejas: an in-depth journey through the history and internals of React that everyone can understand. If you want to reinforce and grow your knowledge of React, then this book will be your new best friend!

—Daniel Afonso, Developer Advocate, OLX

The most in-depth explanation of React and how it works I have ever seen. Every React developer should read this book to learn the framework inside out. And I'm not saying this for the sake of a beautiful praise quote!

—Sergii Kirianov, Developer Advocate, Vue Storefront

Tejas Kumar's *Fluent React* has not only deepened my grasp of complex concepts like hydration, memoization, and server components but has also honed my ability to strategize my code's behavior, enhancing my development process even before the first line is written.

—*Kenneth Quiggins, Software Developer*

Where most React books only teach you how to use React, this book teaches how React works. Tejas has done a great job to also cover the difficult details most other authors just gloss over. Not only that, but he also put himself in the vulnerable position to have some of the greatest of the community review his work, learned from them, and put that new knowledge back into the book. Big kudos to him!"

—*Lenz Weber-Tronic,*
Comaintainer of Apollo Client & Redux Toolkit

Fluent React

*Build Fast, Performant, and
Intuitive Web Applications*

Tejas Kumar
Foreword by Kent C. Dodds

Beijing · Boston · Farnham · Sebastopol · Tokyo

Fluent React

by Tejas Kumar

Published by O'Reilly Media, Inc., 1005 Gravenstein Highway North, Sebastopol, CA 95472.

O'Reilly books may be purchased for educational, business, or sales promotional use. Online editions are also available for most titles (*http://oreilly.com*). For more information, contact our corporate/institutional sales department: 800-998-9938 or *corporate@oreilly.com*.

Acquisition Editor: Amanda Quinn	**Indexer:** Potomac Indexing, LLC
Development Editor: Shira Evans	**Interior Designer:** David Futato
Production Editor: Beth Kelly	**Cover Designer:** Karen Montgomery
Copyeditor: Sonia Saruba	**Illustrator:** Kate Dullea
Proofreader: Piper Editorial, LLC	

February 2024:   First Edition

Revision History for the First Edition

2024-02-13:   First Release

See *http://oreilly.com/catalog/errata.csp?isbn=9781098138714* for release details.

978-1-098-13871-4

[LSI]

Table of Contents

Foreword

There is so much you need to understand as a web developer to build applications that users will love. In the React space in particular, there's a wealth of material available to you, and that's part of the problem. Not all of it is consistent, and you have to make your own path wading through all of the tutorials and blog posts available, hoping you'll piece together a curriculum that is free of contradictions and won't leave gaping holes in your knowledge. And you'll always worry that what you're learning is out of date.

This is where Tejas Kumar comes in with this book. Tejas has had years of React experience and has gone to great lengths to go in depth on topics that will give you a solid foundation of knowledge. He's an experienced engineer and fountain of knowledge that will help you feel confident with React. I have been blessed to associate with Tejas over the years in various capacities in open source, conference speaking, educational content creation, and on a personal level, and I hope you understand you hold in your hand a book that has been crafted by a talented individual who is also a fantastic person.

In this book, you'll dive into subjects you would likely not otherwise be exposed to that will help you "think in React" with the proper mental model. You'll come to understand the purpose of React's existence in the first place, which will give you a good frame of reference when considering React as a tool to solve problems. React wasn't invented in a vacuum, and understanding the origin story will help you know the problems React is intended to solve so you can avoid putting a round peg in a square hole.

You will understand foundational concepts like JSX, the virtual DOM, reconciliation, and concurrent React, which will help you use this tool more efficiently. I've always believed that the best way to level up your experience with a tool is to understand how the tool works. So even if you've been using React for years at this point, these sections will open your mind to new possibilities and understanding as you come to really *understand* React, rather than just piecing things together and hoping (fingers crossed) the result is positive.

You'll discover patterns that the pros use to build effective and powerful abstractions. React itself is a very fast UI library, but there are times when you're building complex applications that you'll need to reach for performance optimizations, and Tejas will show you how with the memoization, lazy loading, and state management techniques available in React. Beyond that, you'll understand how the best libraries in the ecosystem work with patterns like compound components, render props, prop getters, state reducers, and control props. These are critical tools in your tool belt as you build React applications. Even if you're just using off-the-shelf solutions, understanding how those powerful abstractions work will help you use them more effectively.

Tejas goes beyond theoretical React though, and you'll be introduced to practical frameworks like Remix and Next.js that will be important for you to take advantage of React's full stack capabilities to make the best user experience possible. With React's server rendering capabilities since the beginning, you can take control of your own destiny as you use React to build your entire user experience on both the frontend and the backend. And you'll also get to know the leading edge tech, like Server Components and Server Actions, that React is using to level up the user experience.

I'm confident that after reading what Tejas has put together for you, you'll have the knowledge you need to be successful at building exceptional applications with React. I wish you the very best on your learning experience with React, the most widely used UI library in the world. Enjoy the journey!

— Kent C. Dodds
https://kentcdodds.com

Preface

This book is not for people who want to learn how to use React. If you're unfamiliar with React and looking for a tutorial, a great place to start is the React documentation over at *react.dev*. Instead, this book is for the curious: people who aren't as interested in how to use React, but who are more interested in *how React works*.

In our time together, we will go on a journey through a number of React concepts and understand their underlying mechanism, exploring how it all fits together to enable us to create applications using React more effectively. In our pursuit of understanding the underlying mechanism, we will develop the mental models necessary to reason about React and its ecosystem with a high degree of fidelity.

This book assumes we have a satisfactory understanding of this statement: browsers render web pages. Web pages are HTML documents that are styled by CSS and made interactive with JavaScript. It also assumes we're somewhat familiar with how to use React, and that we've built a React app or two in our time. Ideally, some of our React apps are in production.

We'll start with an introduction to React and recap its history, casting our minds back to 2013 when it was first released as open source software. From there, we'll explore the core concepts of React, including the component model, the virtual DOM, and reconciliation. We'll dive into the compiler theory of how JSX works, talk about fibers, and understand its concurrent programming model in depth. This way we'll glean powerful takeaways that will help us more fluently memoize what ought to be memoized and defer rendering work that ought to be deferred through powerful primitives like `React.memo` and `useTransition`.

In the second half of this book, we'll explore React frameworks: what problems they solve, and the mechanisms by which they solve them. We'll do so by writing our own framework that solves three salient problems across nearly all web applications: server rendering, routing, and data fetching.

Once we solve these problems for ourselves, understanding how frameworks solve them becomes far more approachable. We'll also dive deep into React Server Components (RSCs) and server actions, understanding the role of next-generation tooling, like bundlers and isomorphic routers.

Finally, we'll zoom out from React and look at alternatives like Vue, Solid, Angular, Qwik, and more. We'll explore signals and fine-grained reactivity in contrast to React's coarser reactivity model. We'll also explore React's response to signals: the Forget toolchain and how it stacks up when compared to signals.

There's so much to get into, so let's not waste any more time. Let's get started!

Conventions Used in This Book

The following typographical conventions are used in this book:

Italic
Indicates new terms, URLs, email addresses, filenames, and file extensions.

`Constant width`
Used for program listings, as well as within paragraphs to refer to program elements such as variable or function names, databases, data types, environment variables, statements, and keywords.

`Constant width bold` *and light gray text*
Used in Chapter 10 of the print edition to highlight diffs in code blocks.

 This element signifies a general note.

O'Reilly Online Learning

 For more than 40 years, *O'Reilly Media* has provided technology and business training, knowledge, and insight to help companies succeed.

Our unique network of experts and innovators share their knowledge and expertise through books, articles, and our online learning platform. O'Reilly's online learning platform gives you on-demand access to live training courses, in-depth learning paths, interactive coding environments, and a vast collection of text and video from O'Reilly and 200+ other publishers. For more information, visit *https://oreilly.com*.

How to Contact Us

Please address comments and questions concerning this book to the publisher:

O'Reilly Media, Inc.
1005 Gravenstein Highway North
Sebastopol, CA 95472
800-889-8969 (in the United States or Canada)
707-827-7019 (international or local)
707-829-0104 (fax)
support@oreilly.com
https://www.oreilly.com/about/contact.html

We have a web page for this book, where we list errata, examples, and any additional information. You can access this page at *https://oreil.ly/fluent-react*.

For news and information about our books and courses, visit *https://oreilly.com*.

Find us on LinkedIn: *https://linkedin.com/company/oreilly-media*

Follow us on Twitter: *https://twitter.com/oreillymedia*

Watch us on YouTube: *https://youtube.com/oreillymedia*

Acknowledgments

This book is the first book that I've ever written, and I am beyond thankful that I did not do it alone. What you're about to read is the combined effort of a number of brilliant people who have worked in concert to make this possible. On this page, we acknowledge these people for their contributions to this body of text.

Please do not skip this, because these people deserve your attention and your gratitude. Let's start off with the people who have helped me directly with this book:

- Number one is always my wife, Lea. I've spent a lot of time writing this book, often at the cost of together time and family time. Because of my joy in the subject matter and my desire to share it with all of you, working on this book has slightly eaten into vacation time and other opportunities to spend time with my wife. She has been nothing but supportive and encouraging, and I am so thankful for her.

- Shira Evans, my development editor on this book. Shira from O'Reilly has been a joy to work with and has been nothing short of supportive, encouraging, and understanding, even when we were faced with a number of delays since new things kept coming up with React, like Forget and server actions. Shira patiently saw us through all of it, and I am so thankful for her.

- My dear friend and brother Kent C. Dodds (*@kentcdodds*) for his continued mentorship outside the capacities of this book, and for his foreword in this book. Kent has been a dear friend and mentor for years, and I am so thankful for his continued support and encouragement.

- The reviewers. This book would not be possible without the incredible care and attention to detail by the reviewers who partnered with me on this book:
  — Adam Rackis (*@adamrackis*)
  — Daniel Afonso (*@danieljcafonso*)
  — Fabien Bernard (*@fabien0102*)
  — Kent C. Dodds (*@kentcdodds*)
  — Mark Erikson (*@acemarke*)
  — Lenz Weber-Tronic (*@phry*)
  — Rick Hanlon II (*@rickhanlonii*)
  — Sergeii Kirianov (*@SergiiKirianov*)
  — Matheus Albuquerque (*@ythecombinator*)

- The React team at Meta for their continued work on React, continuing to push the boundaries of what's possible with React and making it a joy to use through their brilliance, ingenuity, and engineering acumen. In particular, Dan Abramov (*@dan_abramov*), who took the time to explain the role of the bundler in the React Server Components architecture, as well as for contributing a significant portion of Chapter 9 on React Server Components.

Finally, I'd like to thank you, the reader, for your interest in this book. I hope you find it as rewarding to read as I have found it to write.

CHAPTER 1

The Entry-Level Stuff

Let's start with a disclaimer: React was made to be used by all. In fact, you could go through life having never read this book and continue to use React without problems! This book dives much deeper into React for those of us who are curious about its underlying mechanism, advanced patterns, and best practices. It lends itself better to knowing how React works instead of learning how to use React. There are plenty of other books that are written with the intent to teach folks how to use React as an end user. In contrast, this book will help you understand React at the level of a library or framework author instead of an end user. In keeping with that theme, let's go on a deep dive together, starting at the top: the higher-level, entry-level topics. We'll start with the basics of React, and then dive deeper and deeper into the details of how React works.

In this chapter, we'll talk about why React exists, how it works, and what problems it solves. We'll cover its initial inspiration and design, and follow it from its humble beginnings at Facebook to the prevalent solution that it is today. This chapter is a bit of a meta chapter (no pun intended), because it's important to understand the context of React before we dive into the details.

Why Is React a Thing?

The answer in one word is: *updates*. In the early days of the web, we had a lot of static pages. We'd fill out forms, hit Submit, and load an entirely new page. This was fine for a while, but eventually web experiences evolved significantly in terms of capabilities. As the capabilities grew, so did our desire for superior user experiences on the web. We wanted to be able to see things update instantly without having to wait for a new page to be rendered and loaded. We wanted the web and its pages to feel *snappier* and more "instant." The problem was that these instant updates were pretty hard to do *at scale* for a number of reasons:

Performance

Making updates to web pages often caused performance bottlenecks because we were prone to perform work that triggered browsers to recalculate a page's layout (called a reflow) and repaint the page.

Reliability

Keeping track of state and making sure that the state was consistent across a rich web experience was hard to do because we had to keep track of state in multiple places and make sure that the state was consistent across all of those places. This was especially hard to do when we had multiple people working on the same codebase.

Security

We had to be sure to sanitize all HTML and JavaScript that we were injecting into the page to prevent exploits like cross-site scripting (XSS) and cross-site request forgery (CSRF).

To fully understand and appreciate how React solves these problems for us, we need to understand the context in which React was created and the world without or before React. Let's do that now.

The World Before React

These were some of the large problems for those of us building web apps before React. We had to figure out how to make our apps feel snappy and instant, but also scale to millions of users and work reliably in a safe way. For example, let's consider a button click: when a user clicks a button, we want to update the user interface to reflect that the button has been clicked. We'll need to consider at least four different states that the user interface can be in:

Pre-click

The button is in its default state and has not been clicked.

Clicked but pending

The button has been clicked, but the action that the button is supposed to perform has not yet completed.

Clicked and succeeded

The button has been clicked, and the action that the button is supposed to perform has completed. From here, we may want to revert the button to its pre-click state, or we may want the button to change color (green) to indicate success.

Clicked and failed

The button has been clicked, but the action that the button is supposed to perform has failed. From here, we may want to revert the button to its pre-click state, or we may want the button to change color (red) to indicate failure.

Once we have these states, we need to figure out how to update the user interface to reflect them. Oftentimes, updating the user interface would require the following steps:

1. Find the button in the host environment (often the browser) using some type of element locator API, such as `document.querySelector` or `document.getElementById`.

2. Attach event listeners to the button to listen for click events.

3. Perform any state updates in response to events.

4. When the button leaves the page, remove the event listeners and clean up any state.

This is a simple example, but it's a good one to start with. Let's say we have a button labeled "Like," and when a user clicks it, we want to update the button to "Liked." How do we do this? To start with, we'd have an HTML element:

```
<button>Like</button>
```

We'd need some way to reference this button with JavaScript, so we'd give it an `id` attribute:

```
<button id="likeButton">Like</button>
```

Great! Now that there's an `id`, JavaScript can work with it to make it interactive. We can get a reference to the button using `document.getElementById`, and then we'll add an event listener to the button to listen for click events:

```
const likeButton = document.getElementById("likeButton");
likeButton.addEventListener("click", () => {
  // do something
});
```

Now that we have an event listener, we can do something when the button is clicked. Let's say we want to update the button to have the label "Liked" when it's clicked. We can do this by updating the button's text content:

```
const likeButton = document.getElementById("likeButton");
likeButton.addEventListener("click", () => {
  likeButton.textContent = "Liked";
});
```

Great! Now we have a button that says "Like," and when it's clicked, it says "Liked." The problem here is that we can't "unlike" things. Let's fix that and update the button to say "Like" again if it's clicked in its "Liked" state. We'd need to add some state to the button to keep track of whether or not it's been clicked. We can do this by adding a data-liked attribute to the button:

```
<button id="likeButton" data-liked="false">Like</button>
```

Now that we have this attribute, we can use it to keep track of whether or not the button has been clicked. We can update the button's text content based on the value of this attribute:

```
const likeButton = document.getElementById("likeButton");
likeButton.addEventListener("click", () => {
  const liked = likeButton.getAttribute("data-liked") === "true";
  likeButton.setAttribute("data-liked", !liked);
  likeButton.textContent = liked ? "Like" : "Liked";
});
```

Wait, but we're just changing the textContent of the button! We're not actually saving the "Liked" state to a database. Normally, to do this we had to communicate over the network, like so:

```
const likeButton = document.getElementById("likeButton");
likeButton.addEventListener("click", () => {
  var liked = likeButton.getAttribute("data-liked") === "true";

  // communicate over the network
  var xhr = new XMLHttpRequest();
  xhr.open("POST", "/like", true);
  xhr.setRequestHeader("Content-Type", "application/json;charset=UTF-8");

  xhr.onload = function () {
    if (xhr.status >= 200 && xhr.status < 400) {
      // Success!
      likeButton.setAttribute("data-liked", !liked);
      likeButton.textContent = liked ? "Like" : "Liked";
    } else {
      // We reached our target server, but it returned an error
      console.error("Server returned an error:", xhr.statusText);
    }
  };

  xhr.onerror = function () {
    // There was a connection error of some sort
    console.error("Network error.");
  };

  xhr.send(JSON.stringify({ liked: !liked }));
});
```

Of course, we're using `XMLHttpRequest` and `var` to be time relevant. React was released as open source software in 2013, and the more common `fetch` API was introduced in 2015. In between `XMLHttpRequest` and `fetch`, we had jQuery that often abstracted away some complexity with primitives like `$.ajax()`, `$.post()`, etc.

If we were to write this today, it would look more like this:

```
const likeButton = document.getElementById("likeButton");
likeButton.addEventListener("click", () => {
  const liked = likeButton.getAttribute("data-liked") === "true";

  // communicate over the network
  fetch("/like", {
    method: "POST",
    body: JSON.stringify({ liked: !liked }),
  }).then(() => {
    likeButton.setAttribute("data-liked", !liked);
    likeButton.textContent = liked ? "Like" : "Liked";
  });
});
```

Without digressing too much, the point now is that we're communicating over the network, but what if the network request fails? We'd need to update the button's text content to reflect the failure. We can do this by adding a `data-failed` attribute to the button:

```
<button id="likeButton" data-liked="false" data-failed="false">Like</button>
```

Now we can update the button's text content based on the value of this attribute:

```
const likeButton = document.getElementById("likeButton");
likeButton.addEventListener("click", () => {
  const liked = likeButton.getAttribute("data-liked") === "true";

  // communicate over the network
  fetch("/like", {
    method: "POST",
    body: JSON.stringify({ liked: !liked }),
  })
    .then(() => {
      likeButton.setAttribute("data-liked", !liked);
      likeButton.textContent = liked ? "Like" : "Liked";
    })
    .catch(() => {
      likeButton.setAttribute("data-failed", true);
      likeButton.textContent = "Failed";
    });
});
```

There's one more case to handle: the process of currently "liking" a thing. That is, the pending state. To model this in code, we'd set yet another attribute on the button for the pending state by adding `data-pending`, like so:

```
<button
  id="likeButton"
  data-pending="false"
  data-liked="false"
  data-failed="false"
>
  Like
</button>
```

Now we can disable the button if a network request is in process so that multiple clicks don't queue up network requests and lead to odd race conditions and server overload. We can do that like so:

```
const likeButton = document.getElementById("likeButton");
likeButton.addEventListener("click", () => {
  const liked = likeButton.getAttribute("data-liked") === "true";
  const isPending = likeButton.getAttribute("data-pending") === "true";

  likeButton.setAttribute("data-pending", "true");
  likeButton.setAttribute("disabled", "disabled");

  // communicate over the network
  fetch("/like", {
    method: "POST",
    body: JSON.stringify({ liked: !liked }),
  })
    .then(() => {
      likeButton.setAttribute("data-liked", !liked);
      likeButton.textContent = liked ? "Like" : "Liked";
      likeButton.setAttribute("disabled", null);
    })
    .catch(() => {
      likeButton.setAttribute("data-failed", "true");
      likeButton.textContent = "Failed";
    })
    .finally(() => {
      likeButton.setAttribute("data-pending", "false");
    });
});
```

We can also make use of powerful techniques like debouncing and throttling to prevent users from performing redundant or repetitive actions.

As a quick aside, we mention debouncing and throttling. For clarity, debouncing delays a function's execution until after a set time has passed since the last event trigger (e.g., waits for users to stop typing to process input), and throttling limits a function to running at most once every set time interval, ensuring it doesn't execute too frequently (e.g., processes scroll events at set intervals). Both techniques optimize performance by controlling function execution rates.

OK, now our button is kind of robust and can handle multiple states—but some questions still remain:

- Is `data-pending` really necessary? Can't we just check if the button is disabled? Probably not, because a disabled button could be disabled for other reasons, like the user not being logged in or not having permission to click the button.

- Would it make more sense to have a `data-state` attribute, where `data-state` can be one of `pending`, `liked`, or `unliked`, instead of so many other data attributes? Probably, but then we'd need to add a large switch/case or similar code block to handle each case. Ultimately, the volume of code to handle both approaches is incomparable: we still end up with complexity and verbosity either way.

- How do we test this button in isolation? Can we?

- Why do we have the button initially written in HTML, and then later work with it in JavaScript? Wouldn't it be better if we could just create the button in JavaScript with `document.createElement('button')` and then `document.append Child(likeButton)`? This would make it easier to test and would make the code more self-contained, but then we'd have to keep track of its parent if its parent isn't `document`. In fact, we might have to keep track of *all* the parents on the page.

React helps us solve some of these problems but not all of them: for example, the question of how to break up state into separate flags (`isPending`, `hasFailed`, etc.) or a single state variable (like `state`) is a question that React doesn't answer for us. It's a question that we have to answer for ourselves. However, React does help us solve the problem of scale: creating a lot of buttons that need to be interactive and updating the user interface in response to events in a minimal and efficient way, and doing this in a testable, reproducible, declarative, performant, predictable, and reliable way.

Moreover, React helps us make state far more predictable by fully owning the state of the user interface and rendering based on that state. This is in stark contrast to having the state be owned and operated on by the browser, whose state can be largely unreliable due to a number of factors like other client-side scripts running on the page, browser extensions, device constraints, and so many more variables.

Our example with the Like button is a very simple example, but it's a good one to start with. So far, we've seen how we can use JavaScript to make a button interactive, but this is a very manual process if we want to do it *well*: we have to find the button in the browser, add an event listener, update the button's text content, and account for myriad edge cases. This is a lot of work, and it's not very scalable. What if we had a lot of buttons on the page? What if we had a lot of buttons that needed to be interactive? What if we had a lot of buttons that needed to be interactive, and we needed to update the user interface in response to events? Would we use event delegation (or event bubbling) and attach an event listener to the higher document? Or should we attach event listeners to each button?

As stated in the Preface, this book assumes we have a satisfactory understanding of this statement: browsers render web pages. Web pages are HTML documents that are styled by CSS and made interactive with JavaScript. This has worked great for decades and still does, but building modern web applications that are intended to service a significant (think millions) amount of users with these technologies requires a good amount of abstraction in order to do it safely and reliably with as little possibility for error as possible. Unfortunately, based on the example of the Like button that we've been exploring, it's clear that we're going to need some help with this.

Let's consider another example that's a little bit more complex than our Like button. We'll start with a simple example: a list of items. Let's say we have a list of items and we want to add a new item to the list. We could do this with an HTML form that looks something like this:

```html
<ul id="list-parent"></ul>

<form id="add-item-form" action="/api/add-item" method="POST">
  <input type="text" id="new-list-item-label" />
  <button type="submit">Add Item</button>
</form>
```

JavaScript gives us access to Document Object Model (DOM) APIs. For the unaware, the DOM is an in-memory model of a web page's document structure: it's a tree of objects that represents the elements on your page, giving you ways to interact with them via JavaScript. The problem is, the DOMs on user devices are like an alien planet: we have no way of knowing what browsers they're using, in what network conditions, and on what operating systems (OS) they're working. The result? We have to write code that is resilient to all of these factors.

As we've discussed, application state becomes quite hard to predict when it updates without some type of state-reconciliation mechanism to keep track of things. To continue with our list example, let's consider some JavaScript code to add a new item to the list:

```javascript
(function myApp() {
  var listItems = ["I love", "React", "and", "TypeScript"];
  var parentList = document.getElementById("list-parent");
  var addForm = document.getElementById("add-item-form");
  var newListItemLabel = document.getElementById("new-list-item-label");

  addForm.onsubmit = function (event) {
    event.preventDefault();
    listItems.push(newListItemLabel.value);
    renderListItems();
  };
```

```
function renderListItems() {
  for (i = 0; i < listItems.length; i++) {
    var el = document.createElement("li");
    el.textContent = listItems[i];
    parentList.appendChild(el);
  }
}

renderListItems();
})();
```

This code snippet is written to look as similar as possible to early web applications. Why does this go haywire over time? Mainly because building applications intended to scale this way over time presents some footguns, making them:

Error prone
> addForm's onsubmit attribute could be easily rewritten by other client-side JavaScript on the page. We could use addEventListener instead, but this presents more questions:
>
> - Where and when would we clean it up with removeEventListener?
>
> - Would we accumulate a lot of event listeners over time if we're not careful about this?
>
> - What penalties will we pay because of it?
>
> - How does event delegation fit into this?

Unpredictable
> Our sources of truth are mixed: we're holding list items in a JavaScript array, but relying on existing elements in the DOM (like an element with id="list-parent") to complete our app. Because of these interdependencies between JavaScript and HTML, we have a few more things to consider:
>
> - What if there are mistakenly multiple elements with the same id?
>
> - What if the element doesn't exist at all?
>
> - What if it's not a ul? Can we append list items (li elements) to other parents?
>
> - What if we use class names instead?
>
>   Our sources of truth are mixed between JavaScript and HTML, making the truth unreliable. We'd benefit more from having a single source of truth. Moreover, elements are added and removed from the DOM by client-side JavaScript all the time. If we rely on the existence of these specific elements, our app has no guarantees of working reliably as the UI keeps updating. Our app in this case is full of "side effects," where its success or failure depends on some userland concern. React has remedied this by advocating a functional

programming-inspired model where side effects are intentionally marked and isolated.

Inefficient

renderListItems renders items on the screen sequentially. Each mutation of the DOM can be computationally expensive, especially where layout shift and reflows are concerned. Since we're on an alien planet with unknown computational power, this can be quite unsafe for performance in case of large lists. Remember, we're intending our large-scale web application to be used by millions worldwide, including those with low-power devices from communities across the world without access to the latest and greatest Apple M3 Max processors. What may be more ideal in this scenario, instead of sequentially updating the DOM per single list item, would be to batch these operations somehow and apply them all to the DOM at the same time. But maybe this isn't worth doing for us as engineers because perhaps browsers will eventually update the way they work with quick updates to the DOM and automatically batch things for us.

These are some of the problems that have plagued web developers for years before React and other abstractions appeared. Packaging code in a way that was maintainable, reusable, and predictable at scale was a problem without much standardized consensus in the industry. This pain of creating reliable and scalable user interfaces was shared by many web companies at the time. It was at this point on the web that we saw the rise of multiple JavaScript-based solutions that aimed to solve this: Backbone, KnockoutJS, AngularJS, and jQuery. Let's look at these solutions in turn and see how they solved this problem. This will help us understand how React is different from these solutions, and may even be superior to them.

jQuery

Let's explore how we solved some of these issues earlier on the web using tools that predate React and thus learn why React is important. We'll start with jQuery, and we'll do so by revisiting our Like button example from earlier.

To recap, we've got a Like button in the browser that we'd like to make interactive:

```
<button id="likeButton">Like</button>
```

With jQuery, we'd add "like" behavior to it as we did earlier, like this:

```
$("#likeButton").on("click", function () {
  this.prop("disabled", true);
  fetch("/like", {
    method: "POST",
    body: JSON.stringify({ liked: this.text() === "Like" }),
  })
    .then(() => {
      this.text(this.text() === "Like" ? "Liked" : "Like");
    })
```

```
      .catch(() => {
        this.text("Failed");
      })
      .finally(() => {
        this.prop("disabled", false);
      });
  });
```

From this example, we observe that we're binding data to the user interface and using this data binding to update the user interface in place. jQuery as a tool is quite active in directly manipulating the user interface itself.

jQuery runs in a heavily "side-effectful" way, constantly interacting with and altering state outside of its own control. We say this is "side-effectful" because it allows direct and global modifications to the page's structure from anywhere in the code, including from other imported modules or even remote script execution! This can lead to unpredictable behavior and complex interactions that are difficult to track and reason about, as changes in one part of the page can affect other parts in unforeseen ways. This scattered and unstructured manipulation makes the code hard to maintain and debug.

Modern frameworks address these issues by providing structured, predictable ways to update the UI without direct DOM manipulation. This pattern was common at the time, and it is difficult to reason about and test because the world around the code, that is, the application state adjacent to the code, is constantly changing. At some point, we'd have to stop and ask ourselves: "what is the state of the app in the browser right now?"—a question that became increasingly difficult to answer as the complexity of our applications grew.

Moreover, this button with jQuery is hard to test because it's just an event handler. If we were to write a test, it would look like this:

```
test("LikeButton", () => {
  const $button = $("#likeButton");
  expect($button.text()).toBe("Like");
  $button.trigger("click");
  expect($button.text()).toBe("Liked");
});
```

The only problem is that `$('#likeButton')` returns `null` in the testing environment because it's not a real browser. We'd have to mock out the browser environment to test this code, which is a lot of work. This is a common problem with jQuery: it's hard to test because it's hard to isolate the behavior it adds. jQuery also depends heavily on the browser environment. Moreover, jQuery shares ownership of the user interface with the browser, which makes it difficult to reason about and test: the browser owns the interface, and jQuery is just a guest. This deviation from the "one-way data flow" paradigm was a common problem with libraries at the time.

Eventually, jQuery started to lose its popularity as the web evolved and the need for more robust and scalable solutions became apparent. While jQuery is still used in many production applications, it's no longer the go-to solution for building modern web applications. Here are some of the reasons why jQuery has fallen out of favor:

Weight and load times

One of the significant criticisms of jQuery is its size. Integrating the full jQuery library into web projects adds extra weight, which can be especially taxing for websites aiming for fast load times. In today's age of mobile browsing, where many users might be on slower or limited data connections, every kilobyte counts. The inclusion of the entire jQuery library can, therefore, negatively impact the performance and experience of mobile users.

A common practice before React was to offer configurators for libraries like jQuery and Mootools where users could cherry-pick the functionality they desired. While this helped ship less code, it did introduce more complexity into the decisions developers had to make, and into the overall development workflow.

Redundancy with modern browsers

When jQuery first emerged, it addressed many inconsistencies across browsers and provided developers with a unified way to handle these differences in the context of selecting and then modifying elements in the browser. As the web evolved, so did web browsers. Many features that made jQuery a must-have, such as consistent DOM manipulation or network-oriented functionality around data fetching, are now natively and consistently supported across modern browsers. Using jQuery for these tasks in contemporary web development can be seen as redundant, adding an unnecessary layer of complexity.

`document.querySelector`, for example, quite easily replaces jQuery's built-in `$` selector API.

Performance considerations

While jQuery simplifies many tasks, it often comes at the cost of performance. Native runtime-level JavaScript methods improve with each browser iteration and thus at some point may execute faster than their jQuery equivalents. For small projects, this difference might be negligible. However, in larger and more complex web applications these complexities can accumulate, leading to noticeable jank or reduced responsiveness.

For these reasons, while jQuery played a pivotal role in the web's evolution and simplified many challenges faced by developers, the modern web landscape offers native solutions that often make jQuery less relevant. As developers, we need to weigh the convenience of jQuery against its potential drawbacks, especially in the context of current web projects.

jQuery, despite its drawbacks, was an absolute revolution in the way we interacted with the DOM at the time. So much so that other libraries emerged that used jQuery but added more predictability and reusability to the mix. One such library was Backbone, which was an attempt to solve the same problems React solves today, but much earlier. Let's dive in.

Backbone

Backbone, developed in the early 2010s, was one of the first solutions to the problems we've been exploring in the world before React: state dissonance between the browser and JavaScript, code reuse, testability, and more. It was an elegantly simple solution: a library that provided a way to create "models" and "views." Backbone had its own take on the traditional MVC (Model-View-Controller) pattern (see Figure 1-1). Let's understand this pattern a little bit to help us understand React and form the basis of a higher-quality discussion.

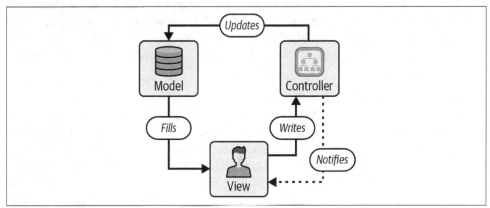

Figure 1-1. Traditional MVC pattern

The MVC pattern

The MVC pattern is a design philosophy that divides software applications into three interconnected components to separate internal representations of information from how that information is presented to or accepted from the user. Here's a breakdown:

Model
> The Model is responsible for the data and the business rules of the application. The Model is unaware of the View and Controller, ensuring that the business logic is isolated from the user interface.

View
> The View represents the user interface of the application. It displays data from the Model to the user and sends user commands to the Controller. The View is passive, meaning it waits for the Model to provide data to display and does not

fetch or save data directly. The View also does not handle user interaction on its own, but delegates this responsibility to the next component: the Controller.

Controller

The Controller acts as an interface between the Model and the View. It takes the user input from the View, processes it (with potential updates to the Model), and returns the output display to the View. The Controller decouples the Model from the View, making the system architecture more flexible.

The primary advantage of the MVC pattern is the separation of concerns, which means that the business logic, user interface, and user input are separated into different sections of the codebase. This not only makes the application more modular but also easier to maintain, scale, and test. The MVC pattern is widely used in web applications, with many frameworks like Django, Ruby on Rails, and ASP.NET MVC offering built-in support for it.

The MVC pattern has been a staple in software design for many years, especially in web development. However, as web applications have evolved and user expectations for interactive and dynamic interfaces have grown, some limitations of the traditional MVC have become apparent. Here's where MVC can fall short and how React addresses these challenges:

Complex interactivity and state management

Traditional MVC architectures often struggle when it comes to managing complex user interfaces with many interactive elements. As an application grows, managing state changes and their effects on various parts of the UI can become cumbersome as controllers pile up, and can sometimes conflict with other controllers, with some controllers controlling views that do not represent them, or the separation between MVC components not accurately scoped in product code.

React, with its component-based architecture and virtual DOM, makes it easier to reason about state changes and their effects on the UI by essentially positing that UI components are like a function: they receive input (props) and return output based on those inputs (elements). This mental model radically simplified the MVC pattern because functions are fairly ubiquitous in JavaScript and much more approachable when compared to an external mental model that is not native to the programming language like MVC.

Two-way data binding

Some MVC frameworks utilize two-way data binding, which can lead to unintended side effects if not managed carefully, where in some cases either the view becomes out of sync with the model or vice versa. Moreover, with two-way data binding the question of data ownership often had a crude answer, with an unclear separation of concerns. This is particularly interesting because while MVC is a proven model for teams that fully understand the appropriate way to separate concerns for their use cases, these separation rules are seldom enforced—especially when faced with high-velocity output and rapid startup growth—and thus separation of concerns, one of the greatest strengths of MVC, is often turned into a weakness by this lack of enforcement.

React leverages a pattern counter to two-way data binding called "unidirectional data flow" (more on this later) to prioritize and even enforce a unidirectional data flow through systems like Forget (which we will also discuss further in the book). These approaches make UI updates more predictable, enable us to separate concerns more clearly, and ultimately are conducive to high-velocity hypergrowth software teams.

Tight coupling

In some MVC implementations, the Model, View, and Controller can become tightly coupled, making it hard to change or refactor one without affecting the others. React encourages a more modular and decoupled approach with its component-based model, enabling and supporting colocation of dependencies close to their UI representations.

We don't need to get too much into the details of this pattern since this is a React book, but for our intents and purposes here, models were conceptually sources of data, and views were conceptually user interfaces that consumed and rendered that data. Backbone exported comfortable APIs to work with these models and views, and provided a way to connect the models and views together. This solution was very powerful and flexible for its time. It was also a solution that was scalable to use and allowed developers to test their code in isolation.

As an example, here's our earlier button example, this time using Backbone:

```
const LikeButton = Backbone.View.extend({
  tagName: "button",
  attributes: {
    type: "button",
  },
  events: {
    click: "onClick",
  },
  initialize() {
    this.model.on("change", this.render, this);
  },
  render() {
    this.$el.text(this.model.get("liked") ? "Liked" : "Like");
    return this;
  },
  onClick() {
    fetch("/like", {
      method: "POST",
      body: JSON.stringify({ liked: !this.model.get("liked") }),
    })
```

```
      .then(() => {
        this.model.set("liked", !this.model.get("liked"));
      })
      .catch(() => {
        this.model.set("failed", true);
      })
      .finally(() => {
        this.model.set("pending", false);
      });
  },
});

const likeButton = new LikeButton({
  model: new Backbone.Model({
    liked: false,
  }),
});

document.body.appendChild(likeButton.render().el);
```

Notice how `LikeButton` extends `Backbone.View` and how it has a `render` method that returns `this`? We'll go on to see a similar `render` method in React, but let's not get ahead of ourselves. It's also worth noting here that Backbone didn't include an actual implementation for `render`. Instead, you either manually mutated the DOM via jQuery, or used a templating system like Handlebars.

Backbone exposed a chainable API that allowed developers to colocate logic as properties on objects. Comparing this to our previous example, we can see that Backbone has made it far more comfortable to create a button that is interactive and updates the user interface in response to events.

It also does this in a more structured way by grouping logic together. Also note that Backbone has made it more approachable to test this button in isolation because we can create a `LikeButton` instance and then call its `render` method to test it.

We test this component like so:

```
test("LikeButton initial state", () => {
  const likeButton = new LikeButton({
    model: new Backbone.Model({
      liked: false, // Initial state set to not liked
    }),
  });
  likeButton.render(); // Ensure render is called to reflect the initial state
  // Check the text content to be "Like" reflecting the initial state
  expect(likeButton.el.textContent).toBe("Like");
});
```

We can even test the button's behavior after its state changes, as in the case of a click event, like so:

```
test("LikeButton", async () => {
  // Mark the function as async to handle promise
  const likeButton = new LikeButton({
    model: new Backbone.Model({
      liked: false,
    }),
  });
  expect(likeButton.render().el.textContent).toBe("Like");

  // Mock fetch to prevent actual HTTP request
  global.fetch = jest.fn(() =>
    Promise.resolve({
      json: () => Promise.resolve({ liked: true }),
    })
  );

  // Await the onClick method to ensure async operations are complete
  await likeButton.onClick();

  expect(likeButton.render().el.textContent).toBe("Liked");

  // Optionally, restore fetch to its original implementation if needed
  global.fetch.mockRestore();
});
```

For this reason, Backbone was a very popular solution at the time. The alternative was to write a lot of code that was hard to test and hard to reason about with no guarantees that the code would work as expected in a reliable way. Therefore, Backbone was a very welcome solution. While it gained popularity in its early days for its simplicity and flexibility, it's not without its criticisms. Here are some of the negatives associated with Backbone.js:

Verbose and boilerplate code
> One of the frequent criticisms of Backbone.js is the amount of boilerplate code developers needed to write. For simple applications, this might not be a big deal, but as the application grows, so does the boilerplate, leading to potentially redundant and hard-to-maintain code.

Lack of two-way data binding
> Unlike some of its contemporaries, Backbone.js doesn't offer built-in two-way data binding. This means that if the data changes, the DOM doesn't automatically update, and vice versa. Developers often need to write custom code or use plugins to achieve this functionality.

Event-driven architecture
> Updates to model data can trigger numerous events throughout the application. This cascade of events can become unmanageable, leading to a situation where it's unclear how changing a single piece of data will affect the rest of the application, making debugging and maintenance difficult. To address these issues,

developers often needed to use careful event management practices to prevent the ripple effect of updates across the entire app.

Lack of composability

Backbone.js lacks built-in features for easily nesting views, which can make composing complex user interfaces difficult. React, in contrast, allows for seamless nesting of components through the children prop, making it much simpler to build intricate UI hierarchies. Marionette.js, an extension of Backbone, attempted to address some of these composition issues, but it does not provide as integrated a solution as React's component model.

While Backbone.js has its set of challenges, it's essential to remember that no tool or framework is perfect. The best choice often depends on the specific needs of the project and the preferences of the development team. It's also worth noting how much web development tools depend on a strong community to thrive, and unfortunately Backbone.js has seen a decline in popularity in recent years, especially with the advent of React. Some would say React killed it, but we'll reserve judgment for now.

KnockoutJS

Let's compare this approach with another popular solution at the time: KnockoutJS. KnockoutJS, developed in the early 2010s, was a library that provided a way to create "observables" and "bindings," making use of dependency tracking whenever state changes.

KnockoutJS was among the first, if not the first, reactive JavaScript libraries, where reactivity is defined as values updating in response to state changes in an observable manner. Modern takes on this style of reactivity are sometimes called "signals" and are prevalent in libraries like Vue.js, SolidJS, Svelte, Qwik, modern Angular, and more. We cover these in Chapter 10 in more detail.

Observables were conceptually sources of data, and bindings were conceptually user interfaces that consumed and rendered that data: observables were like models, and bindings were like views.

However, as a bit of an evolution of the MVC pattern we discussed previously, KnockoutJS instead worked more along a Model-View-ViewModel or MVVM-style pattern (see Figure 1-2). Let's understand this pattern in some detail.

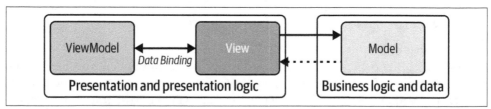

Figure 1-2. MVVM pattern

MVVM pattern

The MVVM pattern is an architectural design pattern that's particularly popular in applications with rich user interfaces, such as those built using platforms like WPF and Xamarin. MVVM is an evolution of the traditional Model-View-Controller (MVC) pattern, tailored for modern UI development platforms where data binding is a prominent feature. Here's a breakdown of the MVVM components:

Model
- Represents the data and business logic of the application.
- Is responsible for retrieving, storing, and processing the data.
- Typically communicates with databases, services, or other data sources and operations.
- Is unaware of the View and ViewModel.

View
- Represents the UI of the application.
- Displays information to the user and receives user input.
- In MVVM, the View is passive and doesn't contain any application logic. Instead, it declaratively binds to the ViewModel, reflecting changes automatically through data binding mechanisms.

ViewModel
- Acts as a bridge between the Model and the View.
- Exposes data and commands for the View to bind to. The data here is often in a format that's display ready.
- Handles user input, often through command patterns.
- Contains the presentation logic and transforms data from the Model into a format that can be easily displayed by the View.
- Notably, the ViewModel is unaware of the specific View that's using it, allowing for a decoupled architecture.

The key advantage of the MVVM pattern is the separation of concerns similar to MVC, which leads to:

Testability
    The decoupling of ViewModel from View makes it easier to write unit tests for the presentation logic without involving the UI.

Reusability
    The ViewModel can be reused across different views or platforms.

Maintainability

With a clear separation, it's easier to manage, extend, and refactor code.

Data binding

The pattern excels in platforms that support data binding, reducing the amount of boilerplate code required to update the UI.

Since we discussed both MVC and MVVM patterns, let's quickly contrast them so that we can understand the differences between them (see Table 1-1).

Table 1-1. Comparison of MVC and MVVM patterns

Criteria	MVC	MVVM
Primary purpose	Primarily for web applications, separating user interface from logic.	Tailored for rich UI applications, especially with two-way data binding, like desktop or SPAs.
Components	Model: data and business logic. View: user interface. Controller: manages user input, updates View.	Model: data and business logic. View: user interface elements. ViewModel: bridge between Model and View.
Data flow	User input is managed by the Controller, which updates the Model and then the View.	The View binds directly to the ViewModel. Changes in the View are automatically reflected in the ViewModel and vice versa.
Decoupling	View is often tightly coupled with the Controller.	High decoupling as ViewModel doesn't know the specific View using it.
User interaction	Handled by the Controller.	Handled through data bindings and commands in the ViewModel.
Platform suitability	Common in web application development (e.g., Ruby on Rails, Django, ASP.NET MVC).	Suited for platforms supporting robust data binding (e.g., WPF, Xamarin).

From this brief comparison, we can see that the real difference between MVC and MVVM patterns is one of coupling and binding: with no Controller between a Model and a View, data ownership is clearer and closer to the user. React further improves on MVVM with its unidirectional data flow, which we'll discuss in a little bit, by getting *even narrower* in terms of data ownership, such that state is owned by specific components that need them. For now, let's get back to KnockoutJS and how it relates to React.

KnockoutJS exported APIs to work with these observables and bindings. Let's look at how we'd implement the Like button in KnockoutJS. This will help us understand "why React" a little better. Here's the KnockoutJS version of our button:

```
function createViewModel({ liked }) {
  const isPending = ko.observable(false);
  const hasFailed = ko.observable(false);
  const onClick = () => {
    isPending(true);
    fetch("/like", {
      method: "POST",
      body: JSON.stringify({ liked: !liked() }),
```

```
      })
        .then(() => {
          liked(!liked());
        })
        .catch(() => {
          hasFailed(true);
        })
        .finally(() => {
          isPending(false);
        });
    };
    return {
      isPending,
      hasFailed,
      onClick,
      liked,
    };
  }

  ko.applyBindings(createViewModel({ liked: ko.observable(false) }));
```

In KnockoutJS, a "view model" is a JavaScript object that contains keys and values that we bind to various elements in our page using the `data-bind` attribute. There are no "components" or "templates" in KnockoutJS, just a view model and a way to bind it to an element in the browser.

Our function `createViewModel` is how we'd create a view model with Knockout. We then use `ko.applyBindings` to connect the view model to the host environment (the browser). The `ko.applyBindings` function takes a view model and finds all the elements in the browser that have a `data-bind` attribute, which Knockout uses to bind them to the view model.

A button in our browser would be bound to this view model's properties like so:

```
<button
  data-bind="click: onClick, text: liked ? 'Liked' : isPending ? [...]
></button>
```

Note that this code has been truncated for simplicity.

We *bind* the HTML element to the "view model" we created using our `createViewModel` function, and the site becomes interactive. As you can imagine, explicitly subscribing to changes in observables and then updating the user interface in response to these changes is a lot of work. KnockoutJS was a great library for its time, but it also required a lot of boilerplate code to get things done.

Moreover, view models often grew to be very large and complex, which led to increasing uncertainty around refactors and optimizations to code. Eventually, we ended up with verbose monolithic view models that were hard to test and reason about. Still, KnockoutJS was a very popular solution and a great library for its time. It was also relatively easy to test in isolation, which was a big plus.

For posterity, here's how we'd test this button in KnockoutJS:

```
test("LikeButton", () => {
  const viewModel = createViewModel({ liked: ko.observable(false) });
  expect(viewModel.liked()).toBe(false);
  viewModel.onClick();
  expect(viewModel.liked()).toBe(true);
});
```

AngularJS

AngularJS was developed by Google in 2010. It was a pioneering JavaScript framework that had a significant impact on the web development landscape. It stood in sharp contrast to the libraries and frameworks we've been discussing by incorporating several innovative features, the ripples of which can be seen in subsequent libraries, including React. Through a detailed comparison of AngularJS with these other libraries and a look at its pivotal features, let's try to understand the path it carved for React.

Two-way data binding

Two-way data binding was a hallmark feature of AngularJS that greatly simplified the interaction between the UI and the underlying data. If the model (the underlying data) changes, the view (the UI) gets updated automatically to reflect the change, and vice versa. This was a stark contrast to libraries like jQuery, where developers had to manually manipulate the DOM to reflect any changes in the data and capture user inputs to update the data.

Let's consider a simple AngularJS application where two-way data binding plays a crucial role:

```
<!DOCTYPE html>
<html>
  <head>
    <script
    src="https://ajax.googleapis.com/ajax/libs/angularjs/1.8.2/angular.min.js">
    </script>
  </head>
  <body ng-app="">
    <p>Name: <input type="text" ng-model="name" /></p>
    <p ng-if="name">Hello, {{name}}!</p>
  </body>
</html>
```

In this application, the `ng-model` directive binds the value of the input field to the variable `name`. As you type into the input field, the model `name` gets updated, and the view—in this case, the greeting `"Hello, {{name}}!"`—gets updated in real time.

Modular architecture

AngularJS introduced a modular architecture that allowed developers to logically separate their application's components. Each module could encapsulate a functionality and could be developed, tested, and maintained independently. Some would call this a precursor to React's component model, but this is debated.

Here's a quick example:

```
var app = angular.module("myApp", [
  "ngRoute",
  "appRoutes",
  "userCtrl",
  "userService",
]);

var userCtrl = angular.module("userCtrl", []);
userCtrl.controller("UserController", function ($scope) {
  $scope.message = "Hello from UserController";
});

var userService = angular.module("userService", []);
userService.factory("User", function ($http) {
  //...
});
```

In the preceding example, the `myApp` module depends on several other modules: `ngRoute`, `appRoutes`, `userCtrl`, and `userService`. Each dependent module could be in its own JavaScript file, and could be developed separately from the main `myApp` module. This concept was significantly different from jQuery and Backbone.js, which didn't have a concept of a "module" in this sense.

We inject these dependencies (`appRoutes`, `userCtrl`, etc.) into our root `app` using a pattern called *dependency injection* that was popularized in Angular. Needless to say, this pattern was prevalent before JavaScript modules were standardized. Since then, `import` and `export` statements quickly took over. To contrast these dependencies with React components, let's talk about dependency injection a little more.

Dependency injection

Dependency injection (DI) is a design pattern where an object receives its dependencies instead of creating them. AngularJS incorporated this design pattern at its core, which was not a common feature in other JavaScript libraries at the time. This had a profound impact on the way modules and components were created and managed, promoting a higher degree of modularity and reusability.

Here is an example of how DI works in AngularJS:

```
var app = angular.module("myApp", []);

app.controller("myController", function ($scope, myService) {
  $scope.greeting = myService.sayHello();
});

app.factory("myService", function () {
  return {
    sayHello: function () {
      return "Hello, World!";
    },
  };
});
```

In the example, `myService` is a service that is injected into the `myController` controller through DI. The controller does not need to know how to create the service. It just declares the service as a dependency, and AngularJS takes care of creating and injecting it. This simplifies the management of dependencies and enhances the testability and reusability of components.

Comparison with Backbone.js and Knockout.js

Backbone.js and Knockout.js were two popular libraries used around the time AngularJS was introduced. Both libraries had their strengths, but they lacked some features that were built into AngularJS.

Backbone.js, for example, gave developers more control over their code and was less opinionated than AngularJS. This flexibility was both a strength and a weakness: it allowed for more customization, but also required more boilerplate code. AngularJS, with its two-way data binding and DI, allowed for more structure. It had more opinions that led to greater developer velocity: something we see with modern frameworks like Next.js, Remix, etc. This is one way AngularJS was far ahead of its time.

Backbone also didn't have an answer to directly mutating the view (the DOM) and often left this up to developers. AngularJS took care of DOM mutations with its two-way data binding, which was a big plus.

Knockout.js was primarily focused on data binding and lacked some of the other powerful tools that AngularJS provided, such as DI and a modular architecture. AngularJS, being a full-fledged framework, offered a more comprehensive solution for building single-page applications (SPAs). While AngularJS was discontinued, today its newer variant called Angular offers the same, albeit enhanced, slew of comprehensive benefits that make it an ideal choice for large-scale applications.

AngularJS trade-offs

AngularJS (1.x) represented a significant leap in web development practices when it was introduced. However, as the landscape of web development continued to evolve rapidly, certain aspects of AngularJS were seen as limitations or weaknesses that contributed to its relative decline. Some of these include:

Performance

> AngularJS had performance issues, particularly in large-scale applications with complex data bindings. The digest cycle in AngularJS, a core feature for change detection, could result in slow updates and laggy user interfaces in large applications. The two-way data binding, while innovative and useful in many situations, also contributed to the performance issues.

Complexity

> AngularJS introduced a range of novel concepts, including directives, controllers, services, dependency injection, factories, and more. While these features made AngularJS powerful, they also made it complex and hard to learn, especially for beginners. A common debate, for example, was "should this be a factory or a service?" leaving a number of developer teams puzzled.

Migration issues to Angular 2+

> When Angular 2 was announced, it was not backward compatible with AngularJS 1.x. and required code to be written in Dart and/or TypeScript. This meant that developers had to rewrite significant portions of their code to upgrade to Angular 2, which was seen as a big hurdle. The introduction of Angular 2+ essentially split the Angular community and caused confusion, paving the way for React.

Complex syntax in templates

> AngularJS's allowance for complex JavaScript expressions within template attributes, such as `on-click="$ctrl.some.deeply.nested.field = 123"`, was problematic because it led to a blend of presentation and business logic within the markup. This approach created challenges in maintainability, as deciphering and managing the intertwined code became cumbersome.

> Furthermore, debugging was more difficult because template layers weren't inherently designed to handle complex logic, and any errors that arose from these inline expressions could be challenging to locate and resolve. Additionally, such practices violated the principle of separation of concerns, which is a fundamental design philosophy advocating for the distinct handling of different aspects of an application to improve code quality and maintainability.

> In theory, a template ought to call a controller method to perform an update, but nothing restricted that.

Absence of type safety

Templates in AngularJS did not work with static type-checkers like TypeScript, which made it difficult to catch errors early in the development process. This was a significant drawback, especially for large-scale applications where type safety is crucial for maintainability and scalability.

Confusing `$scope` *model*

The `$scope` object in AngularJS was often found to be a source of confusion due to its role in binding data and its behavior in different contexts because it served as the glue between the view and the controller, but its behavior was not always intuitive or predictable.

This led to complexities, especially for newcomers, in understanding how data was synchronized between the model and the view. Additionally, `$scope` could inherit properties from parent scopes in nested controllers, making it difficult to track where a particular `$scope` property was originally defined or modified.

This inheritance could cause unexpected side effects in the application, particularly when dealing with nested scopes where parent and child scopes could inadvertently affect each other. The concept of scope hierarchy and the prototypal inheritance on which it was based were often at odds with the more traditional and familiar lexical scoping rules found in JavaScript, adding another layer of learning complexity.

React, for example, colocates state with the component that needs it, and thus avoids this problem entirely.

Limited development tools

AngularJS did not offer extensive developer tools for debugging and performance profiling, especially when compared to the DevTools available in React like Replay.io, which allows extensive capabilities around time-travel debugging for React applications.

Enter React

It was around this time that React rose to prominence. One of the core ideas that React presented was the component-based architecture. Although the implementation is different, the underlying idea is similar: it is optimal to build user interfaces for the web and other platforms by composing reusable components.

While AngularJS used directives to bind views to models, React introduced JSX and a radically simpler component model. Yet, without the ground laid by AngularJS in promoting a component-based architecture through Angular modules, some would argue the transition to React's model might not have been as smooth.

In AngularJS, the two-way data binding model was the industry standard; however, it also had some downsides, such as potential performance issues on large applications. React learned from this and introduced a unidirectional data flow pattern, giving developers more control over their applications and making it easier to understand how data changes over time.

React also introduced the virtual DOM as we'll read about in Chapter 3: a concept that improved performance by minimizing direct DOM manipulation. AngularJS, on the other hand, often directly manipulated the DOM, which could lead to performance issues and other inconsistent state issues we recently discussed with jQuery.

That said, AngularJS represented a significant shift in web development practices, and we'd be remiss if we didn't mention that AngularJS not only revolutionized the web development landscape when it was introduced, but also paved the way for the evolution of future frameworks and libraries, React being one of them.

Let's explore how React fits into all of this and where React came from at this point in history. At this time, UI updates were still a relatively hard and unsolved problem. They're far from solved today, but React has made them noticeably less hard, and has inspired other libraries like SolidJS, Qwik, and more to do so. Meta's Facebook was no exception to the problem of UI complexity and scale. As a result, Meta created a number of internal solutions complementary to what already existed at the time. Among the first of these was BoltJS: a tool Facebook engineers would say "bolted together" a bunch of things that they liked. A combination of tools was assembled to make updates to Facebook's web user interface more intuitive.

Around this time, Facebook engineer Jordan Walke had a radical idea that did away with the status quo of the time and entirely replaced minimal portions of web pages with new ones as updates happened. As we've seen previously, JavaScript libraries would manage relationships between views (user interfaces) and models (conceptually, sources of data) using a paradigm called two-way data binding. In light of this model's limitations, as we've discussed earlier, Jordan's idea was to instead use a paradigm called one-way data flow. This was a much simpler paradigm, and it was much easier to keep the views and models in sync. This was the birth of the unidirectional architecture that would go on to be the foundation of React.

React's Value Proposition

OK, history lesson's over. Hopefully we now have enough context to begin to understand why React is a thing. Given how easy it was to fall into the pit of unsafe, unpredictable, and inefficient JavaScript code at scale, we needed a solution to steer us toward a pit of success where we *accidentally win*. Let's talk about exactly how React does that.

Declarative versus imperative code

React provides a declarative abstraction on the DOM. We'll talk more about how it does this in more detail later in the book, but essentially it provides us a way to write code that expresses *what we want to see*, while then taking care of *how it happens*, ensuring our user interface is created and works in a safe, predictable, and efficient manner.

Let's consider the list app that we created earlier. In React, we could rewrite it like this:

```
function MyList() {
  const [items, setItems] = useState(["I love"]);

  return (
    <div>
      <ul>
        {items.map((i) => (
          <li key={i /* keep items unique */}>{i}</li>
        ))}
      </ul>
      <NewItemForm onAddItem={(newItem) => setItems([...items, newItem])} />
    </div>
  );
}
```

Notice how in the `return`, we literally write something that looks like HTML: it looks like what we want to see. I want to see a box with a `NewItemForm`, and a list. Boom. How does it get there? That's for React to figure out. Do we batch list items to add chunks of them at once? Do we add them sequentially, one by one? React deals with *how* this is done, while we merely describe *what* we want done. In further chapters, we'll dive into React and explore exactly how it does this at the time of writing.

Do we then depend on class names to reference HTML elements? Do we `getElement ById` in JavaScript? Nope. React creates unique "React elements" for us under the hood that it uses to detect changes and make incremental updates so we don't need to read class names and other identifiers from user code whose existence we cannot guarantee: our source of truth becomes exclusively JavaScript with React.

We export our `MyList` component to React, and React gets it on the screen for us in a way that is safe, predictable, and performant—no questions asked. The component's job is to just return a description of what this piece of the UI should look like. It does this by using a *virtual DOM* (vDOM), which is a lightweight description of the intended UI structure. React then compares the virtual DOM *after an update happens* to the virtual DOM *before an update happens*, and turns that into small, performant updates to the real DOM to make it match the virtual DOM. This is how React is able to make updates to the DOM.

The virtual DOM

The virtual DOM is a programming concept that represents the real DOM but as a JavaScript object. If this is a little too in the weeds for now, don't worry: Chapter 3 is dedicated to this and breaks things down in a little more detail. For now, it's just important to know that the virtual DOM allows developers to update the UI without directly manipulating the actual DOM. React uses the virtual DOM to keep track of changes to a component and rerenders the component only when necessary. This approach is faster and more efficient than updating the entire DOM tree every time there is a change.

In React, the virtual DOM is a lightweight representation of the actual DOM tree. It is a plain JavaScript object that describes the structure and properties of the UI elements. React creates and updates the virtual DOM to match the actual DOM tree, and any changes made to the virtual DOM are applied to the actual DOM using a process called *reconciliation*.

Chapter 4 is dedicated to this, but for our contextual discussion here, let's look at a small summary with a few examples. To understand how the virtual DOM works, let's bring back our example of the Like button. We will create a React component that displays a Like button and the number of likes. When the user clicks the button, the number of likes should increase by one.

Here is the code for our component:

```
import React, { useState } from "react";

function LikeButton() {
  const [likes, setLikes] = useState(0);

  function handleLike() {
    setLikes(likes + 1);
  }

  return (
    <div>
      <button onClick={handleLike}>Like</button>
      <p>{likes} Likes</p>
    </div>
  );
}

export default LikeButton;
```

In this code, we have used the useState hook to create a state variable likes, which holds the number of likes. To recap what we might already know about React, a hook is a special function that allows us to use React features, like state and lifecycle methods, within functional components. Hooks enable us to reuse stateful logic without changing the component hierarchy, making it easy to extract and share hooks among components or even with the community as self-contained open source packages.

We have also defined a function `handleLike` that increases the value of likes by one when the button is clicked. Finally, we render the Like button and the number of likes using JSX.

Now, let's take a closer look at how the virtual DOM works in this example.

When the `LikeButton` component is first rendered, React creates a virtual DOM tree that mirrors the actual DOM tree. The virtual DOM contains a single `div` element that contains a `button` element and a `p` element:

```
{
  $$typeof: Symbol.for('react.element'),
  type: 'div',
  props: {},
  children: [
    {
      $$typeof: Symbol.for('react.element'),
      type: 'button',
      props: { onClick: handleLike },
      children: ['Like']
    },
    {
      $$typeof: Symbol.for('react.element'),
      type: 'p',
      props: {},
      children: [0, ' Likes']
    }
  ]
}
```

The `children` property of the `p` element contains the value of the `Likes` state variable, which is initially set to zero.

When the user clicks the Like button, the `handleLike` function is called, which updates the `likes` state variable. React then creates a new virtual DOM tree that reflects the updated state:

```
{
  type: 'div',
  props: {},
  children: [
    {
      type: 'button',
      props: { onClick: handleLike },
      children: ['Like']
    },
    {
      type: 'p',
      props: {},
```

```
        children: [1, ' Likes']
      }
    ]
  }
```

Notice that the virtual DOM tree contains the same elements as before, but the `chil dren` property of the `p` element has been updated to reflect the new value of likes, going from 0 to 1. What follows is a process called *reconciliation* in React, where the new vDOM is compared with the old one. Let's briefly discuss this process.

After computing a new virtual DOM tree, React performs a process called reconciliation to understand the differences between the new tree and the old one. Reconciliation is the process of comparing the old virtual DOM tree with the new virtual DOM tree and determining which parts of the actual DOM need to be updated. If you're interested in *how* exactly this is done, Chapter 4 goes into a lot of detail about this. For now, let's consider our Like button.

In our example, React compares the old virtual DOM tree with the new virtual DOM tree and finds that the `p` element has changed: specifically that its props or state or both have changed. This enables React to mark the component as "dirty" or "should be updated." React then computes a minimal effective set of updates to make on the actual DOM to reconcile the state of the new vDOM with the DOM, and eventually updates the actual DOM to reflect the changes made to the virtual DOM.

React updates only the necessary parts of the actual DOM to minimize the number of DOM manipulations. This approach is much faster and more efficient than updating the entire DOM tree every time there is a change.

The virtual DOM has been a powerful and influential invention for the modern web, with newer libraries like Preact and Inferno adopting it once it was proven in React. We will cover more of the virtual DOM in Chapter 4, but for now, let's move on to the next section.

The component model

React highly encourages "thinking in components": that is, breaking your app into smaller pieces and adding them to a larger tree to compose your application. The component model is a key concept in React, and it's what makes React so powerful. Let's talk about why:

- It encourages reusing the same thing everywhere so that if it breaks, you fix it in one place and it's fixed everywhere. This is called DRY (Don't Repeat Yourself) development and is a key concept in software engineering. For example, if we have a `Button` component, we can use it in many places in our app, and if we need to change the style of the button, we can do it in one place and it's changed everywhere.

- React is more easily able to keep track of components and do performance magic like memoization, batching, and other optimizations under the hood if it's able to identify specific components over and over and track updates to the specific components over time. This is called *keying*. For example, if we have a `Button` component, we can give it a key prop and React will be able to keep track of the `Button` component over time and "know" when to update it, or when to skip updating it and continue making minimal changes to the user interface. Most components have implicit keys, but we can also explicitly provide them if we want to.

- It helps us separate concerns and colocate logic closer to the parts of the user interface that the logic affects. For example, if we have a `RegisterButton` component, we can put the logic for what happens when the button is clicked in the same file as the `RegisterButton` component, instead of having to jump around to different files to find the logic for what happens when the button is clicked. The `RegisterButton` component would wrap a more simple `Button` component, and the `RegisterButton` component would be responsible for handling the logic for what happens when the button is clicked. This is called *composition*.

React's component model is a fundamental concept that underpins the framework's popularity and success. This approach to development has numerous benefits, including increased modularity, easier debugging, and more efficient code reuse.

Immutable state

React's design philosophy emphasizes a paradigm wherein the state of our application is described as a set of immutable values. Each state update is treated as a new, distinct snapshot and memory reference. This immutable approach to state management is a core part of React's value proposition, and it has several advantages for developing robust, efficient, and predictable user interfaces.

By enforcing immutability, React ensures that the UI components reflect a specific state at any given point in time. When the state changes, rather than mutating it directly, you return a new object that represents the new state. This makes it easier to track changes, debug, and understand your application's behavior. Since state transitions are discrete and do not interfere with each other, the chances of subtle bugs caused by a shared mutable state are significantly reduced.

In coming chapters, we'll explore how React batches state updates and processes them asynchronously to optimize performance. Because state must be treated immutably, these "transactions" can be safely aggregated and applied without the risk of one update corrupting the state for another. This leads to more predictable state management and can improve app performance, especially during complex state transitions.

The use of immutable state further reinforces best practices in software development. It encourages developers to think functionally about their data flow, reducing side effects and making the code easier to follow. The clarity of an immutable data flow simplifies the mental model for understanding how an application works.

Immutability also enables powerful developer tools, such as time-travel debugging with tools like Replay.io, where developers can step forward and backward through the state changes of an application to inspect the UI at any point in time. This is only feasible if every state update is kept as a unique and unmodified snapshot.

React's commitment to immutable state updates is a deliberate design choice that brings numerous benefits. It aligns with modern functional programming principles, enabling efficient UI updates, optimizing performance, reducing the likelihood of bugs, and improving the overall developer experience. This approach to state management underpins many of React's advanced features and will continue to be a cornerstone as React evolves.

Releasing React

Unidirectional data flow was a radical departure from the way we had been building web apps for years, and it was met with skepticism. The fact that Facebook was a large company with a lot of resources, a lot of users, and a lot of engineers with opinions made its upward climb a steep one. After much scrutiny, React was an internal success. It was adopted by Facebook and then by Instagram.

It was then made open source in 2013 and released to the world where it was met with a tremendous amount of backlash. People heavily criticized React for its use of JSX, accusing Facebook of "putting HTML in JavaScript" and breaking separation of concerns. Facebook became known as the company that "rethinks best practices" and breaks the web. Eventually, after slow and steady adoption by companies like Netflix, Airbnb, and *The New York Times*, React became the de facto standard for building user interfaces on the web.

A number of details are left out of this story because they fall out of the scope of this book, but it's important to understand the context of React before we dive into the details: specifically the class of technical problems React was created to solve. Should you be more interested in the story of React, there is a full documentary on the history of React that is freely available on YouTube under *React.js: The Documentary* by Honeypot.

Given that Facebook had a front-row seat to these problems at enormous scale, React pioneered a component-based approach to building user interfaces that would solve these problems and more, where each component would be a self-contained unit of code that could be reused and composed with other components to build more complex user interfaces.

A year after React was released as open source software, Facebook released Flux: a pattern for managing data flow in React applications. Flux was a response to the challenges of managing data flow in large-scale applications, and it was a key part of the React ecosystem. Let's take a look at Flux and how it fits into the React.

The Flux Architecture

Flux is an architectural design pattern for building client-side web applications, popularized by Facebook (now Meta) (see Figure 1-3). It emphasizes a unidirectional data flow, which makes the flow of data within the app more predictable.

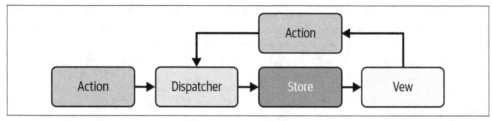

Figure 1-3. The Flux architecture

Here are the key concepts of the Flux architecture:

Actions

Actions are simple objects containing new data and an identifying type property. They represent the external and internal inputs to the system, like user interactions, server responses, and form inputs. Actions are dispatched through a central dispatcher to various stores:

```
// Example of an action object
{
  type: 'ADD_TODO',
  text: 'Learn Flux Architecture'
}
```

Dispatcher

The dispatcher is the central hub of the Flux architecture. It receives actions and dispatches them to the registered stores in the application. It manages a list of callbacks, and every store registers itself and its callback with the dispatcher. When an action is dispatched, it is sent to all registered callbacks:

```
// Example of dispatching an action
Dispatcher.dispatch(action);
```

Stores

Stores contain the application state and logic. They are somewhat similar to models in the MVC architecture, but they manage the state of many objects. They register with the dispatcher and provide callbacks to handle the actions. When a store's state is updated, it emits a change event to alert the views that something has changed:

```
// Example of a store
class TodoStore extends EventEmitter {
  constructor() {
    super();
    this.todos = [];
  }

  handleActions(action) {
    switch (action.type) {
      case "ADD_TODO":
        this.todos.push(action.text);
        this.emit("change");
        break;
      default:
      // no op
    }
  }
}
```

Views

Views are React components. They listen to change events from the stores and update themselves when the data they depend on changes. They can also create new actions to update the system state, forming a unidirectional cycle of data flow.

The Flux architecture promotes a unidirectional data flow through a system, which makes it easier to track changes over time. This predictability can later be used as the basis for compilers to further optimize code, as is the case with React Forget (more on this later).

Benefits of the Flux Architecture

The Flux architecture brings about a variety of benefits that help manage complexity and improve the maintainability of web applications. Here are some of the notable benefits:

Single source of truth

Flux emphasizes having a single source of truth for the application's state, which is stored in the stores. This centralized state management makes the application's behavior more predictable and easier to understand. It eliminates the complications that come with having multiple, interdependent sources of truth, which can lead to bugs and inconsistent state across the application.

Testability

Flux's well-defined structures and predictable data flow make the application highly testable. The separation of concerns among different parts of the system (like actions, dispatcher, stores, and views) allows for unit testing each part in isolation. Moreover, it's easier to write tests when the data flow is unidirectional and when the state is stored in specific, predictable locations.

Separation of concerns (SoC)

Flux clearly separates the concerns of different parts of the system, as described earlier. This separation makes the system more modular, easier to maintain, and easier to reason about. Each part has a clearly defined role, and the unidirectional data flow makes it clear how these parts interact with each other.

The Flux architecture provides a solid foundation for building robust, scalable, and maintainable web applications. Its emphasis on a unidirectional data flow, single source of truth, and Separation of Concerns leads to applications that are easier to develop, test, and debug.

Wrap-Up: So…Why Is React a Thing?

React is a thing because it allows developers to build user interfaces with greater pre-dictability and reliability, enabling us to declaratively express *what we'd like on the screen* while React takes care of the *how* by making incremental updates to the DOM in an efficient manner. It also encourages us to think in components, which helps us separate concerns and reuse code more easily. It is battle-tested at Meta and designed to be used at scale. It's also open source and free to use.

React also has a vast and active ecosystem, with a wide range of tools, libraries, and resources available to developers. This ecosystem includes tools for testing, debugging, and optimizing React applications, as well as libraries for common tasks such as data management, routing, and state management. Additionally, the React community is highly engaged and supportive, with many online resources, forums, and communities available to help developers learn and grow.

React is platform-agnostic, meaning that it can be used to build web applications for a wide range of platforms, including desktop, mobile, and virtual reality. This flexibility makes React an attractive option for developers who need to build applications for multiple platforms, as it allows them to use a single codebase to build applications that run across multiple devices.

To conclude, React's value proposition is centered around its component-based archi-tecture, declarative programming model, virtual DOM, JSX, extensive ecosystem, platform agnostic nature, and backing by Meta. Together, these features make React an attractive option for developers who need to build fast, scalable, and maintainable web applications. Whether you're building a simple website or a complex enterprise application, React can help you achieve your goals more efficiently and effectively than many other technologies. Let's review.

Chapter Review

In this chapter, we covered a brief history of React, its initial value proposition, and how it solves the problems of unsafe, unpredictable, and inefficient user interface updates at scale. We also talked about the component model and why it has been revolutionary for interfaces on the web. Let's recap what we've learned. Ideally, after this chapter you are more informed about the roots of React and where it comes from as well as its main strengths and value proposition.

Review Questions

Let's make sure you've fully grasped the topics we covered. Take a moment to answer the following questions:

1. What was the motivation to create React?
2. How does React improve on prior patterns like MVC and MVVM?
3. What's so special about the Flux architecture?
4. What are the benefits of declarative programming abstractions?
5. What's the role of the virtual DOM in making efficient UI updates?

If you have trouble answering these questions, this chapter may be worth another read. If not, let's explore the next chapter.

Up Next

In Chapter 2 we will dive a little deeper into this declarative abstraction that allows us to express what we want to see on the screen: the syntax and inner workings of JSX—the language that looks like HTML in JavaScript that got React into a lot of trouble in its early days, but ultimately revealed itself to be the ideal way to build user interfaces on the web, influencing a number of future libraries for building user interfaces.

CHAPTER 2

JSX

In Chapter 1, we learned about the basics of React and its origin story, comparing it to other popular JavaScript libraries and frameworks of its time. We learned about the true value proposition of React and why it's a thing.

In this chapter, we'll learn about JSX, which is a syntax extension for JavaScript that allows us to write HTML-like code within our JavaScript code. Back when React was introduced in 2013, it was the first thing people noticed and heavily criticized, so it makes sense to zero in on it this early in the book. With that, let's dive deep into this language extension, how it works, and how we can conceptually make our own code.

To begin our discussion, let's understand what JSX stands for. We already know that JS is JavaScript. Does that mean JSX is JavaScript version 10? Like Mac OS X? Is it JS Xtra? We may think the X in JSX means 10 or Xtra, which would both be good guesses! But the X in JSX stands for *JavaScript Syntax eXtension*. It's also sometimes called *JavaScript XML*.

JavaScript XML?

If you've been around the web for a while, you might remember the term *AJAX*, or *Asynchronous JavaScript and XML*, from around the 2000s. AJAX was essentially a new way of using existing technologies to create highly interactive web pages that updated asynchronously and in place, instead of the status quo at the time: each state change would load an entire new page.

Using tools like `XMLHttpRequest` in the browser, it would initiate an asynchronous (that is, nonblocking) request over HTTP (HyperText Transfer Protocol). The response to this request traditionally would be a response in XML. Today, we tend to respond with JSON instead. This is likely one of the reasons why `fetch` has overtaken `XMLHTTPRequest`, since `XMLHttpRequest` has XML in the name.

JSX is a syntax extension for JavaScript that allows developers to write HTML-like code within their JavaScript code. It was originally developed by Meta to be used with React, but it has since been adopted by other libraries and frameworks as well. JSX is not a separate language, but rather a syntax extension that is transformed into regular JavaScript code by a compiler or transpiler. When JSX code is compiled, it is transformed into plain JavaScript code. We'll get into the details of this later.

While JSX syntax looks similar to HTML, there are some key differences. For example, JSX uses curly braces {} to embed JavaScript expressions within the HTML-like code. Additionally, JSX attributes are written in camel case instead of HTML attributes: `onclick` in HTML is `onClick` in JSX. HTML elements are written in lowercase instead of title case like custom JSX elements or components: `div` is HTML, `Div` is a React component.

Further, we should mention that it is possible to create React applications without JSX, but the code tends to become hard to read, reason about, and maintain. Still, if we want to, we can. Let's look at a React component expressed with JSX and without.

Here's an example of a list with JSX:

```
const MyComponent = () => (
  <section id="list">
    <h1>This is my list!</h1>
    <p>Isn't my list amazing? It contains amazing things!</p>
    <ul>
      {amazingThings.map((t) => (
        <li key={t.id}>{t.label}</li>
      ))}
    </ul>
  </section>
);
```

Here's an example of the same list without JSX:

```
const MyComponent = () =>
  React.createElement(
    "section",
    { id: "list" },
    React.createElement("h1", {}, "This is my list!"),
    React.createElement(
      "p",
      {},
      "Isn't my list amazing? It contains amazing things!"
    ),
    React.createElement(
      "ul",
```

```
      {},
      amazingThings.map((t) =>
        React.createElement("li", { key: t.id }, t.label)
      )
    )
  )
);
```

For the sake of clarity, we've used an earlier JSX transform to illustrate how React was written without JSX. We'll get into transforms in detail later in this chapter, but for now let's establish that a transform is something that takes syntax A and turns it into syntax B.

Nowadays, React ships with a newer transform introduced in React 17 that automatically imports some special functions to essentially do the same thing. This is a minor detail in the grand scheme of things, but with the newer transformer, we'd express the list without JSX like so:

```
import { jsx as _jsx } from "react/jsx-runtime";
import { jsxs as _jsxs } from "react/jsx-runtime";

const MyComponent = () =>
  _jsxs("section", {
    id: "list",
    children: [
      _jsx("h1", {
        children: "This is my list!",
      }),
      _jsx("p", {
        children: "Isn't my list amazing? It contains amazing things!",
      }),
      _jsx("ul", {
        children: amazingThings.map((t) =>
          _jsx(
            "li",
            {
              children: t.label,
            },
            t.id
          )
        ),
      }),
    ],
  });
```

Either way, do you see the difference between examples with and without JSX? You might find the first example with JSX far more readable and maintainable than the latter. The former is JSX, the latter is vanilla JS. Let's talk about its trade-offs.

Benefits of JSX

There are several benefits to using JSX in web development:

Easier to read and write
> JSX syntax is easier to read and write, especially for developers who are familiar with HTML.

Improved security
> JSX code can be compiled into safer JavaScript code that produces HTML strings that have dangerous characters removed, like < and >, which could create new elements. Instead, these HTML strings replace the angular brackets with the less-than and greater-than signs in this scenario to make things safer. This process is called sanitization.

Strong typing
> JSX allows for strong typing, which can help catch errors before they occur. This is because JSX can be expressed with TypeScript, but even without TypeScript it can still benefit from enhanced type safety through the use of JSDoc-style comments and `propTypes`.

Encourages component-based architecture
> JSX encourages a component-based architecture, which can help make code more modular and easier to maintain.

Widely used
> JSX is widely used in the React community and is also supported by other libraries and frameworks.

Drawbacks of JSX

There are also some drawbacks to using JSX:

Learning curve
> Developers who are not familiar with JSX may find it difficult to learn and understand.

Requires tooling
> JSX code must be compiled into regular JavaScript code before it can be executed, which adds an extra step to the development toolchain. Other alternatives, like Vue.js, for example, can work immediately in a browser environment when included as nothing more than a `<script>` tag in a page.

Mixing of concerns
> Some developers argue that JSX mixes concerns by combining HTML-like code with JavaScript code, making it harder to separate presentation from logic.

Partial JavaScript compatibility

> JSX supports inline expressions, but not inline blocks. That is, inside a tree of JSX elements, we can have inline expression, but not if or switch blocks. This can be somewhat difficult to reason about for engineers newer to JSX.

Despite its drawbacks, JSX has become a popular choice for web developers, particularly those of us working with React. It offers a powerful and flexible way to create components and build user interfaces, and has been embraced by a large and active community. In addition to its use with React, JSX has also been adopted by other libraries and frameworks, including Vue.js, Solid, Qwik, and more. This shows that JSX has wider applications beyond just React, and its popularity is likely to continue to grow in the coming years, even breaking out of the React and web ecosystem by influencing implementations like SwiftUI in the iOS space and more.

Overall, JSX is a powerful and flexible tool that can help us build dynamic and responsive user interfaces. JSX was created with one job: make expressing, presenting, and maintaining the code for React components simple while preserving powerful capabilities such as iteration, computation, and inline execution.

JSX becomes vanilla JavaScript before it makes it to the browser. How does it accomplish this? Let's take a look under the hood!

Under the Hood

How does one make a language extension? How do they work? To answer these questions, we need to understand a little bit about programming languages. Specifically, we need to explore how, exactly, code like this outputs 3:

```
const a = 1;
let b = 2;

console.log(a + b);
```

Understanding this will help us understand JSX better, which will in turn help us understand React better, thereby increasing our fluency with React.

How Does Code Work?

The code snippet we just saw is literally just text. How is this interpreted by a computer and then executed? For starters, it's not a big, clever RegExp (regular expression) that can identify key words in a text file. I once tried to build a programming language this way and failed miserably, because regular expressions are often hard to get right, harder still to read back and mentally parse, and quite difficult to maintain because of the readability issues. For example, what follows is a regular expression to identify a valid email address. At first glance, it's almost impossible to know its purpose:

```
\[(?:[a-z0-9!#\$%&'\*\+-/=\?\^_`{\|}~]+(?:\.[a-z0-9!#\$%&'\*\+-/=\?\^_`{\|}~]+)\
*|"(?:[\x01-\x08\x0b\x0c\x0e-\x1f\x21\x23-\x5b\x5d-\x7f]|\\[\x01-\x09\x0b\x0c\x0
e-\x7f])\*")@(?:(?:[a-z0-9](?:[a-z0-9-]\*?[a-z0-9])?\.)\*?[a-z0-9](?:[a-z0-9-]\*
?[a-z0-9])?|\[(?:(?:25[0-5]|2[0-4][0-9]|[01]?[0-9][0-9]?)\.){3}(?:25[0-5]|2[0-4]
[0-9]|[01]?[0-9][0-9]?|[a-z0-9-]\*?[a-z0-9]:(?:[\x01-\x08\x0b\x0c\x0e-\x1f\x21-\
x5a\x53-\x7f]|\\[\x01-\x09\x0b\x0c\x0e-\x7f])\+)\])\]
```

That regular expression isn't even fully valid because the full version doesn't fit on the page! This is why instead of using regular expressions, code is compiled using a *compiler*. A compiler is a piece of software that translates source code written in a high-level programming language into a syntax tree (literally, a tree data structure like a JavaScript object) according to specific rules. The process of compiling code involves several steps, including lexical analysis, parsing, semantic analysis, optimization, and code generation. Let's explore each of these steps in more detail and discuss the role of compilers in the modern software development landscape.

A compiler uses a three-step process (at least in JavaScript anyway) that is in play here. These steps are called *tokenization, parsing,* and *code generation*. Let's look at each of these steps in more detail:

Tokenization

Essentially breaking up a string of characters into meaningful *tokens*. When a tokenizer is stateful and each token contains state about its parents and/or children, a tokenizer is called a *lexer*. This is a necessary simplification for the purposes of our discussion here: lexing is essentially stateful tokenization.

Lexers have *lexer rules* that, in some cases, indeed use a regular expression or similar to detect key tokens like variable names, object keys and values, and more in a text string representing a programming language. The lexer then maps these key words to some type of enumerable value, depending on its implementation. For example, `const` becomes 0, `let` becomes 1, `function` becomes 2, etc.

Once a string is tokenized or lexed, we move on to the next step, parsing.

Parsing

The process of taking the tokens and converting them into a syntax tree. The syntax tree is a data structure that represents the structure of the code. For example, the code snippet we looked at earlier would be represented as a syntax tree, like this:

```
{
type: "Program",
body: [
    {
    type: "VariableDeclaration",
    declarations: [
        {
        type: "VariableDeclarator",
        id: {
```

```
                    type: "Identifier",
                    name: "a"
                },
                init: {
                    type: "Literal",
                    value: 1,
                    raw: "1"
                }
            }
        ],
        kind: "const"
    },
    {
    type: "VariableDeclaration",
    declarations: [
            {
            type: "VariableDeclarator",
            id: {
                    type: "Identifier",
                    name: "b"
                },
                init: {
                    type: "Literal",
                    value: 2,
                    raw: "2"
                }
            }
        ],
        kind: "let"
    },
    {
    type: "ExpressionStatement",
    expression: {
            type: "CallExpression",
            callee: {
            type: "Identifier",
            name: "console"
                },
                arguments: [
                {
                    type: "BinaryExpression",
                    left: {
                    type: "Identifier",
                    name: "a"
                    },
                    right: {
                    type: "Identifier",
                    name: "b"
                    },
                    operator: "+"
                }
            ]
```

```
          }
        }
      ]
    }
```

The string, thanks to the parser, becomes a JSON object. As programmers, when we have a data structure like this, we can do some really fun things. Language engines use these data structures to complete the process with the third step, code generation.

Code generation
This is where the compiler generates machine code from the abstract syntax tree (AST). This involves translating the code in the AST into a series of instructions that can be executed directly by the computer's processor. The resulting machine code is then executed by the JavaScript engine. Overall, the process of converting an AST into machine code is complex and involves many different steps. However, modern compilers are highly sophisticated and can produce highly optimized code that runs efficiently on a wide range of hardware architectures.

There are several types of compilers, each with different characteristics and use cases. Some of the most common types of compilers include:

Native compilers
These compilers produce machine code that can be executed directly by the target platform's processor. Native compilers are typically used to create standalone applications or system-level software.

Cross-compilers
These compilers produce machine code for a different platform than the one on which the compiler is running. Cross-compilers are often used in embedded systems development or when targeting specialized hardware.

Just-in-Time (JIT) compilers
These compilers translate code into machine code at runtime, rather than ahead of time. JIT compilers are commonly used in virtual machines, such as the Java virtual machine, and can offer significant performance advantages over traditional interpreters.

Interpreters
These programs execute source code directly, without the need for compilation. Interpreters are typically slower than compilers, but offer greater flexibility and ease of use.

To execute JavaScript code efficiently, many modern environments, including web browsers, utilize JIT compilers. In these systems, JavaScript source code might first be translated into an intermediate representation, such as bytecode. The JIT compiler then dynamically compiles this bytecode into machine code as the program runs.

This on-the-fly compilation allows the engine to make optimizations based on real-time information, such as variable types and frequently executed code paths. Some engines employ multiple stages of compilation, starting with a quick, nonoptimized compilation to begin execution swiftly, followed by more optimized compilation for frequently executed code segments. This dynamic approach allows JavaScript engines to achieve impressive performance for a wide range of applications.

Runtimes usually interface with engines to provide more contextual helpers and features for their specific environment. The most popular JavaScript runtime, by far, is the common web browser, such as Google Chrome: it ships the Chromium *runtime* that interfaces with the engine. Similarly, on the server side we use the Node.js runtime that still uses the v8 *engine*. What more engines and runtimes can you identify in the wild?

Runtimes give JavaScript engines context, like the `window` object and the `document` object that browser runtimes ship with. If you've worked with both browsers and Node.js before, you may have noticed Node.js does not have a global `window` object. This is because it's a different runtime and, as such, provides different context. Cloudflare created a similar runtime called *Workers* whose sole responsibility is executing JavaScript on globally distributed machines called edge servers, with Bun and Deno being even more alternative runtimes—but we're digressing. How does this all relate to JSX?

Extending JavaScript Syntax with JSX

Now that we understand how we would extend JavaScript syntax, how does JSX work? How would we do it? To extend JavaScript syntax, we'd need to either have a different engine that can understand our new syntax, or deal with our new syntax before it reaches the engine. The former is nearly impossible to do because engines require a lot of thought to create and maintain since they tend to be widely used. If we decided to go with that option, it might take years or decades before we can use our extended syntax! We'd then have to make sure our "bespoke special engine" is used everywhere. How would we convince browser vendors and other stakeholders to switch to our unpopular new thing? This wouldn't work.

The latter is quicker: let's explore how we can deal with our new syntax before it reaches the engine. To do this, we need to create our own lexer and parser that can understand our extended language: that is, take a text string of code and understand it. Then, instead of generating machine code as is traditional, we can take this syntax tree and instead generate plain old regular vanilla JavaScript that all current engines can understand. This is precisely what *Babel* in the JavaScript ecosystem does, along with other tools like TypeScript, Traceur, and swc (see Figure 2-1).

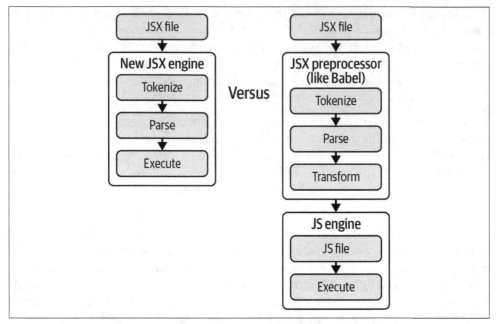

Figure 2-1. Creating a new JSX engine versus using a JS preprocessor

Because of this, JSX cannot be used directly in the browser, but instead requires a "build step" where a custom parser runs against it, then compiles it into a syntax tree. This code is then transformed into vanilla JavaScript in a final, distributable bundle. This is called *transpilation*: transformed, then compiled code.

To be clear, transpilation is the process of taking source code written in one language and transforming it into another language that has a similar level of abstraction. That's why it's also known as *source-to-source compilation*.

Formally, it's a type of translator. This generic term could refer to a compiler, assembler, or interpreter, for example. Conceptually, it's near-identical to compiling, except the target language is something on a similar abstraction level like the source language.

For example, TypeScript is a high-level language that, when transpiled, is turned into JavaScript (another high-level language). Babel's transpilation of ES6 JavaScript code into ES5 JavaScript is another example.

Now that we understand how we can build our own extension of JavaScript, let's look at what we can do with this specific extension JSX.

The JSX Pragma

It all starts with <, which, on its own, is an unrecognizable character in JavaScript when used outside of comparison operations. When a JavaScript engine encounters this, it throws a `SyntaxError: Unexpected token '<'`. In JSX, this "JSX pragma" can be transpiled into a function call. A pragma is a compiler directive to provide additional information to the compiler, usually beyond what is conveyed in the language itself. It can, for example, tell the compiler how it should handle some contents of a file.

Examples of this in JavaScript are the "use strict" pragmas that we sometimes see atop older modules, and the recent "use client" pragma in the context of React Server Components (RSCs). More on those in Chapter 9.

The name of the function to call when a parser sees a < pragma is configurable, and defaults to the function `React.createElement` or `_jsxs` with the newer transform, as discussed earlier. The signature of this function is expected to be this:

```
function pragma(tag, props, ...children)
```

That is, it receives `tag`, `props`, and `children` as arguments. Here's how JSX maps to regular JavaScript syntax. The following JSX code:

```
<MyComponent prop="value">contents</MyComponent>
```

becomes the following JavaScript code:

```
React.createElement(MyComponent, { prop: "value" }, "contents");
```

Notice the mapping between the tag (MyComponent), the props (prop="value"), and the children ("contents"). This is essentially the role of the JSX pragma: syntax sugar over multiple, recursive function calls. The JSX pragma is effectively an alias: < instead of `React.createElement`.

Expressions

One of the most powerful features of JSX is the ability to execute code inside a tree of elements. To iterate over a list as we did in "Under the Hood" on page 43, we can put executable code inside curly braces like we did with our `map` earlier in this chapter. If we want to show a sum of two numbers in JSX, we'd do it like this:

```
const a = 1;
const b = 2;

const MyComponent = () => <Box>Here's an expression: {a + b}</Box>;
```

This will render `Here's an expression: 3`, because the stuff inside curly brackets is executed as an expression. Using JSX expressions, we can iterate over lists and

execute a variety of expressions, including conditional checks with ternary operations, string replacement, and more.

Here's another example with a conditional check using a ternary operation:

```
const a = 1;
const b = 2;

const MyComponent = () => <Box>Is b more than a? {b > a ? "YES" : "NO"}</Box>;
```

This will render Is b more than a? YES since the comparison is an evaluated
expression. For posterity, it's worth mentioning here that JSX expressions are exactly
that—expressions. It's not possible to execute statements inside of a JSX element tree.
This will not work:

```
const MyComponent = () => <Box>Here's an expression: {
    const a = 1;
    const b = 2;

    if (a > b) {
        3
    }
}</Box>;
```

It doesn't work because statements do not return anything and are considered side
effects: they set state without yielding a value. After statements and computations,
how would we print a value inline? Notice that in the example, we just put the number 3 in there on line 6. How is our renderer supposed to know we intend to print 3?
This is why expressions are evaluated, but statements are not.

Chapter Review

OK, we've covered a fair amount of ground on the topic of JSX. We should be feeling
pretty confident (or even fluent, if you will) about the topic, to the point where we
can confidently explain aspects of it.

Review Questions

Let's make sure you've fully grasped the topics we covered. Take a moment to answer
the following questions:

1. What is JSX? What are some of its pros and cons?
2. What is the difference between JSX and HTML?
3. How does a string of text become machine code?
4. What are JSX expressions, and what benefits do they provide?

If you have trouble answering these questions, this chapter may be worth another read. If not, let's explore the next chapter.

Up Next

Now that we're pretty fluent with JSX, let's turn our attention to the next aspect of React and see how we can squeeze the most knowledge out of it to further boost our fluency. Let's explore the virtual DOM.

CHAPTER 3

The Virtual DOM

In this chapter, we'll dive deep into the concept of virtual DOM, sometimes called vDOM, and its significance in React. We'll also explore how React uses the virtual DOM to make web development easier and more efficient.

As web applications become more complex, it becomes increasingly difficult to manage the "real DOM," which is a complex and error-prone process as we'll see soon enough, and as we crudely covered in Chapter 1. React's virtual DOM provides a solution to this problem.

Throughout this chapter, we'll explore the workings of React's virtual DOM, its advantages over the real DOM, and how it is implemented. We'll also cover how React optimizes performance around the real DOM using the virtual DOM and how it all fits together.

Through a series of code examples and detailed explanations, we'll understand the virtual DOM's role in React and how to take advantage of its benefits to create robust and efficient web applications. Let's get started!

An Intro to the Virtual DOM

The virtual DOM, like the DOM, is an HTML document modeled as a JavaScript object: this is literally what Document Object Model (DOM) means. The DOM itself is the browser runtime's model of the document. The virtual DOM is a lightweight copy of this, with the key difference that while the real DOM is made up of Node objects, the virtual DOM is made up of plain JS objects that act as descriptions. It allows web developers to create user interfaces in a more efficient and performant way, as we'll discover in this chapter.

In React, whenever we tell it to make a change to the UI via `setState` or some other mechanism, the virtual DOM is updated first, and then the real DOM is updated to match the changes in the virtual DOM. This process is called *reconciliation*, the subject of Chapter 4.

The reason for updating the virtual DOM first is that updates to the real DOM can be somewhat slow and expensive. We'll cover this in the next section, but the gist of it is that every time a change is made to the real DOM, the browser has to recalculate the layout of the page, repaint the screen, and perform other operations that can be time-consuming.

For example, just reading an element's `offsetWidth` can trigger a reflow, which is a process where the browser recalculates the layout of all or part of the document, potentially affecting performance and making direct DOM interactions less efficient:

```
const btn = document.getElementById("myButton");
const width = btn.offsetWidth; // This can trigger a reflow
```

On the other hand, updating the virtual DOM is much faster because it doesn't involve any changes to the actual page layout. Instead, it is a simple JavaScript object that can be manipulated quickly and efficiently through various algorithmic approaches that can make the best use of the JavaScript engine available and increase its efficiency over time, decoupled from the browsers and other host environments.

When updates are made to the virtual DOM, React uses a diffing algorithm to identify the differences between the old and new versions of the virtual DOM. This algorithm then determines the minimal set of changes required to update the real DOM, and these changes are applied in a batched and optimized way to minimize the performance impact.

In this chapter, we will explore the differences between the virtual DOM and the real DOM, the pitfalls of the real DOM, and how the virtual DOM helps create better user interfaces. We will also dive into React's implementation of the virtual DOM and the algorithms it uses for efficient updates.

The Real DOM

When an HTML page is loaded into a web browser, it is parsed and converted into a tree of nodes and objects—an *object model*—which is the DOM: just a big JavaScript object. The DOM is a live representation of the web page, meaning that it is constantly being updated as users interact with the page.

Here is an example of the real DOM for a simple HTML page:

```
<!DOCTYPE html>
<html>
  <head>
    <title>Example Page</title>
```

```
    </head>
    <body>
      <h1 class="heading">Welcome to my page!</h1>
      <p>This is an example paragraph.</p>
      <ul>
        <li>Item 1</li>
        <li>Item 2</li>
        <li>Item 3</li>
      </ul>
    </body>
  </html>
```

In this example, the real DOM is represented by a tree-like structure that consists of nodes for each HTML element in the page. This is what the tree structure could look like, though it's oversimplified for the purposes of understanding. The actual DOM has far more properties and methods per node. Still, this should help us understand how a document is modeled as an object:

```
const dom = {
  type: "document",
  doctype: "html",
  children: [
    {
      type: "element",
      tagName: "html",
      children: [
        {
          type: "element",
          tagName: "head",
          children: [
            {
              type: "element",
              tagName: "title",
              children: "Example Page",
            },
          ],
        },
        {
          type: "element",
          tagName: "body",
          children: [
            {
              type: "element",
              tagName: "h1",
              innerHTML: "Welcome to my page!",
              children: [],
              className: "heading",
            },
            {
              type: "element",
              tagName: "p",
              children: "This is an example paragraph.",
```

```
    },
    {
      type: "element",
      tagName: "ul",
      children: [
        {
          type: "element",
          tagName: "li",
          children: "Item 1",
        },
        {
          type: "element",
          tagName: "li",
          children: "Item 2",
        },
        // ...you can fill in the rest
      ],
    },
  ],
},
  ],
};
```

Each node in the tree represents an HTML element, and it contains properties and methods that allow it to be manipulated through JavaScript. For example, we can use the document.querySelector() method to retrieve a specific node from the real DOM and modify its contents:

```
// Retrieve the <h1> node
const h1Node = document.querySelector(".heading");

// Modify its contents
if (h1Node) {
  h1Node.innerHTML = "Updated Heading!";
}

console.log(h1Node);
```

In this example, we retrieve the h1 element with the class of "heading" using the document.querySelector() method. We then modify the contents of the element by setting its innerHTML property to "Updated Heading!". This changes the text displayed on the page from "Welcome to my page!" to "Updated Heading!".

That doesn't seem too complicated, but there are a few things to note here. First, we are using the document.querySelector() method to retrieve the element from the real DOM. This method accepts a CSS selector as an argument and returns the first element that matches the selector. In this case, we are passing in the class selector .heading, which matches the h1 element with the class of "heading".

There's a bit of a danger here, because while the `document.querySelector` method is a powerful tool for selecting elements in the real DOM based on CSS selectors, one potential performance issue with this method is that it can be slow when working with large and complex documents. The method has to start at the top of the document and traverse downward to find the desired element, which can be a time-consuming process.

When we call `document.querySelector()` with a CSS selector, the browser has to search the entire document tree for matching elements. This means that the search can be slow, especially if the document is large and has a complex structure. In addition, the browser has to evaluate the selector itself, which can be a complex process, depending on the complexity of the selector.

In contrast, `document.getElementById` does not require validation like CSS selectors, and has increased specificity since `id` attributes are expected to be unique, so it is generally more efficient.

In terms of runtime complexity using Big O notation, `getElementById` is often approximated as $(O(1))$ in modern browsers, given that they likely employ hashing mechanisms, such as hash tables, for efficient ID→element mapping. While ideal hash table lookups are $(O(1))$ on average, it's important to consider that worst-case scenarios, like hash collisions, can lead to longer lookups. Given that browsers don't really enforce ID uniqueness, these hash collisions can be more than likely.

Nevertheless, with advanced hashing functions and resizing strategies in modern browsers, these cases are rare.

 For those of us who didn't go to computer school and maybe don't understand Big O, it's a handy tool used by developers to gauge how fast or slow a piece of code will run, especially as the amount of data the code has to work with increases. Essentially, Big O notation gives a high-level understanding of algorithms in terms of both time complexity (how the execution time grows with the size of the input) and space complexity (how the amount of memory used grows with the size of the input). It's often expressed using terms like $(O(1))$, $(O(n))$, $(O(n\ n))$, or $(O(n^2))$, where (n) is the size of the input. So when developers talk about code being "efficient" or "scalable," they're often referring to these Big O values, aiming for algorithms with lower time and space complexity to ensure that their software remains performant even as it handles more and more data.

Also, since IDs are supposed to be unique, they're not really well suited to having multiple reusable components on a page. This is where `querySelector` shines, as it can be used to select multiple elements with the same class name, for example.

That said, `querySelector`, which can accept a broad range of CSS selectors, has a variable complexity. In the worst-case scenario, where the method may need to traverse the entire DOM to ensure a match or the absence thereof, its complexity can be $(O(n))$, where (n) is the number of elements in the DOM. However, the actual runtime can be less than $(O(n))$ for more specific selectors or if a match is found early in the DOM tree. That said, there's still the added computational cost of parsing and validating the selectors themselves.

It's worth noting that the performance difference between `document.getElementById` and `document.querySelector` may be negligible in small documents or when searching for elements in specific areas of the document tree. However, in larger and more complex documents, the difference can become more pronounced.

Some would say that this whole "CPU efficiency" argument is overblown, and that it's not worth worrying about. While this may or may not be true, no one can question the additional value that React's virtual DOM provides with being able to componentize logic and avoid worrying about managing state in an environment as volatile as the DOM. We say the DOM is volatile because it is affected by so many things, including user interactions, network requests, client-side scripts, and other events that can cause it to change at any time. React, through the virtual DOM, protects us from this environment using the virtual DOM.

We're diving deep into these nuanced details because to be truly fluent with React, it's important to understand the overall complexity of the DOM. Working intelligently with the DOM is no small feat, and with React, we have a choice to either navigate this minefield ourselves and occasionally step on landmines, or to use a tool that helps us navigate the DOM safely using the virtual DOM.

While we've discussed some small nuances in how we select elements here, we haven't had an opportunity to dive deeper into the pitfalls of working with the DOM directly. Let's do this quickly to fully understand the value that React's virtual DOM provides.

Pitfalls of the Real DOM

The real DOM has several pitfalls that can make it difficult to build a high-performance web application. Some of these pitfalls include performance issues, cross-browser compatibility, and security vulnerabilities, where manipulating the DOM directly could present cross-site scripting (XSS) vulnerabilities.

Performance

One of the biggest issues with the real DOM is its performance. Whenever a change is made to the DOM, such as adding or removing an element, or changing the text or attributes of an element, the browser has to recalculate the layout and repaint the affected parts of the page. This can be a slow and resource-intensive process, especially for large and complex web pages.

As mentioned earlier, reading a DOM element's `offsetWidth` property may seem like a simple operation, but it can actually trigger a costly recalculation of the layout by the browser. This is because `offsetWidth` is a computed property that depends on the layout of the element and its ancestors, which means that the browser needs to ensure that the layout information is up-to-date before it can return an accurate value.

In the worst-case scenario, reading an element's `offsetWidth` property with Big O notation would be estimated as ($O(n)$). This is because accessing this property can potentially trigger a reflow in the browser, which involves recalculating layout positions for a number of elements on the page. In this context, (n) represents the number of DOM elements affected by the reflow. Even though the direct property access is quick, the associated side effects, like a reflow, can make the operation scale with the number of elements on the page.

If you're looking to avoid the potential reflow triggered by accessing layout properties like `offsetWidth`, we can employ certain techniques to make the operation more performant. Here's one approach using the `getBoundingClientRect()` method, which can batch layout reads and writes:

```
// Accessing layout properties in a more performant way
function getOffsetWidthWithoutTriggeringReflow(element) {
  let width;

  // Batch all reading operations
  const rect = element.getBoundingClientRect();
  width = rect.width;

  // ... any other reading operations

  // Followed by writing operations, if any

  return width;
}

const element = document.querySelector(".myElement");
const width = getOffsetWidthWithoutTriggeringReflow(element);
console.log(width);
```

By using `getBoundingClientRect()`, we retrieve multiple layout properties in a single call, reducing the chances of triggering multiple reflows. Additionally, by batching reading and writing operations separately, we can further minimize *layout thrashing*, which is the repeated and unnecessary recalculations of layout caused by frequent interleaved reading and writing of layout properties (see Figure 3-1). This thrashing can significantly degrade the performance of a web page, leading to a sluggish user experience. By strategically accessing layout properties and batching our operations, we can keep our web interactions smooth and responsive.

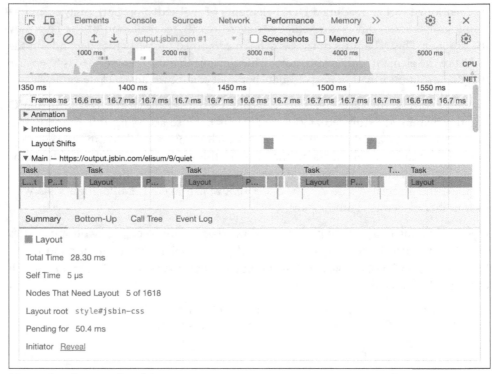

Figure 3-1. Layout thrashing

However, even `getBoundingClientRect()` can cause a reflow if there are pending layout changes. The key to performance here is to minimize the number of times you force the browser to recalculate layout, and when you do, try to retrieve as much information as you need in one go.

React handles all of this for us out of the box using the virtual DOM as an intermediate layer between real DOM operations.

Consider the following example, where we have a simple HTML document with a single `div` element:

```
<!DOCTYPE html>
<html>
  <head>
    <title>Reading offsetWidth example</title>
    <style>
      #my-div {
        width: 100px;
        height: 100px;
```

```
        background-color: red;
      }
    </style>
  </head>
  <body>
    <div id="my-div"></div>
    <script>
      var div = document.getElementById("my-div");
      console.log(div.offsetWidth);
    </script>
  </body>
</html>
```

When we load this document in a browser and open the developer console, we can see that the `offsetWidth` property of the `div` element is logged to the console. However, what we don't see is the behind-the-scenes work that the browser has to do to compute the value of `offsetWidth`.

To understand this work, we can use the Performance panel in our developer tools to record a timeline of the browser's activities as it loads and renders the page. When we do that, we can see that the browser is performing several layout and paint operations as it processes the document. In particular, we can see that there are two layout operations that correspond to reading `offsetWidth` in the script.

Each of these layout operations takes some time to complete (in this case, about 2 ms), even though they are just reading the value of a property. This is because the browser needs to ensure that the layout information is up-to-date before it can return an accurate value, which requires it to perform a full layout of the document. Although 2 milliseconds might not seem like a big deal, at scale it adds up.

In general, we should be careful when reading layout-dependent properties like `offsetWidth`, because they can cause unexpected performance problems. If we need to read the value of such properties multiple times, we should consider caching the value in a variable to avoid triggering unnecessary layout recalculations. Alternatively, we can use the `requestAnimationFrame` API to defer the reading of the property until the next animation frame, when the browser has already performed the necessary layout calculations.

To understand more about accidental performance issues with the real DOM, let's take a look at some examples. Consider the following HTML document:

```
<!DOCTYPE html>
<html>
  <head>
    <title>Example</title>
  </head>
  <body>
    <ul id="list">
      <li>Item 1</li>
```

```
      <li>Item 2</li>
      <li>Item 3</li>
    </ul>
  </body>
</html>
```

Suppose we want to add a new item to the list using JavaScript. We might write the following code:

```
const list = document.getElementById("list");
const newItem = document.createElement("li");
newItem.textContent = "Item 4";
list.appendChild(newItem);
```

Notice we're using `getElementById` instead of `querySelector` here because:

- We know the ID
- We know the performance trade-offs

Let's keep going.

This code selects the `ul` element with the ID `"list"`, creates a new `li` element, sets its text content to `"Item 4"`, and appends it to the list. When we run this code, the browser has to recalculate the layout and repaint the affected parts of the page to display the new item.

This process can be slow and resource intensive, especially for larger lists. For example, suppose we have a list with 1,000 items, and we want to add a new item to the end of the list. We might write the following code:

```
const list = document.getElementById("list");
const newItem = document.createElement("li");
newItem.textContent = "Item 1001";
list.appendChild(newItem);
```

When we run this code, the browser has to recalculate the layout and repaint the entire list, even though only one item has been added. This can take a significant amount of time and resources, especially on slower devices or with larger lists.

To further illustrate this issue, consider the following example:

```
<!DOCTYPE html>
<html>
  <head>
    <title>Example</title>
    <style>
      #list li {
        background-color: #f5f5f5;
      }
      .highlight {
        background-color: yellow;
      }
```

```
      </style>
    </head>
    <body>
      <ul id="list">
        <li>Item 1</li>
        <li>Item 2</li>
        <li>Item 3</li>
      </ul>
      <button onclick="highlight()">Highlight Item 2</button>
      <script>
        function highlight() {
          const item = document.querySelector("#list li:nth-child(2)");
          item.classList.add("highlight");
        }
      </script>
    </body>
  </html>
```

In this example, we have a list with three items and a button that highlights the second item when clicked. When the button is clicked, the browser has to recalculate the layout and repaint the entire list, even though only one item has changed. This can cause a noticeable delay or flicker in the UI, which can be frustrating for users.

Overall, the performance issues of the real DOM can be a significant challenge for us, especially when dealing with large and complex web pages. While there are techniques for mitigating these issues, such as optimizing selectors, using event delegation, batching read/write DOM operations, or using CSS animations, they can be complex and difficult to implement.

As a result, many of us have turned to the virtual DOM as a solution to these issues. The virtual DOM allows us to create UIs that are more efficient and performant by abstracting away the complexities of the real DOM and providing a more lightweight way of representing the UI.

But...is it really necessary to save a few milliseconds? Well, CPU/processing performance is a critical factor that can greatly impact the success of an application. In today's digital age, where users expect fast and responsive websites, it's essential for us web developers to prioritize CPU efficiency to ensure that our applications run smoothly and responsively. An excellent article titled "Milliseconds make millions" (*https://oreil.ly/BtXCh*) on the Google web develpment blog adds further credibility to these claims.

Direct DOM manipulation that triggers layout recalculation (called reflows) and repaints can lead to increased CPU usage and processing times, which can cause delays and even crashes for users. This can be particularly problematic for users on low-powered devices, such as smartphones or tablets, which may have limited processing power and memory. In many parts of the world, users may be accessing our web apps on older or less capable devices, which can further compound the problem.

By prioritizing CPU efficiency, we can create applications that are accessible to users on a wide range of devices, regardless of their processing power or memory. This can lead to increased engagement, higher conversion rates, and ultimately, a more successful online presence.

React's virtual DOM has enabled building CPU-efficient web applications; using its efficient rendering algorithms can help minimize processing times and improve overall performance.

Cross-browser compatibility

Another issue with the real DOM is cross-browser compatibility. Different browsers model documents differently, which can lead to inconsistencies and bugs in web applications. This was far more common when React was released and is far less common now. Still, this can and did make it difficult for developers to create web applications that work seamlessly across different browsers and platforms.

One of the primary issues with cross-browser compatibility is that certain DOM elements and attributes may not be supported by all browsers. As a result, we had to spend additional time and effort implementing workarounds and fallbacks to ensure that applications function correctly on all target platforms.

This is exactly what React solves using its synthetic event system. `SyntheticEvent` is a wrapper around browsers' native events, designed to ensure consistency across different browsers. It addresses inconsistencies between browsers using the following mechanisms:

Unified interface
   In raw JavaScript, handling browser events can be tricky due to inconsistencies. For instance, accessing event properties might differ across browsers. Some might use `event.target`, while others use `event.srcElement`. `SyntheticEvent` abstracts these differences, providing a consistent way to interact with events and ensuring that developers don't have to write browser-specific code:

```
// Without React, developers might need checks for
// browser-specific properties
const targetElement = event.target || event.srcElement;

// In React, thanks to SyntheticEvent, it's consistent
function handleClick(event) {
  const target = event.target;
  // ... rest of the code
}
```

By wrapping native events into the `SyntheticEvent` system, React shields developers from many of the inconsistencies and quirks of the native browser event systems.

Event delegation

Instead of attaching event listeners directly to elements, React listens for events at the root level. This approach sidesteps issues where some events might not be available on certain elements in older browsers.

Cross-functional enhancements

One of the areas where native browser events exhibit inconsistencies is in how they handle certain events across different input elements. A notable example is the onChange event:

- In raw JavaScript, the behavior of the onChange event differs between input types:
  - For `<input type="text">`, the onChange event in some browsers might trigger only after the input loses focus, rather than immediately upon value change.
  - For `<select>`, it might trigger whenever an option is selected, even if it's the same as the previous one.
  - In other cases, especially in older browsers, the onChange event might not trigger reliably for all user interactions on certain form elements.
- React's SyntheticEvent system normalizes the behavior of the onChange event across these input elements. In React:
  - The onChange event for a text input (`<input type="text">`) consistently fires with every keystroke, giving real-time feedback.
  - For `<select>`, it reliably triggers whenever a new option is chosen.
  - React ensures that onChange provides a consistent experience across other form elements as well.

    By doing so, React frees developers from dealing with these native inconsistencies, allowing them to focus on their application logic without worrying about browser-specific quirks.

Access to native events

If developers need the original browser event, it's available via event.native Event, ensuring flexibility without sacrificing the benefits of the abstraction.

In essence, SyntheticEvent offers a stable event system, ironing out the quirks and differences of native browser events. This is just one specific way that React uses its virtual DOM to provide conveniences to UI development.

So far, we've been discussing how working with the DOM directly can cause performance issues and cross-browser compatibility problems. Let's now explore a way to natively get around these issues in a more performant manner using document fragments, which can be considered something of a native precursor to understanding React's virtual DOM.

Document Fragments

As we've seen, direct manipulation of the DOM can be performance intensive, especially when multiple changes are involved. Every time the DOM is updated, the browser may need to perform layout recalculations, repaint the UI, and update the view, which can slow down the application. This is where document fragments come into play.

A *document fragment* is a lightweight container that holds DOM nodes. It acts like a temporary staging area where you can make multiple changes without affecting the main DOM. Once you're done, you can append the document fragment to the DOM, triggering a single reflow and repaint. Document fragments are very close to React's virtual DOM in this way.

Because document fragments are lightweight containers that allow us to batch updates, they present a number of performance benefits:

Batched updates
> Instead of making multiple individual updates to the live DOM, you can batch all your changes in a document fragment. This means only one reflow and repaint occurs, regardless of how many elements or changes you've made inside the fragment.

Memory efficiency
> When nodes are added to a document fragment, they're removed from their current parent in the DOM. This can help in optimizing memory usage, especially when reordering large sections of a document.

No redundant rendering
> Since the document fragment is not part of the active document tree, changes to it don't affect the live document, and styles and scripts aren't applied until the fragment is appended to the actual DOM. This avoids redundant style recalculations and script executions.

Consider a scenario where you need to add multiple list items to a list:

```
const fragment = document.createDocumentFragment();
for (let i = 0; i < 100; i++) {
  const li = document.createElement("li");
  li.textContent = `Item ${i + 1}`;
  fragment.appendChild(li);
}
document.getElementById("myList").appendChild(fragment);
```

In this example, the 100 list items are first appended to the document fragment. Only when all items are added does the fragment get appended to the main list. This results in a single update to the live DOM instead of 100 separate updates.

In this way, document fragments offer a way to efficiently manipulate the DOM by batching multiple changes together, thus reducing the number of costly reflows and repaints. For developers aiming for optimal performance in their web applications, leveraging document fragments can lead to smoother interactions and faster render times.

React's virtual DOM can be likened to an advanced implementation of the document fragment concept. Here's a brief connection:

Batched updates
> Similar to document fragments, React's virtual DOM batches multiple changes together. Instead of directly altering the live DOM on every state or prop change, React compiles these changes in the virtual DOM first.

Efficient diffs
> React then determines the differences (or "diffs") between the current virtual DOM and the real DOM. This diffing process ensures that only the necessary changes are made to the real DOM, analogous to how document fragments reduce direct DOM manipulations.

Single render
> Once the diffs are identified, React updates the actual DOM in a single batch, much like appending a fully populated document fragment. This minimizes costly reflows and repaints.

In essence, while document fragments offer a way to group and optimize a set of changes before updating the live DOM, React's virtual DOM takes this a step further by intelligently diffing and batching updates across the entire application's UI, ensuring maximal efficiency in rendering. Moreover, React turns all of this document fragment stuff into an implementation detail that we as everyday developers need not concern ourselves with, enabling us to build our products with more focus. With that, let's look at how the virtual DOM works in detail.

How the Virtual DOM Works

The virtual DOM is a technique that helps to mitigate the pitfalls of the real DOM. By creating a virtual representation of the DOM in memory, changes can be made to the virtual representation without directly modifying the real DOM, similar to document fragments. This allows the framework or library to update the real DOM in a more efficient and performant way, without causing the browser to do any work in recomputing the layout of the page and repainting the elements.

The virtual DOM also helps to improve the authoring experience of elements and their updates by providing a consistent API that abstracts away the differences between different browser implementations of the real DOM. For example, if docu ment.appendChild is different in another runtime, it doesn't matter when using JSX and the virtual DOM. This makes it easier for developers to create web applications that work seamlessly across different browsers and platforms.

React uses the virtual DOM to build user interfaces. In this section, we will explore how React's implementation of the virtual DOM works.

React Elements

In React, user interfaces are represented as a tree of *React elements*, which are light-weight representations of a component or HTML element. They are created using the React.createElement function and can be nested to create complex user interfaces.

Here is an example of a React element:

```
const element = React.createElement(
  "div",
  { className: "my-class" },
  "Hello, world!"
);
```

This creates a React element that represents a <div> element with a className of my-class and the text content Hello, world!.

From here, we can see the actual created element if we use console.log(element). It looks like this:

```
{
  $$typeof: Symbol(react.element),
  type: "div",
  key: null,
  ref: null,
  props: {
    className: "my-class",
    children: "Hello, world!"
  },
  _owner: null,
  _store: {}
}
```

This is a representation of a React element. React elements are the smallest building blocks of a React application, and they describe what should appear on the screen. Each element is a plain JavaScript object that describes the component it represents, along with any relevant props or attributes.

The React element shown in the code block is represented as an object with several properties:

$$typeof
> This is a symbol used by React to ensure that an object is a valid React element. In this case, it is `Symbol(react.element)`. `$$typeof` can have other values, depending on the type of the element:

> `Symbol(react.fragment)`
>> When the element represents a React fragment.

> `Symbol(react.portal)`
>> When the element represents a React portal.

> `Symbol(react.profiler)`
>> When the element represents a React profiler.

> `Symbol(react.provider)`
>> When the element represents a React context provider.

> In general, `$$typeof` serves as a type marker that identifies the type of the React element. We'll cover more of these in more detail later in the book.

type
> This property represents the type of the component that the element represents. In this case, it is `"div"`, indicating that this is a `<div>` DOM element, called a "host component." The `type` property of a React element can be either a string or a function (or a class, but we don't talk about that because it's being phased out). If it is a string, it represents the HTML tag name, like `"div"`, `"span"`, `"button"`, etc. When it is a function, it represents a custom React component, which is essentially just a JavaScript function that returns JSX.

> Here is an example of an element with a custom component type:

```
const MyComponent = (props) => {
  return <div>{props.text}</div>;
};

const myElement = <MyComponent text="Hello, world!" />;
```

> In this case, the type property of `myElement` is `MyComponent`, which is a function that defines a custom component. The value of `myElement` as a React element object would be:

```
{
  $$typeof: Symbol(react.element),
  type: MyComponent,
  key: null,
  ref: null,
```

```
      props: {
        text: "Hello, world!"
      },
      _owner: null,
      _store: {}
}
```

Note that type is set to the `MyComponent` function, which is the type of the component that the element represents, and `props` contains the props passed to the component, in this case `{ text: "Hello, world!" }`.

When React encounters an element with a function type, it will invoke that function with the element's `props`, and the return value will be used as the element's `children`, in this case, a `div`. This is how custom React components are rendered: React continually goes deeper and deeper and deeper with elements until scalar values are reached, which are then rendered as text nodes, or if `null` or `undefined` is reached, nothing is rendered.

Here is an example of an element with a string type:

```
const myElement = <div>Hello, world!</div>;
```

In this case, the type property of `myElement` is `"div"`, which is a string that represents an HTML tag name. When React encounters an element with a string type, it will create a corresponding HTML element with that tag name and render its children within that element.

ref

This property lets the parent component request a reference to the underlying DOM node. It is generally used in cases where direct manipulation of the DOM is necessary. In this case, the `ref` is `null`.

props

This property is an object that contains all of the attributes and props that were passed to the component. In this case, it has two properties: `className` and `children`. `className` specifies the class name of the element, and `children` contains the content of the element.

_owner

This property, only accessible in nonproduction builds of React, is used internally by React to track the component that created this element. This information is used to determine which component should be responsible for updating the element when its props or state change.

Here is an example that demonstrates how the _owner property is used:

```
function Parent() {
  return <Child />;
}

function Child() {
  const element = <div>Hello, world!</div>;
  console.log(element._owner); // Parent
  return element;
}
```

In this example, the Child component creates a React element representing a <div> element with the text "Hello, world!". The _owner property of this element is set to the Parent component, which is the component that created the Child component.

React uses this information to determine which component should be responsible for updating the element when its props or state change. In this case, if the Parent component updates its state or receives new props, React will update the Child component and its associated element.

It's important to note that the _owner property is an internal implementation detail of React and should not be relied upon in application code.

_store

The _store property of a React element object is an object that is used internally by React to store additional data about the element. The specific properties and values stored in _store are not part of the public API and should not be accessed directly.

Here's an example of what the _store property might look like:

```
{
  validation: null,
  key: null,
  originalProps: { className: 'my-class', children: 'Hello, world!' },
  props: { className: 'my-class', children: 'Hello, world!' },
  _self: null,
  _source: { fileName: 'MyComponent.js', lineNumber: 10 },
  _owner: {
    _currentElement: [Circular], _debugID: 0, stateNode: [MyComponent]
  },
  _isStatic: false,
  _warnedAboutRefsInRender: false,
}
```

As you can see, _store includes various properties such as validation, key, originalProps, props, _self, _source, _owner, _isStatic, and _warned AboutRefsInRender. These properties are used by React internally to track various aspects of the element's state and context.

For example, _source in development mode is used to track the filename and line number where the element was created, which can be helpful for debugging. _owner is used to track the component that created the element, as discussed earlier. And props and originalProps are used to store the props passed to the component.

Again, it's important to note that _store is an internal implementation detail of React and should not be accessed directly in application code, and for this exact reason, we will refrain from going deeper here.

Virtual DOM Versus Real DOM

The React.createElement function and the DOM's built-in createElement method are similar in that they both create new elements; however, React.createElement creates React elements and document.createElement creates DOM nodes. They're vastly different in their implementation, but conceptually they're similar.

React.createElement is a function provided by React that creates a new virtual element in memory, whereas document.createElement is a method provided by the DOM API that creates a new element also in memory until it is attached to the DOM with APIs like document.appendChild or similar. Both functions take a tag name as their first argument, while React.createElement takes additional arguments to specify props and children.

For example, let's compare how we'd create a <div> element using both methods:

```
// Using React's createElement
const divElement = React.createElement(
  "div",
  { className: "my-class" },
  "Hello, World!"
);

// Using the DOM API's createElement
const divElement = document.createElement("div");
divElement.className = "my-class";
divElement.textContent = "Hello, World!";
```

The virtual DOM in React is similar in concept to the real DOM in that both represent a tree-like structure of elements. When a React component is rendered, React creates a new virtual DOM tree, compares it to the previous virtual DOM tree, and calculates the minimum number of changes needed to update the old tree to match the new. This is known as the *reconciliation process*. Here's an example of how this might work in a React component:

```
function App() {
  const [count, setCount] = useState(0);

  return (
    <div>
      <h1>Count: {count}</h1>
      <button onClick={() => setCount(count + 1)}>Increment</button>
    </div>
  );
}
```

For clarity, this component can also be expressed like so:

```
function App() {
  const [count, setCount] = React.useState(0);

  return React.createElement(
    "div",
    null,
    React.createElement("h1", null, "Count: ", count),
    React.createElement(
      "button",
      { onClick: () => setCount(count + 1) },
      "Increment"
    )
  );
}
```

In the `createElement` calls, the first argument is the name of the HTML tag or React component, the second argument is an object of properties (or `null` if no properties are needed), and any additional arguments represent child elements.

When the component is first rendered, React creates a virtual DOM tree like so:

```
div
├ h1
│  └ "Count: 0"
└ button
   └ "Increment"
```

When the button is clicked, React creates a new virtual DOM tree that looks like this:

```
div
├ h1
│  └ "Count: 1"
└ button
   └ "Increment"
```

React then calculates that only the text content of the h1 element needs to be updated, and updates only that part of the real DOM.

The use of a virtual DOM in React allows for efficient updates to the real DOM, as well as allowing React to work seamlessly with other libraries that also manipulate the DOM directly.

Efficient Updates

When a React component's state or props change, React creates a new tree of React elements that represents the updated user interface. This new tree is then compared to the previous tree to determine the minimal set of changes required to update the real DOM using a diffing algorithm.

This algorithm compares the new tree of React elements with the previous tree and identifies the differences between the two. It is a recursive comparison. If a node has changed, React updates the corresponding node in the real DOM. If a node has been added or removed, React adds or removes the corresponding node in the real DOM.

Diffing involves comparing the new tree with the old one node by node to find out which parts of the tree have changed.

React's diffing algorithm is highly optimized and aims to minimize the number of changes that need to be made to the real DOM. The algorithm works as follows:

- If the nodes at the root level of the two trees are different, React will replace the entire tree with the new one.
- If the nodes at the root level are the same, React will update the attributes of the node if they have changed.
- If the children of a node are different, React will update only the children that have changed. React does not re-create the entire subtree; it only updates the nodes that have changed.
- If the children of a node are the same, but their order has changed, React will reorder the nodes in the real DOM without actually re-creating them.
- If a node is removed from the tree, React will remove it from the real DOM.
- If a new node has been added to the tree, React will add it to the real DOM.
- If a node's type has changed (e.g., from a div to a span), React will remove the old node and create a new node of the new type.
- If the node has a key prop, React uses it to know if it should replace the node or not. It can be useful when you need to reset the state of the components.

React's diffing algorithm is efficient and allows React to update the real DOM quickly and with minimal changes. This helps to improve the performance of React applications and makes it easier to build complex, dynamic user interfaces.

Unnecessary rerenders

While React's diffing algorithm indeed plays a crucial role in efficiently updating the real DOM by minimizing the changes needed, there's a common challenge that developers may encounter: unnecessary rerenders.

This is the way React works by design: when a component's state changes, React rerenders the component and all of its descendants. By rerendering, we mean that React calls each function component recursively, passing each function component its props as an argument. React does not skip components whose props have not changed, but calls all function components that are children of a parent whose state or props change. This is because React doesn't know which components depend on the state of the component that changed, so it has to rerender all of them to ensure that the UI stays consistent.

This can present some significant performance challenges, especially when dealing with large and complex user interfaces. For example, ChildComponent in the following snippet will rerender every time the ParentComponent's state changes, even if the props passed to ChildComponent do not:

```
import React, { useState } from "react";

const ChildComponent = ({ message }) => {
  return <div>{message}</div>;
};

const ParentComponent = () => {
  const [count, setCount] = useState(0);

  return (
    <div>
      <button onClick={() => setCount(count + 1)}>Increment</button>
      <ChildComponent message="This is a static message" />
    </div>
  );
};

export default ParentComponent;
```

In this example:

- ParentComponent has a state variable count that is incremented every time the button is clicked.
- ChildComponent receives a static prop called message. Since this prop doesn't change, ideally, we wouldn't want ChildComponent to rerender every time Parent Component's state changes.
- However, due to React's default behavior, ChildComponent will rerender every time the ParentComponent rerenders, which happens on every state change.

- This is inefficient because `ChildComponent` does not depend on the `count` state from `ParentComponent`.

- Since `ChildComponent`'s props and state haven't changed, the render was pointless: it presumably returned the same result as last time, so this was wasted effort.

This is the problem that we often need to optimize, especially in larger applications where many components might be rerendering unnecessarily, leading to potential performance issues. Addressing this issue requires a thoughtful approach to managing component rerenders, ensuring that changes in state or props at a higher level in the component hierarchy do not result in widespread, unnecessary rerenders among descendant components. Through mindful structuring of components and judicious use of React's optimization features like `memo` and `useMemo`, developers can better manage rerenders and maintain high performance in their applications.

We cover this in more detail in Chapter 5.

Chapter Review

Throughout this chapter, we have explored the differences between the real DOM and the virtual DOM in web development, as well as the advantages of using the latter in React.

We first talked about the real DOM and its limitations, such as slow rendering times and cross-browser compatibility issues, which can make it difficult for developers to create web applications that work seamlessly across different browsers and platforms. To illustrate this, we examined how to create a simple web page using the real DOM APIs, and how these APIs can quickly become unwieldy and difficult to manage as the complexity of the page increases.

Next, we dove into the virtual DOM and how it addresses many of the limitations of the real DOM. We explored how React leverages the virtual DOM to improve performance by minimizing the number of updates needed to the real DOM, which can be expensive in terms of rendering time. We also looked at how React uses elements to compare the virtual DOM with the previous version and calculate the most efficient way to update the real DOM.

To illustrate the benefits of the virtual DOM, we examined how to create the same simple web page using React components. We compared this approach to the real DOM approach and saw how React components were more concise and easier to manage, even as the complexity of the page increased.

We also looked at the differences between `React.createElement` and `document.crea teElement`, and we saw how we could create components using JSX, which provides a syntax similar to HTML, making it easier to reason about the structure of the virtual DOM.

Finally, we looked at how React's diffing algorithm can lead to unnecessary rerenders, which can be a significant performance challenge, especially when dealing with large and complex user interfaces, and alluded to Chapter 5, where we'll explore how we can optimize this by using React's memo and useMemo features.

Overall, we have learned about the benefits of using the virtual DOM in web development, and how React leverages this concept to make building web applications easier and more efficient.

Review Questions

Let's take a moment to answer the following questions:

1. What is the DOM, and how does it compare to the virtual DOM?
2. What are document fragments, and how are they similar and different to React's virtual DOM?
3. What are some issues with the DOM?
4. How does the virtual DOM provide a faster way of performing user interface updates?
5. How does React rendering work? What potential problems can arise from this?

Up Next

In Chapter 4, we will dive deep into React reconciliation and its Fiber architecture.

CHAPTER 4

Inside Reconciliation

To be truly fluent in React, we need to understand *what* its functions do. So far, we've understood JSX and `React.createElement`. We've also understood the virtual DOM in some appreciable level of detail. Let's explore the practical applications of it in React in this chapter, and understand what `ReactDOM.createRoot(element).render()` does. Specifically, we'll explore *how* React builds its virtual DOM and then updates the real DOM through a process called reconciliation.

Understanding Reconciliation

As a quick recap, React's virtual DOM is a blueprint of our desired UI state. React takes this blueprint and, through a process called *reconciliation*, makes it a reality in a given host environment; usually a web browser, but possibly other environments like shells, native platforms like iOS and Android, and more.

Consider the following code snippet:

```
import { useState } from "react";

const App = () => {
  const [count, setCount] = useState(0);

  return (
    <main>
      <div>
        <h1>Hello, world!</h1>
        <span>Count: {count}</span>
        <button onClick={() => setCount(count + 1)}>Increment</button>
      </div>
    </main>
  );
};
```

This code snippet contains a declarative description of what we want our UI state to be: a tree of elements. Both our teammates *and* React can read this and understand we're trying to create a counter app with an increment button that increments the counter. To understand reconciliation, let's understand what React does on the inside when faced with a component like this.

First, the JSX becomes a tree of React elements. This is what we saw in Chapter 3. When invoked, the App component returns a React element whose children are further React elements. React elements are immutable (to us) and represent the desired state of the UI. They are not the actual UI state. React elements are created by React.createElement or the JSX < symbol, so this would be transpiled into:

```
const App = () => {
  const [count, setCount] = useState(0);

  return React.createElement(
    "main",
    null,
    React.createElement(
      "div",
      null,
      React.createElement("h1", null, "Hello, world!"),
      React.createElement("span", null, "Count: ", count),
      React.createElement(
        "button",
        { onClick: () => setCount(count + 1) },
        "Increment"
      )
    )
  );
};
```

This would give us a tree of created React elements that looks something like this:

```
{
  type: "main",
  props: {
    children: {
      type: "div",
      props: {
        children: [
          {
            type: "h1",
            props: {
              children: "Hello, world!",
            },
          },
          {
            type: "span",
            props: {
              children: ["Count: ", count],
```

```
            },
          },
          {
            type: "button",
            props: {
              onClick: () => setCount(count + 1),
              children: "Increment",
            },
          },
        ],
      },
    },
  },
}
```

This snippet represents the virtual DOM that comes from our Counter component. Since this is the first render, this tree is now committed to the browser using minimal calls to imperative DOM APIs. How does React ensure minimal calls to imperative DOM APIs? It does so by batching vDOM updates into one real DOM update, and touching the DOM as little as possible for reasons discussed in earlier chapters. Let's dive into this in some more detail to fully understand batching.

Batching

In Chapter 3, we discussed document fragments in browsers as part of the DOM's built-in APIs: lightweight containers that hold collections of DOM nodes that act like a temporary staging area where you can make multiple changes without affecting the main DOM until you finally append the document fragment to the DOM, triggering a single reflow and repaint.

In a similar vein, React batches updates to the real DOM during reconciliation, combining multiple vDOM updates into a single DOM update. This reduces the number of times the real DOM has to be updated and therefore lends itself to better performance for web applications.

To understand this, let's consider a component that updates its state multiple times in quick succession:

```
function Example() {
  const [count, setCount] = useState(0);

  const handleClick = () => {
    setCount((prevCount) => prevCount + 1);
    setCount((prevCount) => prevCount + 1);
    setCount((prevCount) => prevCount + 1);
  };

  return (
    <div>
```

```
        <p>Count: {count}</p>
        <button onClick={handleClick}>Increment</button>
      </div>
    );
  }
```

In this example, the handleClick function calls setCount three times in quick succession. Without batching, React would update the real DOM three separate times, even though the value of count only changed once. This would be wasteful and slow.

However, because React batches updates, it makes *one* update to the DOM with count + 3 instead of three updates to the DOM with count + 1 each time.

To calculate the most efficient batched update to the DOM, React will create a new vDOM tree as a fork of the current vDOM tree with the updated values, where count is 3. This tree will need to be *reconciled* with what is currently in the browser, effectively turning 0 into 3. React will then calculate that just one update is required to the DOM using the new vDOM value 3 instead of manually updating the DOM three times. This is how batching fits into the picture, and it is a part of the broader topic we're about to dive into: reconciliation, or the process of reconciling the next expected DOM state with the current DOM.

Before we understand what modern-day React does under the hood, let's explore how React used to perform reconciliation before version 16, with the legacy "stack" reconciler. This will help us understand the need for today's popular Fiber reconciler.

 At this point, it's worth mentioning that all of the topics we're about to discuss are implementation details in React that can and likely will change over time. Here, we are isolating the mechanism of how React works from actual practical usage of React. The goal is that by understanding React's internal mechanisms, we'll have a better understanding of how to use React effectively in applications.

Prior Art

Previously, React used a stack data structure for rendering. To make sure we're on the same page, let's briefly discuss the stack data structure.

Stack Reconciler (Legacy)

In computer science, a stack is a linear data structure that follows the last in, first out (LIFO) principle. This means that the last element added to the stack will be the first one to be removed. A stack has two fundamental operations, push and pop, that allow elements to be added and removed from the top of the stack, respectively.

A stack can be visualized as a collection of elements that are arranged vertically, with the topmost element being the most recently added one. Here's an ASCII illustration of a stack with three elements:

```
- - - - -
| 3 |
|___|
| 2 |
|___|
| 1 |
|___|
```

In this example, the most recently added element is 3, which is at the top of the stack. The element 1, which was added first, is at the bottom of the stack.

In this stack, the push operation adds an element to the top of the stack. In code, this can be executed in JavaScript using an array and the push method, like this:

```
const stack = [];

stack.push(1); // stack is now [1]
stack.push(2); // stack is now [1, 2]
stack.push(3); // stack is now [1, 2, 3]
```

The pop operation removes the top element from the stack. In code, this can be executed in JavaScript using an array and the pop method, like this:

```
const stack = [1, 2, 3];

const top = stack.pop(); // top is now 3, and stack is now [1, 2]
```

In this example, the pop method removes the top element (3) from the stack and returns it. The stack array now contains the remaining elements (1 and 2).

React's original reconciler was a stack-based algorithm that was used to compare the old and new virtual trees and update the DOM accordingly. While the stack reconciler worked well in simple cases, it presented a number of challenges as applications grew in size and complexity.

Let's take a quick look at why this was the case. To do so, we'll consider an example where we've got a list of updates to make:

1. A nonessential computationally expensive component consumes CPU and renders.

2. A user types into an input element.

3. Button becomes enabled if the input is valid.

4. A containing Form component holds the state, so it rerenders.

In code, we'd express this like so:

```
import React, { useReducer } from "react";

const initialState = { text: "", isValid: false };

function Form() {
  const [state, dispatch] = useReducer(reducer, initialState);

  const handleChange = (e) => {
    dispatch({ type: "handleInput", payload: e.target.value });
  };

  return (
    <div>
      <ExpensiveComponent />
      <input value={state.text} onChange={handleChange} />
      <Button disabled={!state.isValid}>Submit</Button>
    </div>
  );
}

function reducer(state, action) {
  switch (action.type) {
    case "handleInput":
      return {
        text: action.payload,
        isValid: action.payload.length > 0,
      };
    default:
      throw new Error();
  }
}
```

In this case, the stack reconciler would render the updates sequentially without being able to pause or defer work. If the computationally expensive component blocks rendering, user input will appear on screen with an observable lag. This leads to poor user experience, since the text field would be unresponsive. Instead, it would be far more pleasant to be able to recognize the user input as a higher-priority update than rendering the nonessential expensive component, and update the screen to reflect the input, deferring rendering the computationally expensive component.

There is a need to be able to bail out of current rendering work if interrupted by higher-priority rendering work, like user input. To do this, React needs to have a sense of priority for certain types of rendering operations over others.

The stack reconciler did not prioritize updates, which meant that less important updates could block more important updates. For example, a low-priority update to a tooltip might block a high-priority update to a text input. Updates to the virtual tree were executed in the order they were received.

In a React application, updates to the virtual tree can have different levels of importance. For example, an update to a form input might be more important than an update to an indicator showing the number of likes on a post, because the user is directly interacting with the input and expects it to be responsive.

In the stack reconciler, updates were executed in the order they were received, which meant that less important updates could block more important updates. For example, if a like counter update was received before a form input update, the like counter update would be executed first and could block the form input update.

If the like counter update takes a long time to execute (e.g., because it's performing an expensive computation), this could result in a noticeable delay or jank in the user interface, especially if the user is interacting with the application during the update.

Another challenge with the stack reconciler was that it did not allow updates to be interrupted or cancelled. What this means is that even if the stack reconciler had a sense of update priority, there were no guarantees that it could work well with various priorities by bailing out of unimportant work when a high-priority update was scheduled.

In any web application, not all updates are created equal: a random unexpected notification appearing is not as important as responding to my click on a button because the latter is a deliberate action that warrants an immediate reaction, whereas the former isn't even expected and may not even be welcome.

In the stack reconciler, updates could not be interrupted or cancelled, which meant that unnecessary updates, like showing a toast, were sometimes made at the expense of user interactions. This could result in unnecessary work being performed on the virtual tree and the DOM, which negatively impacted the performance of the application.

The stack reconciler presented a number of challenges as applications grew in size and complexity. The main challenges were centered around jank and user interfaces being slow to respond. To address these challenges, the React team developed a new reconciler called the Fiber reconciler, which is based on a different data structure called a Fiber tree. Let's explore this data structure in the next section.

The Fiber Reconciler

The Fiber reconciler involves the use of a different data structure called a "Fiber" that represents a single unit of work for the reconciler. Fibers are created from React elements that we covered in Chapter 3, with the key difference being that they are stateful and long-lived, while React elements are ephemeral and stateless.

Mark Erikson, the maintainer of Redux and a prominent React expert, describes Fibers as "React's internal data structure that represents the actual component tree at a point in time." Indeed, this is a good way to think about Fibers, and it's on-brand for Mark who, at the time of writing, works on time-travel debugging React apps full time with Replay: a tool that allows you to rewind and replay your app's state for debugging. If you haven't already, check out Replay.io for more information.

Similar to how the vDOM is a tree of elements, React uses a Fiber tree in reconciliation which, as the name suggests, is a tree of Fibers that is directly modeled after the vDOM.

Fiber as a Data Structure

The Fiber data structure in React is a key component of the Fiber reconciler. The Fiber reconciler allows updates to be prioritized and executed concurrently, which improves the performance and responsiveness of React applications. Let's explore the Fiber data structure in more detail.

At its core, the Fiber data structure is a representation of a component instance and its state in a React application. As discussed, the Fiber data structure is designed to be a mutable instance and can be updated and rearranged as needed during the reconciliation process.

Each instance of a Fiber node contains information about the component it represents, including its props, state, and child components. The Fiber node also contains information about its position in the component tree, as well as metadata that is used by the Fiber reconciler to prioritize and execute updates.

Here's an example of a simple Fiber node:

```
{
  tag: 3, // 3 = ClassComponent
  type: App,
  key: null,
  ref: null,
  props: {
    name: "Tejas",
    age: 30
  },
  stateNode: AppInstance,
  return: FiberParent,
  child: FiberChild,
  sibling: FiberSibling,
  index: 0,
  //...
}
```

In this example, we have a Fiber node that represents a ClassComponent called App. The Fiber node contains information about the component's:

---

tag
> In this case it's 3, which React uses to identify class components. Each type of component (class components, function components, Suspense and error boundaries, fragments, etc.) has its own numerical ID as Fibers.

type
> App refers to the function or class component that this Fiber represents.

props
> ({name: "Tejas", age: 30}) represent the input props to the component, or input arguments to the function.

stateNode
> The instance of the App component that this Fiber represents.
>
> Its position in the component tree: return, child, sibling, and index each give the Fiber reconciler a way to "walk the tree," identifying parents, children, siblings, and the Fiber's index.

Fiber reconciliation involves comparing the current Fiber tree with the next Fiber tree and figuring out which nodes need to be updated, added, or removed.

During the reconciliation process, the Fiber reconciler creates a Fiber node for each React element in the virtual DOM. There is a function called createFiberFrom TypeAndProps that does this. Of course, another way of saying "type and props" is by calling them React elements. As we recall, a React element is this: type and props:

```
{
  type: "div",
  props: {
    className: "container"
  }
}
```

This function returns a Fiber derived from elements. Once the Fiber nodes have been created, the Fiber reconciler uses a *work loop* to update the user interface. The work loop starts at the root Fiber node and works its way down the component tree, marking each Fiber node as "dirty" if it needs to be updated. Once it reaches the end, it walks back up, creating a new DOM tree in memory, detached from the browser, that will eventually be committed (flushed) to the screen. This is represented by two functions: beginWork walks downward, marking components as "need to update," and completeWork walks back up, constructing a tree of real DOM elements detached from the browser. This off-screen rendering process can be interrupted and thrown away at any time, since the user doesn't see it.

The Fiber architecture takes inspiration from a concept called "double buffering" in the game world, where the next screen is prepared offscreen and then "flushed" to the current screen. To better grasp the Fiber architecture, let's understand this concept in a little more detail before we move further.

Double Buffering

Double buffering is a technique used in computer graphics and video processing to reduce flicker and improve perceived performance. The technique involves creating two buffers (or memory spaces) for storing images or frames, and switching between them at regular intervals to display the final image or video.

Here's how double buffering works in practice:

1. The first buffer is filled with the initial image or frame.
2. While the first buffer is being displayed, the second buffer is updated with new data or images.
3. When the second buffer is ready, it is switched with the first buffer and displayed on the screen.
4. The process continues, with the first and second buffers being switched at regular intervals to display the final image or video.

By using double buffering, flicker and other visual artifacts can be reduced, since the final image or video is displayed without interruptions or delays.

Fiber reconciliation is similar to double buffering such that when updates happen, the current Fiber tree is forked and updated to reflect the new state of a given user interface. This is called *rendering*. Then, when the alternate tree is ready and accurately reflects the state a user expects to see, it is swapped with the current tree similarly to how video buffers are swapped in double buffering. This is called the *commit phase* of reconciliation or a *commit*.

By using a work-in-progress tree, the Fiber reconciler presents a number of benefits:

- It can avoid making unnecessary updates to the real DOM, which can improve performance and reduce flicker.
- It can compute the new state of a UI off-screen, and throw it away if a newer higher-priority update needs to happen.
- Since reconciliation happens off-screen, it can even pause and resume without messing up what the user currently sees.

With the Fiber reconciler, two trees are derived from a user-defined tree of JSX elements: one tree containing "current" Fibers, and another tree containing work-in-progress Fibers. Let's explore these trees a little more.

Fiber Reconciliation

Fiber reconciliation happens in two phases: the render phase and the commit phase. This two-phase approach, shown in Figure 4-1, allows React to do rendering work that can be disposed of at any time before committing it to the DOM and showing a new state to users: it makes rendering interruptible. To be a little bit more detailed, what makes rendering feel interruptible are the heuristics employed by the React scheduler of yielding the execution back to the main thread every 5 ms, which is smaller than a single frame even on 120 fps devices.

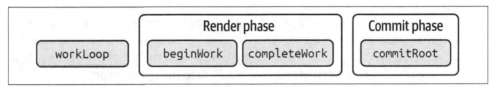

Figure 4-1. Reconciliation flow in the Fiber reconciler

We'll dive more into the details around the scheduler in Chapter 7 as we explore React's concurrent features. For now, though, let's walk through these phases of reconciliation.

The render phase

The *render phase* starts when a state-change event occurs in the current tree. React does the work of making the changes *off-screen* in the alternate tree by recursively stepping through each Fiber and setting flags that signal updates are pending (see Figure 4-2). As we alluded to earlier, this happens in a function called beginWork internally in React.

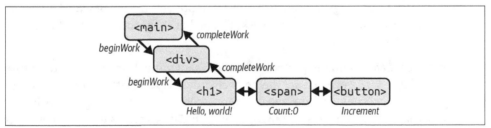

Figure 4-2. Call order of the render phase

beginWork. beginWork is responsible for setting flags on Fiber nodes in the work-in-progress tree about whether or not they should update. It sets a bunch of flags and then recursively goes to the next Fiber node, doing the same thing until it reaches the bottom of the tree. When it finishes, we start calling completeWork on the Fiber nodes and walk back up.

The signature of `beginWork` is as follows:

```
function beginWork(
  current: Fiber | null,
  workInProgress: Fiber,
  renderLanes: Lanes
): Fiber | null;
```

More on `completeWork` later. For now, let's dive into `beginWork`. Its signature includes the following arguments:

`current`

A reference to the Fiber node in the current tree that corresponds to the work-in-progress node being updated. This is used to determine what has changed between the previous version and the new version of the tree, and what needs to be updated. This is *never* mutated and is only used for comparison.

`workInProgress`

The Fiber node being updated in the work-in-progress tree. This is the node that will be marked as "dirty" if updated and returned by the function.

`renderLanes`

Render lanes is a new concept in React's Fiber reconciler that replaces the older `renderExpirationTime`. It's a bit more complex than the old `renderExpiration Time` concept, but it allows React to better prioritize updates and make the update process more efficient. Since `renderExpirationTime` is deprecated, we'll focus on `renderLanes` in this chapter.

It is essentially a bitmask that represents "lanes" in which an update is being processed. Lanes are a way of categorizing updates based on their priority and other factors. When a change is made to a React component, it is assigned a lane based on its priority and other characteristics. The higher the priority of the change, the higher the lane it is assigned to.

The `renderLanes` value is passed to the `beginWork` function in order to ensure that updates are processed in the correct order. Updates that are assigned to higher-priority lanes are processed before updates that are assigned to lower-priority lanes. This ensures that high-priority updates, such as updates that affect user interaction or accessibility, are processed as quickly as possible.

In addition to prioritizing updates, `renderLanes` also helps React better manage concurrency. React uses a technique called "time slicing" to break up long-running updates into smaller, more manageable chunks. `renderLanes` plays a key role in this process, as it allows React to determine which updates should be processed first, and which updates can be deferred until later.

After the render phase is complete, the `getLanesToRetrySynchronouslyOnError` function is called to determine if any deferred updates were created during the render phase. If there are deferred updates, the `updateComponent` function starts a new work loop to handle them, using `beginWork` and `getNextLanes` to process the updates and prioritize them based on their lanes.

We dive much deeper into render lanes in Chapter 7, the upcoming chapter on concurrency. For now, let's continue following the Fiber reconciliation flow.

completeWork. The `completeWork` function applies updates to the work-in-progress Fiber node and constructs a new real DOM tree that represents the updated state of the application. It constructs this tree detached from the DOM out of the plane of browser visibility.

If the host environment is a browser, this means doing things like `document.createElement` or `newElement.appendChild`. Keep in mind, this tree of elements is not yet attached to the in-browser document: React is just creating the next version of the UI off-screen. Doing this work off-screen makes it interruptible: whatever next state React is computing is not yet painted to the screen, so it can be thrown away in case some higher-priority update gets scheduled. This is the whole point of the Fiber reconciler.

The signature of `completeWork` is as follows:

```
function completeWork(
  current: Fiber | null,
  workInProgress: Fiber,
  renderLanes: Lanes
): Fiber | null;
```

Here, the signature is the same signature as `beginWork`.

The `completeWork` function is closely related to the `beginWork` function. While `beginWork` is responsible for setting flags about "should update" state on a Fiber node, `completeWork` is responsible for constructing a new tree to be committed to the host environment. When `completeWork` reaches the top and has constructed the new DOM tree, we say that "the render phase is completed." Now, React moves on to the commit phase.

The commit phase

The *commit phase* (see Figure 4-3) is responsible for updating the actual DOM with the changes that were made to the virtual DOM during the render phase. During the commit phase, the new virtual DOM tree is committed to the host environment, and the work-in-progress tree is replaced with the current tree. It's in this phase that all effects are also run. The commit phase is divided into two parts: the mutation phase and the layout phase.

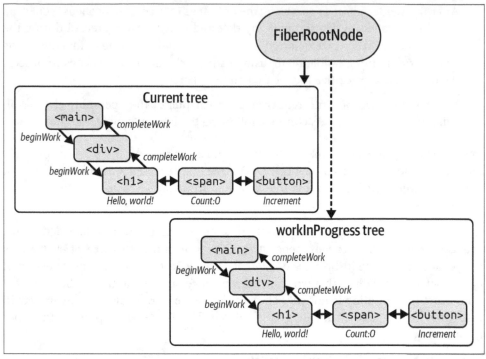

Figure 4-3. The commit phase with `FiberRootNode`

The mutation phase. The mutation phase is the first part of the commit phase, and it is responsible for updating the actual DOM with the changes that were made to the virtual DOM. During this phase, React identifies updates that need to be made and calls a special function called `commitMutationEffects`. This function applies the updates that were made to Fiber nodes in the alternate tree during the render phase to the actual DOM.

Here's an full-pseudocode example of how `commitMutationEffects` might be implemented:

```
function commitMutationEffects(Fiber) {
  switch (Fiber.tag) {
    case HostComponent: {
      // Update DOM node with new props and/or children
      break;
    }
    case HostText: {
      // Update text content of DOM node
      break;
    }
    case ClassComponent: {
      // Call lifecycle methods like componentDidMount and componentDidUpdate
```

```
      break;
    }
    // ... other cases for different types of nodes
  }
}
```

During the mutation phase, React also calls other special functions, such as commit Unmount and commitDeletion, to remove nodes from the DOM that are no longer needed.

The layout phase.   The layout phase is the second part of the commit phase, and it is responsible for calculating the new layout of the updated nodes in the DOM. During this phase, React calls a special function called commitLayoutEffects. This function calculates the new layout of the updated nodes in the DOM.

Like commitMutationEffects, commitLayoutEffects is also a massive switch statement that calls different functions, depending on the type of node being updated.

Once the layout phase is complete, React has successfully updated the actual DOM to reflect the changes that were made to the virtual DOM during the render phase.

By dividing the commit phase into two parts (mutation and layout), React is able to apply updates to the DOM in an efficient manner. By working in concert with other key functions in the reconciler, the commit phase helps to ensure that React applications are fast, responsive, and reliable, even as they become more complex and handle larger amounts of data.

Effects.   During the commit phase of React's reconciliation process, side effects are performed in a specific order, depending on the type of effect. There are several types of effects that can occur during the commit phase, including:

Placement effects
> These effects occur when a new component is added to the DOM. For example, if a new button is added to a form, a placement effect will occur to add the button to the DOM.

Update effects
> These effects occur when a component is updated with new props or state. For example, if the text of a button changes, an update effect will occur to update the text in the DOM.

Deletion effects
> These effects occur when a component is removed from the DOM. For example, if a button is removed from a form, a deletion effect will occur to remove the button from the DOM.

Layout effects

These effects occur before the browser has a chance to paint, and are used to update the layout of the page. Layout effects are managed using the `useLayoutEf fect` hook in function components and the `componentDidUpdate` lifecycle method in class components.

In contrast to these commit-phase effects, passive effects are user-defined effects that are scheduled to run after the browser has had a chance to paint. Passive effects are managed using the `useEffect` hook.

Passive effects are useful for performing actions that are not critical to the initial rendering of the page, such as fetching data from an API or performing analytics tracking. Because passive effects are not performed during the render phase, they do not affect the time required to compute a minimal set of updates required to bring a user interface into the developer's desired state.

Putting everything on the screen

React maintains a `FiberRootNode` atop both trees that points to one of the two trees: the `current` or the `workInProgress` tree. The `FiberRootNode` is a key data structure that is responsible for managing the commit phase of the reconciliation process.

When updates are made to the virtual DOM, React updates the `workInProgress` tree, while leaving the current tree unchanged. This allows React to continue rendering and updating the virtual DOM, while also preserving the current state of the application.

When the rendering process is complete, React calls a function called `commitRoot`, which is responsible for committing the changes made to the `workInProgress` tree to the actual DOM. `commitRoot` switches the pointer of the `FiberRootNode` from the current tree to the `workInProgress` tree, making the `workInProgress` tree the new current tree.

From this point on, any future updates are based on the new current tree. This process ensures that the application remains in a consistent state, and that updates are applied correctly and efficiently.

All of this appears to happen instantly in the browser. This is the work of reconciliation.

Chapter Review

In this chapter, we explored the concept of React reconciliation and learned about the Fiber reconciler. We also learned about Fibers, which enable efficient and interruptible rendering in concert with a powerful scheduler. We also learned about the render phase and the commit phase, which are the two main phases of the reconciliation process. Finally, we learned about the `FiberRootNode`: a key data structure responsible for managing the commit phase of the reconciliation process.

Review Questions

Let's ask ourselves a few questions to test our understanding of the concepts in this chapter:

1. What is React reconciliation?
2. What's the role of the Fiber data structure?
3. Why do we need two trees?
4. What happens when an application updates?

If we can answer these questions, we should be well on our way to understanding the Fiber reconciler and the reconciliation process in React.

Up Next

In Chapter 5, we'll look at common questions in React and explore some advanced patterns. We'll answer questions around how often to use `useMemo` and when to use `React.lazy`. We'll also explore how to use `useReducer` and `useContext` to manage state in React applications.

See you there!

Common Questions and Powerful Patterns

Now that we're more aware of what React does and how it works under the hood, let's explore its practical applications a little deeper in how we write React applications. In this chapter, we'll explore the answers to common React questions to boost our fluency around memoization, lazy loading, and performance. Let's get started by talking about memoization.

Memoization with React.memo

Memoization is a technique used in computer science to optimize the performance of functions by caching their previously computed results. In simple terms, memoization stores the output of a function based on its inputs so that if the function is called again with the same inputs, it returns the cached result rather than recomputing the output. This significantly reduces the time and resources needed to execute a function, especially for functions that are computationally expensive or called frequently. Memoization relies on function purity, which is defined as a function predictably returning the same outputs for given inputs. An example of a pure function is:

```
function add(num1, num2) {
  return num1 + num2;
}
```

This add function always returns 3 when given arguments 1 and 2, and therefore can be memoized safely. If the function relies on some side effect like network communication, it wouldn't be memoizable. Consider, for example:

```
async function addToNumberOfTheDay(num) {
  const todaysNumber = await fetch("https://number-api.com/today")
    .then((r) => r.json())
    .then((data) => data.number);
  return num + todaysNumber;
}
```

Given an input 2, this function will return a different result every day and therefore cannot be memoized. A silly example perhaps, but through it we crudely understand basic memoization.

Memoization is particularly useful when dealing with expensive calculations or when rendering large lists of items. Consider a function:

```
let result = null;
const doHardThing = () => {
  if (result) return result;

  // ...do hard stuff

  result = hardStuff;
  return hardStuff;
};
```

Calling `doHardThing` once might take a few minutes to do the hard thing, but calling it a second, third, fourth, or *nth* time doesn't actually do the hard thing but instead returns the stored result. This is the gist of memoization.

In the context of React, memoization can be applied to functional components using the `React.memo` component. This function returns a new component that only rerenders if its props have changed. Based on Chapter 4, ideally now we know that to "rerender" means to reinvoke the function component. If wrapped in `React.memo`, the function is not called again during reconciliation unless its props have changed. By memoizing functional components, we can prevent unnecessary rerenders, which can improve the overall performance of our React application.

We already know that React components are functions that are invoked for reconciliation, as discussed in Chapter 4. React calls function components with their props recursively to create a vDOM tree that is then used as the basis of two Fiber trees that are reconciled. Sometimes, rendering (that is, invoking a component function) can take a long time due to intense computations within the function component, or intense computations when applying it to the DOM via placement or update effects, as covered in Chapter 4. This slows down our application and presents a laggy user experience. Memoization is a way to avoid this by storing the results of expensive computations and returning them when the same inputs are passed to the function, or the same props are passed to the component.

To understand why `React.memo` is important, let's consider a common scenario where we have a list of items that need to be rendered in a component. For example, let's say we have a to do list that we want to display in a component, like this:

```
function TodoList({ todos }) {
  return (
    <ul>
      {todos.map((todo) => (
```

```
        <li key={todo.id}>{todo.title}</li>
      ))}
    </ul>
  );
}
```

Now, let's compose this component into another component that rerenders on user input:

```
function App() {
  const todos = Array.from({ length: 1000000 });
  const [name, setName] = useState("");

  return (
    <div>
      <input value={name} onChange={(e) => setName(e.target.value)} />
      <TodoList todos={todos} />
    </div>
  );
}
```

In our App component, on every keystroke in the input field, TodoList will rerender: the TodoList function component will be reinvoked with its props on every keystroke. This can and probably will present performance problems, but is central to how React works: when a state change occurs in a component, every function component from that component down the tree is reinvoked during reconciliation.

If the to do list is large, and the component is rerendered frequently, this can cause a performance bottleneck in the application. One way to optimize this component is to memoize it using React.memo:

```
const MemoizedTodoList = React.memo(function TodoList({ todos }) {
  return (
    <ul>
      {todos.map((todo) => (
        <li key={todo.id}>{todo.title}</li>
      ))}
    </ul>
  );
});
```

By wrapping the TodoList component with React.memo, React will only rerender the component if its props have changed. Surrounding state changes will not affect it. This means that if the to do list remains the same, the component will not rerender, and its cached output will be used instead. This can save significant resources and time, especially when the component is complex and the to do list is large.

Let's consider another example where we have a complex component with multiple nested components that are expensive to render:

```
function Dashboard({ data }) {
  return (
    <div>
      <h1>Dashboard</h1>
      <UserStats user={data.user} />
      <RecentActivity activity={data.activity} />
      <ImportantMessages messages={data.messages} />
    </div>
  );
}
```

If the data prop changes frequently, this component can be expensive to render, especially if the nested components are also complex. We can optimize this component using React.memo to memoize each nested component:

```
const MemoizedUserStats = React.memo(function UserStats({ user }) {
  // ...
});

const MemoizedRecentActivity = React.memo(function RecentActivity({
  activity,
}) {
  // ...
});

const MemoizedImportantMessages = React.memo(function ImportantMessages({
  messages,
}) {
  // ...
});

function Dashboard({ data }) {
  return (
    <div>
      <h1>Dashboard</h1>
      <MemoizedUserStats user={data.user} />
      <MemoizedRecentActivity activity={data.activity} />
      <MemoizedImportantMessages messages={data.messages} />
    </div>
  );
}
```

By memoizing each nested component, React will only rerender the components that have changed, and the cached outputs will be used for the components that have not changed. This can significantly improve the performance of the Dashboard component and reduce unnecessary rerenders. Thus, we can see that React.memo is an essential tool for optimizing the performance of functional components in React. This can be particularly useful for components that are expensive to render or have complex logic.

Getting Fluent in React.memo

Let's briefly walk through how `React.memo` works. When an update happens in React, your component is compared with the results of the vDOM returned from its previous render. If these results are different—i.e., if its props change—the reconciler runs an update effect if the element already exists in the host environment (usually the browser DOM), or a placement effect if it doesn't. If its props are the same, the component still rerenders and the DOM is still updated.

This is what `React.memo` is good for: avoiding unnecessary rerenders when a component's props are identical between renders. Since we can do this in React, it begs the question: how much and how often should we memoize stuff? Surely if we memoize every component, our application might be faster overall, no?

Memoized Components That Still Rerender

`React.memo` performs what is called a *shallow* comparison of the props to determine whether they've changed or not. The problem with this is while scalar types can be compared quite accurately in JavaScript, nonscalars cannot. To have a high-quality discussion, let's break down briefly what scalar and nonscalar types are, and how they behave in comparison operations.

Scalars (primitive types)

Scalar types, also known as primitive types, are foundational. These types represent singular, indivisible values. Unlike more complex data structures like arrays and objects, scalars do not possess properties or methods, and they are immutable by nature. This means that once a scalar value is set, it cannot be altered without creating a completely new value. JavaScript has several scalar types, including numbers, strings, booleans, and others like symbols, BigInts, undefined, and null. Each of these types serves a unique purpose. For instance, while numbers are self-explanatory, symbols provide a way to create unique identifiers, and undefined and null allow developers to represent the absence of a value in different contexts. When comparing scalar values, we're often interested in their actual content or value.

Nonscalars (reference types)

Moving beyond the simplicity of scalars, we encounter nonscalar or reference types. These types don't store data, but rather a reference or a pointer to where the data is stored in memory. This distinction is crucial because it impacts how these types are compared, manipulated, and interacted with in code. In JavaScript, the most common nonscalar types are objects and arrays. Objects allow us to store structured data with key-value pairs, while arrays provide ordered collections. Functions, too, are considered reference types in JavaScript. A key characteristic of nonscalars is that multiple references can point to the same memory location. This means that modifying data through one reference can impact other references pointing to the same data. When it comes to comparison, nonscalar types are compared by their memory reference, not by their content. This can sometimes lead to unexpected results for those not familiar with this nuance. For example, two arrays with identical content but different memory locations will be considered unequal when compared using the strict equality operator.

Consider the following example:

```
// Scalar types
"a" === "a"; // string; true
3 === 3; // number; true

// Non-scalar types
[1, 2, 3] === [1, 2, 3]; // array; false
{ foo: "bar"} === { foo: "bar" } // object; false
```

With this array comparison, the arrays, objects, and other nonscalar types are compared *by reference*: as in, does the lefthand-side array's reference to its position in the computer's memory equal the righthand-side's memory location. This is why the comparison returns `false`. The same is true for objects. What we're doing with the object comparison is creating two different objects in memory on the lefthand side and the righthand side—of course they're not equal, they're two different objects that live in two different places in memory! They just have the same content.

This is why `React.memo` can be tricky to use. Consider a functional component `List` that takes in an array of items as a prop and renders them:

```
const List = React.memo(function List({ items }) {
  return (
    <ul>
      {items.map((item) => (
        <li key={item}>{item}</li>
      ))}
    </ul>
  );
});
```

Now, imagine using this component within a parent component and passing a new array instance each time the parent renders:

```
function ParentComponent({ allFruits }) {
  const [count, setCount] = React.useState(0);
  const favoriteFruits = allFruits.filter((fruit) => fruit.isFavorite);

  return (
    <div>
      <button onClick={() => setCount(count + 1)}>Increment</button>
      <List items={favoriteFruits} />
    </div>
```

```
  );
}
```

Every time the Increment button is clicked, the ParentComponent rerenders. Even though the items passed to List haven't changed in value, a new array instance is created, with ['apple', 'banana', 'cherry'] each time. Since React.memo performs a shallow comparison of props, it will see this new array instance as a different prop from the previous render's array, causing the List component to rerender unnecessarily.

To fix this, we could memoize the array using the useMemo hook:

```
function ParentComponent({ allFruits }) {
  const [count, setCount] = React.useState(0);
  const favoriteFruits = React.useMemo(
    () => allFruits.filter((fruit) => fruit.isFavorite),
    []
  );

  return (
    <div>
      <button onClick={() => setCount(count + 1)}>Increment</button>
      <List items={favoriteFruits} />
    </div>
  );
}
```

Now, the array is only created once and retains the same reference across rerenders, preventing unnecessary rerenders of the List component.

This example underscores the importance of understanding reference comparisons when working with React.memo and nonscalar props. If not used cautiously, we could inadvertently introduce performance issues instead of optimizations.

React.memo often also gets circumvented quite commonly by another nonscalar type: functions. Consider the following case:

```
<MemoizedAvatar
  name="Tejas"
  url="https://github.com/tejasq.png"
  onChange={() => save()}
/>
```

While the props don't appear to change or depend on enclosing state with props name, url, and onChange all having constant values, if we compare the props we see the following:

```
"Tejas" === "Tejas"; // <- `name` prop; true
"https://github.com/tejasq.png" === "https://github.com/tejasq.png";

(() => save()) === (() => save()); // <- `onChange` prop; false
```

Once again, this is because we're comparing functions *by reference*. Remember that as long as props differ, our component will not be memoized. We can combat this by using the useCallback hook inside MemoizedAvatar's parent:

```
const Parent = ({ currentUser }) => {
  const onAvatarChange = useCallback(
    (newAvatarUrl) => {
      updateUserModel({ avatarUrl: newAvatarUrl, id: currentUser.id });
    },
    [currentUser]
  );

  return (
    <MemoizedAvatar
      name="Tejas"
      url="https://github.com/tejasq.png"
      onChange={onAvatarChange}
    />
  );
};
```

Now we can be confident that onAvatarChange will never change unless one of the things in its dependency array (second argument) changes, like the current user ID. With this, our memoization is fully complete and reliable. This is the recommended way to memoize components that have functions as props.

Great! This now means that our memoized components will never unnecessarily rerender. Right? Wrong! There's one more thing we need to be aware of.

It's a Guideline, Not a Rule

React uses React.memo as a hint to its reconciler that we don't want our components to rerender if their props stay the same. The function just hints to React. Ultimately, what React does is up to React. React.memo is consistent about avoiding rerenders that cascade from the parent, and that's its one purpose. It's not a guarantee that a component will never rerender. To echo back to the beginning of this book, React is intended to be a declarative abstraction of our user interface where we describe *what* we want, and React figures out the best way *how* to do it. React.memo is a part of this.

React.memo does not guarantee consistently avoided rerenders, because React may decide to rerender a memoized component for various reasons, such as changes to the component tree or changes to the global state of the application.

To understand this more, let's take a look at some code snippets from React's source code.

First, let's look at the implementation of React.memo:

```
function memo(type, compare) {
  return {
    $$typeof: REACT_MEMO_TYPE,
    type,
    compare: compare === undefined ? null : compare,
  };
}
```

In this implementation, React.memo returns a new object that represents the memo-ized component. The object has a $$typeof property that identifies it as a memoized component, a type property that references the original component, and a compare property that specifies the comparison function to use for memoization.

Next, let's look at how React.memo is used in the reconciler:

```
function updateMemoComponent(
  current: Fiber | null,
  workInProgress: Fiber,
  Component: any,
  nextProps: any,
  renderLanes: Lanes
): null | Fiber {
  if (current === null) {
    const type = Component.type;
    if (
      isSimpleFunctionComponent(type) &&
      Component.compare === null &&
      // SimpleMemoComponent codepath doesn't resolve outer props either.
      Component.defaultProps === undefined
    ) {
      let resolvedType = type;
      if (__DEV__) {
        resolvedType = resolveFunctionForHotReloading(type);
      }
      // If this is a plain function component without default props,
      // and with only the default shallow comparison, we upgrade it
      // to a SimpleMemoComponent to allow fast path updates.
      workInProgress.tag = SimpleMemoComponent;
      workInProgress.type = resolvedType;
      if (__DEV__) {
        validateFunctionComponentInDev(workInProgress, type);
      }
      return updateSimpleMemoComponent(
        current,
        workInProgress,
        resolvedType,
        nextProps,
        renderLanes
      );
    }
    if (__DEV__) {
      const innerPropTypes = type.propTypes;
```

```
    if (innerPropTypes) {
      // Inner memo component props aren't currently validated in createElement
      // We could move it there, but we'd still need this for lazy code path.
      checkPropTypes(
        innerPropTypes,
        nextProps, // Resolved props
        "prop",
        getComponentNameFromType(type)
      );
    }
    if (Component.defaultProps !== undefined) {
      const componentName = getComponentNameFromType(type) || "Unknown";
      if (!didWarnAboutDefaultPropsOnFunctionComponent[componentName]) {
        console.error(
          "%s: Support for defaultProps will be removed from components " +
            "in a future release. Use JavaScript default parameters instead.",
          componentName
        );
        didWarnAboutDefaultPropsOnFunctionComponent[componentName] = true;
      }
    }
  }
  const child = createFiberFromTypeAndProps(
    Component.type,
    null,
    nextProps,
    null,
    workInProgress,
    workInProgress.mode,
    renderLanes
  );
  child.ref = workInProgress.ref;
  child.return = workInProgress;
  workInProgress.child = child;
  return child;
}
if (__DEV__) {
  const type = Component.type;
  const innerPropTypes = type.propTypes;
  if (innerPropTypes) {
    // Inner memo component props aren't currently validated in createElement
    // We could move it there, but we'd still need this for lazy code path.
    checkPropTypes(
      innerPropTypes,
      nextProps, // Resolved props
      "prop",
      getComponentNameFromType(type)
    );
  }
}
// This is always exactly one child
const currentChild = ((current.child: any): Fiber);
```

```
    const hasScheduledUpdateOrContext = checkScheduledUpdateOrContext(
      current,
      renderLanes
    );
    if (!hasScheduledUpdateOrContext) {
      // This will be the props with resolved defaultProps,
      // unlike current.memoizedProps which will be the unresolved ones.
      const prevProps = currentChild.memoizedProps;
      // Default to shallow comparison
      let compare = Component.compare;
      compare = compare !== null ? compare : shallowEqual;
      if (compare(prevProps, nextProps) && current.ref === workInProgress.ref) {
        return bailoutOnAlreadyFinishedWork(current, workInProgress, renderLanes);
      }
    }
  }
  // React DevTools reads this flag.
  workInProgress.flags |= PerformedWork;
  const newChild = createWorkInProgress(currentChild, nextProps);
  newChild.ref = workInProgress.ref;
  newChild.return = workInProgress;
  workInProgress.child = newChild;
  return newChild;
}
```

Here's a breakdown of what's happening:

1. Initial check

The function `updateMemoComponent` takes several parameters, including the current and work-in-progress Fibers, the component, new props, and render lanes (which, as discussed, indicate priority and timing of updates). The initial check (`if (current === null)`) determines if this is the initial render of the component. If `current` is `null`, the component is being mounted for the first time.

2. Type and fast path optimization

It then checks if the component is a simple function component and eligible for a fast path update by checking `Component.compare` and `Component.defaultProps`. If these conditions are met, it sets the work-in-progress Fiber's tag to `SimpleMemo Component`, indicating a simpler component type that can be updated more efficiently.

3. Development mode checks

In development mode (`__DEV__`), the function performs additional checks, like validating prop types and warning about deprecated features (like `defaultProps` in function components).

4. Creating new Fiber

If it's the initial render, a new Fiber is created with `createFiberFromTypeAnd Props`. This Fiber represents the unit of work for React's renderer. It sets up references and returns the child (new Fiber).

5. Updating existing Fiber

If the component is updating (`current !== null`), it performs similar development mode checks. It then checks if the component needs an update by comparing the old props with new props using a shallow comparison (`shallowEqual`) or a custom comparison function, if provided.

6. Bailing out of update

If the props are equal and the ref hasn't changed, it can bail out of the update using `bailoutOnAlreadyFinishedWork`, which means no further rendering work is needed for this component.

7. Updating work-in-progress Fiber

If an update is needed, the function flags the work-in-progress Fiber with `PerformedWork` and creates a new work-in-progress child Fiber based on the current child, but with new props.

To summarize, this function is responsible for determining whether a memoized component (a component wrapped with `React.memo`) needs to be updated or if it can skip updating to optimize performance. It handles both the initial render and updates, performing different operations based on whether it's creating a new Fiber or updating an existing one.

Here's what parts of this function tell us about the conditions under which a `React.memo` component would rerender or not:

No previous render (initial mount)

If `current === null`, the component is being mounted for the first time and thus it cannot skip rendering. A new Fiber is created and returned for the component to render.

Simple function component optimization

If the component is a simple function component (without default props and without a custom comparison function), React will optimize it to a `SimpleMemo Component`. This allows React to use a fast path for updates because it can assume that the component only depends on its props and nothing else, and a shallow comparison is sufficient to determine if it should update.

Comparison function

If there is a previous render, the component will only update if the comparison function returns `false`. This comparison function can be custom if supplied or default to a shallow equality check (`shallowEqual`). If the comparison function determines that the new props are equal to the previous props and the `ref` is the same, the component will not rerender, and the function will bail out of the rendering process.

Default props and prop types in development
> In development mode (`__DEV__`), there are checks for `defaultProps` and `prop Types`. The use of `defaultProps` will trigger a warning in development mode because future versions of React plan to deprecate `defaultProps` on function components. Prop types are checked for validation purposes.

Bailout conditions
> If there are no scheduled updates or context changes (`hasScheduledUpdateOr Context` is `false`), the comparison function deems the old and new props to be equal, and the `ref` hasn't changed, then the function will return the result of `bai loutOnAlreadyFinishedWork`, effectively skipping the rerender.
>
> However, if there are scheduled context updates, the component will rerender—even if its props don't change. This is because context updates are considered to be outside the scope of the component's props. State changes, context changes, and scheduled updates can also trigger rerenders.

Performed work flag
> If an update is necessary, the `PerformedWork` flag is set on the `workInProgress` Fiber, indicating that this Fiber has performed work during the current render.

Thus, `React.memo` components will not rerender if the comparison between the old and new props (using either the custom provided comparison function or the default shallow comparison) determines that the props are equal, and there are no updates scheduled due to state or context changes. If the props are determined to be different, or if there are state or context changes, the component will rerender.

Memoization with useMemo

`React.memo` and the `useMemo` hook are both tools for memoization, but with very different purposes. `React.memo` memoizes an entire component to keep it from rerendering. `useMemo` memoizes a specific calculation inside a component, to avoid expensive recalculations and preserve a consistent reference for the result.

Let's briefly delve into `useMemo`. Consider a component:

```
const People = ({ unsortedPeople }) => {
  const [name, setName] = useState("");
  const sortedPeople = unsortedPeople.sort((a, b) => b.age - a.age);
```

```
  // ... rest of the component
};
```

This component can potentially slow down our application due to its sorting operation. The sorting operation has a time complexity that's typically O(n log n) for average and worst-case scenarios. If our list has, say, one million people, it can involve
significant computational overhead on each render. In computer science terms, the
sorting operation's efficiency is largely determined by the number of items, n, hence
the O(n log n) time complexity.

To optimize this, we would use the useMemo hook to avoid sorting the people array on
every render, especially when the unsortedPeople array hasn't changed.

The current implementation of the component presents a significant performance
issue. Every time the state updates, which happens on every keystroke inside the
input field, the component rerenders. If a name is entered with 5 characters and our
list contains 1,000,000 people, the component will rerender 5 times. For each render,
it will sort the list, which involves on the order of 1,000,000 × log(1,000,000) operations due to the time complexity of sorting. This amounts to many millions of operations just for entering a five-character name! Fortunately, this inefficiency can be
mitigated using the useMemo hook, ensuring that the sorting operation is only executed when the unsortedPeople array changes.

Let's rewrite that code snippet a little bit:

```
const People = ({ unsortedPeople }) => {
  const [name, setName] = useState("");
  const sortedPeople = useMemo(
    // Spreading so we don't mutate the original array
    () => [...unsortedPeople].sort((a, b) => b.age - a.age),
    [unsortedPeople]
  );

  return (
    <div>
      <div>
        Enter your name:{" "}
        <input
          type="text"
          placeholder="Obinna Ekwuno"
          onChange={(e) => setName(e.target.value)}
        />
      </div>
      <h1>Hi, {name}! Here's a list of people sorted by age!</h1>
      <ul>
        {sortedPeople.map((p) => (
          <li key={p.id}>
            {p.name}, age {p.age}
          </li>
        ))}
```

```
        </ul>
      </div>
    );
  };
```

There! Much better! We wrapped the value of `sortedPeople` in a function that was passed to the first argument of `useMemo`. The second argument we pass to `useMemo` represents an array of values that, if changed, re-sorts the array. Since the array contains only `unsortedPeople`, it will only sort the array once, and every time the list of people changes—not whenever someone types in the name input field. This is a great example of how to use `useMemo` to avoid unnecessary rerenders.

useMemo Considered Harmful

While it might be tempting to wrap all variable declarations inside a component with `useMemo`, this isn't always beneficial. `useMemo` is particularly valuable for memoizing computationally expensive operations or maintaining stable references to objects and arrays. For scalar values, such as strings, numbers, or booleans, using `useMemo` is typically unnecessary. This is because these scalar values are passed and compared by their actual value in JavaScript, not by reference. So every time you set or compare a scalar value, it's the actual value you're working with, not a reference to a memory location that might change.

In these cases, loading and executing the `useMemo` function may be more expensive than the actual operation it's trying to optimize. For instance, consider the following example:

```
const MyComponent = () => {
  const [count, setCount] = useState(0);
  const doubledCount = useMemo(() => count * 2, [count]);

  return (
    <div>
      <p>Count: {count}</p>
      <p>Doubled count: {doubledCount}</p>
      <button onClick={() => setCount((oldCount) => oldCount + 1)}>
        Increment
      </button>
    </div>
  );
};
```

In this example, the `doubledCount` variable is memoized using the `useMemo` hook. However, since `count` is a scalar value, it's not necessary to memoize it. Instead, we can simply compute the doubled count directly in the JSX:

```
const MyComponent = () => {
  const [count, setCount] = useState(0);
```

```
    return (
      <div>
        <p>Count: {count}</p>
        <p>Doubled count: {count * 2}</p>
        <button onClick={() => setCount((oldCount) => oldCount + 1)}>
          Increment
        </button>
      </div>
    );
  };
```

Now, doubledCount is no longer memoized, but the component still performs the same computation with less memory consumption and overhead since we're not importing and invoking useMemo. This is a good example of how to avoid using use Memo when it's not necessary.

What may present an additional performance problem, however, is that we're re-creating the onClick handler on the button on every render since it's passed by memory reference. But is this really a problem? Let's look closer.

Some suggest that we should memoize the onClick handler using useCallback:

```
const MyComponent = () => {
  const [count, setCount] = useState(0);
  const doubledCount = useMemo(() => count * 2, [count]);
  const increment = useCallback(
    () => setCount((oldCount) => oldCount + 1),
    [setCount]
  );

  return (
    <div>
      <p>Count: {count}</p>
      <p>Doubled count: {doubledCount}</p>
      <button onClick={increment}>Increment</button>
    </div>
  );
};
```

Should we, though? The answer is no. There is no benefit in having the increment function memoized here, since <button> is a browser-native element and not a React function component that can be called. Also, there are no further components below it that React would continue on to render.

Moreover, in React, built-in or "host" components (like div, button, input, etc.) are treated slightly differently from custom components when it comes to props, including function props.

Here's what happens with function props on built-in components:

Direct pass-through

When you pass a function prop (such as an `onClick` handler) to a built-in component, React passes it through directly to the actual DOM element. It does not create any wrappers or perform any additional work on these functions.

However, in the case of `onClick` and event-based props, React uses event delegation for handling events, not direct attachment of event handlers to DOM elements. This means that when you provide an `onClick` handler to a built-in React element like a `<button>`, React does not attach the `onClick` handler directly to the button's DOM node. Instead, React listens for all events at the top level using a single event listener. This is attached to the root of the document (or the root of the React application), and it relies on event bubbling to catch events that originate from individual elements. This approach is efficient because it reduces the memory footprint and the initial setup time for event handlers. Rather than having to attach and manage individual handlers for each instance of an event on each element, React can handle all events of a particular type (like clicks) with a single real event listener. When an event occurs, React maps it to the appropriate component and calls the handlers you've defined in a way that follows the expected propagation path. So even though the events are being caught at the top level, they will behave as if they were attached directly to the specific elements. This event delegation system is mostly transparent when you're writing a React application; you define `onClick` handlers the same way you would if they were being attached directly. Under the hood, however, React is optimizing event handling for you.

Rerendering behavior

Built-in components do not rerender due to changes in function props unless they are part of a higher component that has rerendered. For example, if a parent component rerenders and provides a new function as a prop to a built-in component, the built-in component will rerender because its props have changed. However, this rerender is typically fast and not something you generally need to optimize unless profiling shows it to be a problem.

No virtual DOM comparison for functions

The virtual DOM comparison for built-in components is based on the identity of the function props. If you pass an inline function (like `onClick={() => doSomething()}`), it will be a new function each time the component renders, but React doesn't do a deep comparison on functions to detect changes. The new function simply replaces the old one on the DOM element, and thus we get performance savings with built-in components.

Event pooling

React uses event pooling for event handlers to reduce memory overhead. The event object that is passed to your event handlers is a synthetic event that is pooled, meaning that it is reused for different events to reduce the garbage collection overhead.

This is a strong contrast to custom components. For custom components, if you pass a new function as a prop, the child component may rerender if it's a pure component or if it has memoization applied (such as with React.memo), because it detects a change in props. But for host components, React doesn't provide such built-in memoization because it would add overhead that isn't beneficial in most cases. The actual DOM elements that React outputs don't have a memoization concept; they simply update with the new function reference when the properties change.

In practice, this means that while you should be cautious about passing new function instances to custom components that might be expensive to rerender, doing so with built-in components is less of a concern. However, it's always good to be mindful of how often you're creating new functions and passing them around, as unnecessary function creation can lead to garbage collection churn, which might be a performance issue in very high-frequency update scenarios.

Thus, useCallback isn't helping here at all, and is in fact worse than useless: not only does it provide no value, it also adds overhead to our application. This is because useCallback has to be imported, invoked, and passed the dependencies, and then it has to compare the dependencies to see if the function should be recomputed. All of this has runtime complexity that can hurt our app more than help it.

What's a good example for useCallback then? useCallback is particularly useful when you have a component that is likely to rerender often and you pass a callback down to a child component, especially if that child component is optimized with React.memo or shouldComponentUpdate. The memoization of the callback ensures that the child component does not rerender unnecessarily when the parent component renders.

Here's an example where useCallback is beneficial:

```
import React, { useState, useCallback } from "react";

const ExpensiveComponent = React.memo(({ onButtonClick }) => {
  // This component is expensive to render and we want
  // to avoid unnecessary renders
  // We're just simulating something expensive here
  const now = performance.now();
  while (performance.now() - now < 1000) {
    // Artificial delay -- block for 1000ms
  }

  return <button onClick={onButtonClick}>Click Me</button>;
});

const MyComponent = () => {
```

```
    const [count, setCount] = useState(0);
    const [otherState, setOtherState] = useState(0);

    // This callback is memoized and will only change if count changes
    const incrementCount = useCallback(() => {
      setCount((prevCount) => prevCount + 1);
    }, []); // Dependency array

    // This state update will cause MyComponent to rerender
    const doSomethingElse = () => {
      setOtherState((s) => s + 1);
    };

    return (
      <div>
        <p>Count: {count}</p>
        <ExpensiveComponent onButtonClick={incrementCount} />
        <button onClick={doSomethingElse}>Do Something Else</button>
      </div>
    );
  };
```

In this example:

- ExpensiveComponent is a child component that is wrapped in React.memo, which means it will only rerender if its props change. This is a case where you want to avoid passing a new function instance on each render.

- MyComponent has two pieces of state: count and otherState.

- incrementCount is a callback that updates count. It is memoized with use Callback, which means the ExpensiveComponent will not rerender when MyCom ponent rerenders due to a change in otherState.

- The doSomethingElse function changes otherState but doesn't need to be memoized with useCallback because it is not passed down to Expensive Component or any other child.

By using useCallback, we ensure that ExpensiveComponent does not rerender unnecessarily when MyComponent rerenders for reasons unrelated to count. This is beneficial in cases where the rendering of the child component is a heavy operation and you want to optimize performance by reducing the number of renders.

This is a good example of how to use useCallback to avoid unnecessary rerenders, ensuring that the function that is passed down to an expensive component is only created once, and it retains the same reference across rerenders. This prevents unnecessary rerenders of the expensive component. useCallback is essentially useMemo for functions.

Let's consider another example:

```
const MyComponent = () => {
  const dateOfBirth = "1993-02-19";
  const isAdult =
    new Date().getFullYear() - new Date(dateOfBirth).getFullYear() >= 18;

  if (isAdult) {
    return <h1>You are an adult!</h1>;
  } else {
    return <h1>You are a minor!</h1>;
  }
};
```

We're not using useMemo here anywhere, mainly because the component is stateless. This is good! But what if we have some input that triggers rerenders like this:

```
const MyComponent = () => {
  const [birthYear, setBirthYear] = useState(1993);
  const isAdult = new Date().getFullYear() - birthYear >= 18;

  return (
    <div>
      <label>
        Birth year:
        <input
          type="number"
          value={birthYear}
          onChange={(e) => setBirthYear(e.target.value)}
        />
      </label>
      {isAdult ? <h1>You are an adult!</h1> : <h1>You are a minor!</h1>}
    </div>
  );
};
```

Now we're recomputing new Date() on every keystroke. Let's fix this with useMemo:

```
const MyComponent = () => {
  const [birthYear, setBirthYear] = useState(1993);
  const today = useMemo(() => new Date(), []);
  const isAdult = today.getFullYear() - birthYear >= 18;

  return (
    <div>
      <label>
        Birth year:
        <input
          type="number"
          value={birthYear}
          onChange={(e) => setBirthYear(e.target.value)}
        />
      </label>
      {isAdult ? <h1>You are an adult!</h1> : <h1>You are a minor!</h1>}
    </div>
```

```
  );
};
```

This is good because `today` will be a reference to the same object every time the component rerenders with the same props, and we assume the component will always rerender in the same day.

 There's a slight edge case here if the user's clock lapses at midnight while they're using this component, but this is a rare edge case that we can ignore for now. Of course, we do better when there's real production code involved.

This example facilitates a bigger question: should we wrap `isAdult`'s value in `useMemo`? What happens if we do? The answer is that we shouldn't because `isAdult` is a scalar value that requires no computation besides memory allocation. We *do* call `.getFullYear` a bunch of times, but we trust the JavaScript engine and the React runtime to handle the performance for us. It's a simple assignment with no further computation, like sorting, filter, or mapping.

In this case, we should not use `useMemo` because it is more likely to slow our app down than speed it up because of the overhead of `useMemo` itself, including importing it, calling it, passing in the dependencies, and then comparing the dependencies to see if the value should be recomputed. All of this has runtime complexity that can hurt our app more than help it. Instead, we assign and trust React to intelligently rerender our component when necessary with its own optimizations.

Our applications are now enjoying performance benefits of faster rerenders even in the face of heavy computations—but can we do more? In the next section, let's take a look at how all of the stuff we've covered so far probably will not even matter in a few years based on some exciting things the React team is working on to automatically consider memoization for us, enabling us to *forget* about the details and instead focus on our applications.

Forget About All of This

React Forget is a new toolchain aimed at automating memoization in React applications, potentially making hooks like `useMemo` and `useCallback` redundant. By automatically handling memoization, React Forget helps optimize component rerendering, improving both user experience (UX) and developer experience (DX). This automation shifts React's rerendering behavior from object identity changes to semantic value changes without deep comparisons, thereby enhancing performance. Introduced at React Conf 2021, React Forget is not yet generally available at the time of writing, but is in use in production at Meta across Facebook, Instagram, and more, and has "exceeded expectations" internally so far.

If there is enough interest, we will cover React Forget in a future edition of this book. Please let us know by posting about it on social media (especially X, formerly Twitter) and tagging the author, *@tejaskumar_*.

Lazy Loading

As our applications grow, we accumulate a lot of JavaScript. Our users then download these massive JavaScript bundles—sometimes going into the double digits on megabytes—only to use a small portion of the code. This is a problem because it slows down our users' initial load time, and it also slows down our users' subsequent page loads because they have to download the entire bundle again, especially when we don't have access to the servers that serve these bundles and cannot add the requisite headers for caching and so on.

One of the main problems with shipping too much JavaScript is that it can slow down page load times. JavaScript files are typically larger than other types of web assets, such as HTML and CSS, and require more processing time to execute. This can lead to longer page load times, especially on slower internet connections or older devices.

For example, consider the following code snippet that loads a large JavaScript file on page load:

```
<!DOCTYPE html>
<html>
  <head>
    <title>My Website</title>
    <script src="https://example.com/large.js"></script>
  </head>
  <body>
    <!-- Page content goes here -->
  </body>
</html>
```

In this example, the *large.js* file is loaded in the <head> of the page, which means that it will be executed before any other content on the page. This can lead to slower page load times, especially on slower internet connections or older devices. A common solution to this problem is to load JavaScript files asynchronously using the `async` attribute:

```
<!DOCTYPE html>
<html>
  <head>
    <title>My Website</title>
    <script async src="https://example.com/large.js"></script>
  </head>
  <body>
    <!-- Page content goes here -->
  </body>
</html>
```

In this example, the *large.js* file is loaded asynchronously using the `async` attribute. This means that it will be downloaded in parallel with other resources on the page, which can help improve page load times.

Another problem with shipping too much JavaScript is that it can increase data usage. JavaScript bundles are typically larger than other types of web assets, which means that they require more data to be transferred over the network. This can be a problem for users with limited data plans or slow internet connections, as it can lead to increased costs and slower page load times.

To mitigate these issues, we can take several steps to reduce the amount of JavaScript that is shipped to users. One approach is to use code splitting to load only the JavaScript that is needed for a particular page or feature. This can help reduce page load times and data usage by only loading the necessary code.

For example, consider the following code snippet that uses code splitting to load only the JavaScript that is needed for a particular page:

```
import("./large.js").then((module) => {
  // Use module here
});
```

In this example, the `import` function is used to asynchronously load the *large.js* file only when it is needed. This can help reduce page load times and data usage by only loading the necessary code.

Another approach is to use lazy loading to defer the loading of noncritical JavaScript until after the page has loaded. This can help reduce page load times and data usage by loading noncritical code only when it is needed.

For example, consider the following code snippet that uses lazy loading to defer the loading of noncritical JavaScript:

```
<!DOCTYPE html>
<html>
  <head>
    <title>My Website</title>
  </head>
  <body>
    <!-- Page content goes here -->
    <button id="load-more">Load more content</button>
    <script>
      document.getElementById("load-more").addEventListener("click", () => {
        import("./non-critical.js").then((module) => {
          // Use module here
        });
      });
    </script>
  </body>
</html>
```

In this example, the `import` function is used to asynchronously load the *non-critical.js* file only when the "Load more content" button is clicked. This can help reduce page load times and data usage by loading noncritical code only when it is needed.

Thankfully, React has a solution that makes this even more straightforward: lazy loading using `React.lazy` and `Suspense`. Let's take a look at how we can use these to improve our application's performance.

Lazy loading is a technique that allows us to load a component only when it's needed, like with the dynamic import in the preceding example. This is useful for large applications that have many components that are not needed on the initial render. For example, if we have a large application with a collapsible sidebar that has a list of links to other pages, we might not want to load the full sidebar if it's collapsed on first load. Instead, we can load it only when the user toggles the sidebar.

Let's explore the following code sample:

```
import Sidebar from "./Sidebar"; // 22MB to import

const MyComponent = ({ initialSidebarState }) => {
  const [showSidebar, setShowSidebar] = useState(initialSidebarState);

  return (
    <div>
      <button onClick={() => setShowSidebar(!showSidebar)}>
        Toggle sidebar
      </button>
      {showSidebar && <Sidebar />}
    </div>
  );
};
```

In this example, `<Sidebar />` is 22 MB of JavaScript. This is a lot of JavaScript to download, parse, and execute, and it's not necessary on the initial render if the sidebar is collapsed. Instead, we can use `React.lazy` to lazy load the component only if `showSidebar` is true. As in, only if we need it:

```
import { lazy, Suspense } from "react";
import FakeSidebarShell from "./FakeSidebarShell"; // 1kB to import

const Sidebar = lazy(() => import("./Sidebar"));

const MyComponent = ({ initialSidebarState }) => {
  const [showSidebar, setShowSidebar] = useState(initialSidebarState);

  return (
    <div>
      <button onClick={() => setShowSidebar(!showSidebar)}>
        Toggle sidebar
      </button>
      <Suspense fallback={<FakeSidebarShell />}>
```

```
        {showSidebar && <Sidebar />}
      </Suspense>
    </div>
  );
};
```

Instead of *statically importing* `./Sidebar`, we *dynamically* import it—that is, we pass a function to `lazy` that returns a promise that resolves to the imported module. A dynamic import returns a promise because the module may not be available immediately. It may need to be downloaded from the server first. React's `lazy` function, which triggers the import, is never called unless the underlying component (in this case, `Sidebar`) is to be rendered. This way, we avoid shipping the 22 MB sidebar until we actually *render* `<Sidebar />`.

You may have also noticed another new import: `Suspense`. We use `Suspense` to wrap the component in the tree. `Suspense` is a component that allows us to show a fallback component while the promise is resolving (read: as the sidebar is downloading). In the snippet, we're showing a fallback component that is a lightweight version of the heavy sidebar while the heavy sidebar is downloading. This is a great way to provide immediate feedback to the user while the sidebar is loading.

Now, when the user clicks the button to toggle the sidebar, they'll see a "skeleton UI" that they can orient themselves around while the sidebar is loaded and rendered.

Greater UI Control with Suspense

React Suspense works like a try/catch block. You know how you can `throw` an exception from literally anywhere in your code, and then catch it with a `catch` block somewhere else—even in a different module? Well, Suspense works in a similar (but not exactly the same) way. You can place lazy-loaded and asynchronous primitives anywhere in your component tree, and then catch them with a `Suspense` component anywhere above it in the tree, even if your Suspense boundary is in a completely different file.

Knowing this, we have the power to choose where we want to show the loading state for our 22 MB sidebar. For example, we can hide the entire application while the sidebar is loading—which is a pretty bad idea because we block our entire app's information from the user just for a sidebar—or we can show a loading state for the sidebar only. Let's take a look at how we can do the former (even though we shouldn't) just to understand `Suspense`'s capabilities:

```
import { lazy, Suspense } from "react";

const Sidebar = lazy(() => import("./Sidebar"));

const MyComponent = () => {
  const [showSidebar, setShowSidebar] = useState(false);
```

```
      return (
        <Suspense fallback={<p>Loading...</p>}>
          <div>
            <button onClick={() => setShowSidebar(!showSidebar)}>
              Toggle sidebar
            </button>
            {showSidebar && <Sidebar />}
            <main>
              <p>Hello hello welcome, this is the app's main area</p>
            </main>
          </div>
        </Suspense>
      );
    };
```

By wrapping the entire component in `Suspense`, we render the `fallback` until all asynchronous children (promises) are resolved. This means that the entire application is hidden until the sidebar is loaded. This can be useful if we want to wait until everything's ready to reveal the user interface to the user, but in this case it might not be the best idea because the user is left wondering what's going on and can't interact with the application at all.

This is why we should only use `Suspense` to wrap the components that need to be lazy loaded, like this:

```
import { lazy, Suspense } from "react";

const Sidebar = lazy(() => import("./Sidebar"));

const MyComponent = () => {
  const [showSidebar, setShowSidebar] = useState(false);

  return (
    <div>
      <button onClick={() => setShowSidebar(!showSidebar)}>
        Toggle sidebar
      </button>
      <Suspense fallback={<p>Loading...</p>}>
        {showSidebar && <Sidebar />}
      </Suspense>
      <main>
        <p>Hello hello welcome, this is the app's main area</p>
      </main>
    </div>
  );
};
```

The Suspense boundary is a very powerful primitive that can remedy layout shift and make user interfaces more responsive and intuitive. It's a great tool to have in your arsenal. Moreover, if high-quality skeleton UI is used in the `fallback`, we can further guide our users to understand what's going on and what to expect while our lazy-loaded components load, thereby orienting them to the interface they're about to interact with before it's ready. Taking advantage of all of this is a great way to improve our applications' performance and fluently get the most out of React.

Next, we'll look at another interesting question that many React developers ask: when should we use useState versus useReducer?

useState Versus useReducer

React exposes two hooks for managing state: useState and useReducer. Both of these hooks are used to manage state in a component. The difference between the two is that useState is a hook that is better suited to manage a single piece of state, whereas useReducer is a hook that manages more complex state. Let's take a look at how we can use useState to manage state in a component:

```
import { useState } from "react";

const MyComponent = () => {
  const [count, setCount] = useState(0);

  return (
    <div>
      <p>Count: {count}</p>
      <button onClick={() => setCount(count + 1)}>Increment</button>
    </div>
  );
};
```

In this example, we're using useState to manage a single piece of state: count. But what if our state's a little more complex?

```
import { useState } from "react";

const MyComponent = () => {
  const [state, setState] = useState({
    count: 0,
    name: "Tejumma",
    age: 30,
  });

  return (
    <div>
      <p>Count: {state.count}</p>
      <p>Name: {state.name}</p>
      <p>Age: {state.age}</p>
      <button onClick={() => setState({ ...state, count: state.count + 1 })}>
        Increment
      </button>
    </div>
```

```
  );
};
```

Now we can see that our state is a little more complex. We have a count, a name, and an age. We can increment the count by clicking the button, which sets the state to *a new object* that has the same properties as the previous state, but with the count incremented by 1. This is a very common pattern in React. The problem with it is that it can raise the possibility of bugs. For example, if we don't carefully spread the old state, we might accidentally overwrite some of the state's properties.

Fun fact: useState uses useReducer internally. You can think of useState as a higher-level abstraction of useReducer. In fact, you can reimplement useState with useReducer if you wish!

Seriously, you'd just do this:

```
import { useReducer } from "react";

function useState(initialState) {
  const [state, dispatch] = useReducer(
    (state, newValue) => newValue,
    initialState
  );
  return [state, dispatch];
}
```

Let's look at the same example, but implemented with useReducer instead:

```
import { useReducer } from "react";

const initialState = {
  count: 0,
  name: "Tejumma",
  age: 30,
};

const reducer = (state, action) => {
  switch (action.type) {
    case "increment":
      return { ...state, count: state.count + 1 };
    default:
      return state;
  }
};

const MyComponent = () => {
  const [state, dispatch] = useReducer(reducer, initialState);

  return (
    <div>
      <p>Count: {state.count}</p>
      <p>Name: {state.name}</p>
```

```
      <p>Age: {state.age}</p>
      <button onClick={() => dispatch({ type: "increment" })}>Increment</button>
    </div>
  );
};
```

Now, some would say this is a tad more verbose than useState, and many would agree, but this is to be expected whenever anyone goes a level lower in an abstraction stack: the lower the abstraction, the more verbose the code. After all, abstractions are intended to replace complex logic with syntax sugar in most cases. So since we can do the same thing with useState as we can with useReducer, why don't we just always use useState since it's simpler?

There are three large benefits to using useReducer to answer this question:

- It separates the logic of updating state from the component. Its accompanying reducer function can be tested in isolation, and it can be reused in other components. This is a great way to keep our components clean and simple, and embrace the *single responsibility principle*.

We can test the reducer like this:

```
describe("reducer", () => {
  test("should increment count when given an increment action", () => {
    const initialState = {
      count: 0,
      name: "Tejumma",
      age: 30,
    };
    const action = { type: "increment" };
    const expectedState = {
      count: 1,
      name: "Tejumma",
      age: 30,
    };
    const actualState = reducer(initialState, action);
    expect(actualState).toEqual(expectedState);
  });

  test("should return the same object when given an unknown action",
    () => {
    const initialState = {
      count: 0,
      name: "Tejumma",
      age: 30,
    };
    const action = { type: "unknown" };
    const expectedState = initialState;
    const actualState = reducer(initialState, action);
    expect(actualState).toBe(expectedState);
```

```
      });
    });
```

In this example, we're testing two scenarios: one where the increment action is dispatched to the reducer, and one where an unknown action is dispatched.

In the first test, we're creating an initial state object with a count value of 0, and an increment action object. We're then expecting the count value in the resulting state object to be incremented to 1. We use the `toEqual` matcher to compare the expected and actual state objects.

In the second test, we're creating an initial state object with a count value of 0, and an unknown action object. We're then expecting the resulting state object to be the same as the initial state object. We use the `toBe` matcher to compare the expected and actual state objects, since we're testing for reference equality.

By testing our reducer in this way, we can ensure that it behaves correctly and produces the expected output when given different input scenarios.

- Our state and the way it changes is always explicit with `useReducer`, and some would argue that `useState` can obfuscate the overall state update flow of a component through layers of JSX trees.

- `useReducer` is an *event sourced* model, meaning it can be used to model events that happen in our application, which we can then keep track of in some type of audit log. This audit log can be used to replay events in our application to reproduce bugs or to implement *time-travel debugging*. It also enables some powerful patterns like undo/redo, optimistic updates, and analytics tracking of common user actions across our interface.

While `useReducer` is a great tool to have in your arsenal, it's not always necessary. In fact, it's often overkill for most use cases. So when should we use `useState` versus `useReducer`? The answer is that it depends on the complexity of your state. But hopefully with all of this information, you can make a more informed decision about which one to use in your application.

Immer and Ergonomics

Immer, a popular React library, is particularly useful when dealing with complex state management in your applications. When your state shape is nested or complex, traditional state updating methods can become verbose and error prone. Immer helps to manage such complexities by allowing you to work with a mutable draft state while ensuring the produced state is immutable.

In a React application, state management is commonly handled using the `useState` or `useReducer` hooks. While `useState` is suitable for simple state, `useReducer` is more suited for complex state management, and that's where Immer shines the most.

When working with useReducer, the reducer function you provide is expected to be pure and always return a new state object. This can lead to verbose code when dealing with nested state objects. However, by integrating Immer with useReducer through useImmerReducer from the use-immer library, you can write reducers that appear to mutate the state directly, while actually operating on a draft state provided by Immer. This way, you get to write simpler and more intuitive reducer functions:

```
import { useImmerReducer } from "use-immer";

const initialState = {
  user: {
    name: "John Doe",
    age: 28,
    address: {
      city: "New York",
      country: "USA",
    },
  },
};

const reducer = (draft, action) => {
  switch (action.type) {
    case "updateName":
      draft.user.name = action.payload;
      break;
    case "updateCity":
      draft.user.address.city = action.payload;
      break;
    // other cases...
    default:
      break;
  }
};

const MyComponent = () => {
  const [state, dispatch] = useImmerReducer(reducer, initialState);

  // ...
};
```

In this example, useImmerReducer simplifies the reducer function significantly, allowing direct assignments to update the nested state properties, which would have required spread or Object.assign operations in a traditional reducer.

Furthermore, Immer is not just limited to useReducer. You can also use it with useState whenever you have a complex state object and want to ensure immutability when updating the state. Immer provides a produce function that you can use to create your next state based on the current state and a set of instructions:

```
import produce from "immer";
import { useState } from "react";

const MyComponent = () => {
  const [state, setState] = useState(initialState);

  const updateName = (newName) => {
    setState(
      produce((draft) => {
        draft.user.name = newName;
      })
    );
  };

  // ...
};
```

In the `updateName` function, Immer's `produce` function takes the current `state` and a function that receives a `draft` of the state. Inside this function, you can work with the draft as if it were mutable, while Immer ensures that the produced state is a new immutable object.

Immer's ability to simplify state updates, especially in complex or nested state structures, makes it a great companion to React's state management hooks, facilitating cleaner, more maintainable, and less error-prone code.

Powerful Patterns

Software design patterns are commonly used solutions to recurring problems in software development. They provide a way to solve problems that have been encountered and solved by other developers, saving time and effort in the software development process. They are often expressed as templates or guidelines for creating software that can be used in different situations. Software design patterns are typically described using a common vocabulary and notation, which makes them easier to understand and communicate among developers. They can be used to improve the quality, maintainability, and efficiency of software systems.

Software design patterns are important for several reasons:

Reusability
: Design patterns provide reusable solutions to common problems, which can save time and effort in software development.

Standardization
: Design patterns provide a standard way of solving problems, which makes it easier for developers to understand and communicate with each other.

Maintainability
> Design patterns provide a way to structure code that is easy to maintain and modify, which can improve the longevity of software systems.

Efficiency
> Design patterns provide efficient solutions to common problems, which can improve the performance of software systems.

Usually, software design patterns naturally arrive over time in response to real-world needs. These patterns solve specific problems that engineers experience, and find their way into an "engineer's arsenal" of tools to use in different use cases. *One pattern is not inherently worse than the other*; each has its place.

Most patterns help us identify ideal levels of abstraction: how we can write code that ages like fine wine instead of accruing extra state and configuration to the point where it becomes unreadable and/or unmaintainable. This is why a common consideration when picking a design pattern is *control*: how much of it we give to users versus how much of it our program handles.

With that, let's dive in to some popular React patterns, following a rough chronological order of when these patterns emerged.

Presentational/Container Components

It's common to see a React design pattern that is a combination of two components: a *presentational component* and a *container component*. The presentational component renders the UI, and the container component handles the state of the UI. Consider a counter. This is how a counter would look when implementing this pattern:

```
const PresentationalCounter = (props) => {
  return (
    <section>
      <button onClick={props.increment}>+</button>
      <button onClick={props.decrement}>-</button>
      <button onClick={props.reset}>Reset</button>
      <h1>Current Count: {props.count}</h1>
    </section>
  );
};

const ContainerCounter = () => {
  const [count, setCount] = useState(0);
  const increment = () => setCount(count + 1);
  const decrement = () => setCount(count - 1);
  const reset = () => setCount(0);

  return (
    <PresentationalCounter
      count={count}
```

```
          increment={increment}
          decrement={decrement}
          reset={reset}
      />
    );
  };
```

In this example, we have two components: `PresentationalCounter` (a presentational component) and `ContainerCounter` (a container component). The presentational component renders the UI, and the container component handles the state.

Why is this a thing? This pattern is quite useful because of the principle of *single responsibility*, which highly encourages us to separate concerns in our applications, enabling them to scale better by being more modular, reusable, and even testable. Instead of having a component be responsible for how it should look and how it should work, we split these concerns. The result? `PresentationalCounter` can be passed between other stateful containers and preserve the look we want, while `ContainerCounter` can be replaced with another stateful container and preserve the functionality we want.

We can also unit test `ContainerCounter` in isolation, and instead visually test (using Storybook or similar) `PresentationalCounter` in isolation. We can also assign engineers or engineering teams more comfortable with visual work to `PresentationalCounter`, while assigning engineers who prefer data structures and algorithms to `ContainerCounter`.

We have so many more options because of this decoupled approach. For these reasons, the container/presentational component pattern has gained quite a lot of popularity and is still in use today. However, the introduction of hooks allowed for far more convenience in adding statefulness to components without needing a container component to provide that state.

Nowadays, in many cases the container/presentational pattern can be replaced with hooks. Although we can still leverage this pattern, even with React Hooks, it can easily be considered overengineering in smaller applications.

Higher-Order Component

According to Wikipedia's definition of a higher-order function (*https://oreil.ly/ Ywx56*):

> In mathematics and computer science, a higher-order function (HOF) is a function that does at least one of the following: takes one or more functions as arguments (i.e., a procedural parameter, which is a parameter of a procedure that is itself a procedure), returns a function as its result.

In the JSX world, a higher-order component (HOC) is basically this: a component that takes another component as an argument and returns a new component that is the result of the composition of the two. HOCs are great for *shared behavior across components that we'd rather not repeat.*

For example, many web applications need to request data from some data source asynchronously. Loading and error states are often inevitable, but we sometimes forget to account for them in our software. If we manually add loading, data, and error props to our components, the chances that we miss a few get even higher. Let's consider a basic to do list app:

```
const App = () => {
  const [data, setData] = useState([]);

  useEffect(() => {
    fetch("https://mytodolist.com/items")
      .then((res) => res.json())
      .then(setData);
  }, []);

  return <BasicTodoList data={data} />;
};
```

This app has a few problems. We don't account for loading or error states. Let's fix this:

```
const App = () => {
  const [isLoading, setIsLoading] = useState(true);
  const [data, setData] = useState([]);
  const [error, setError] = useState([]);

  useEffect(() => {
    fetch("https://mytodolist.com/items")
      .then((res) => res.json())
      .then((data) => {
        setIsLoading(false);
        setData(data);
      })
      .catch(setError);
  }, []);

  return isLoading ? (
    "Loading..."
  ) : error ? (
    error.message
  ) : (
    <BasicTodoList data={data} />
  );
};
```

Yikes. This got pretty unruly, pretty fast. Moreover, *this solves the problem for just one component*. Do we need to add these pieces of state (i.e., loading, data, and error) to each component that interacts with a foreign data source? This is a *cross-cutting concern*, and exactly where HOCs shine.

Instead of repeating this loading, error, and data pattern for each component that talks to a foreign data source asynchronously, we can use an HOC factory to deal with these states for us. Let's consider a `withAsync` HOC factory that remedies this:

```
const TodoList = withAsync(BasicTodoList);
```

`withAsync` will deal with loading and error states, and render any component when data is available. Let's look at its implementation:

```
const withAsync = (Component) => (props) => {
  if (props.loading) {
    return "Loading...";
  }

  if (props.error) {
    return error.message;
  }

  return (
    <Component
      // Pass through whatever other props we give `Component`.
      {...props}
    />
  );
};
```

So now, when any `Component` is passed into `withAsync`, we get a new component that renders appropriate pieces of information based on its props. This changes our initial component into something more workable:

```
const TodoList = withAsync(BasicTodoList);

const App = () => {
  const [isLoading, setIsLoading] = useState(true);
  const [data, setData] = useState([]);
  const [error, setError] = useState([]);

  useEffect(() => {
    fetch("https://mytodolist.com/items")
      .then((res) => res.json())
      .then((data) => {
        setIsLoading(false);
        setData(data);
      })
      .catch(setError);
  }, []);
```

```
    return <TodoList loading={isLoading} error={error} data={data} />;
};
```

No more nested ternaries, and the TodoList itself can show appropriate information depending on whether it's loading, has an error, or has data. Since the withAsync HOC factory deals with this cross-cutting concern, we can wrap any component that talks to an external data source with it and get back a new component that responds to loading and error props. Consider a blog:

```
const Post = withAsync(BasicPost);
const Comments = withAsync(BasicComments);

const Blog = ({ req }) => {
  const { loading: isPostLoading, error: postLoadError } = usePost(
    req.query.postId
  );
  const { loading: areCommentsLoading, error: commentLoadError } = useComments({
    postId: req.query.postId,
  });

  return (
    <>
      <Post
        id={req.query.postId}
        loading={isPostLoading}
        error={postLoadError}
      />
      <Comments
        postId={req.query.postId}
        loading={areCommentsLoading}
        error={commentLoadError}
      />
    </>
  );
};
```

```
export default Blog;
```

In this example, both Post and Comments use the withAsync HOC pattern, which returns a newer version of BasicPost and BasicComments, respectively, that now responds to loading and error props. The behavior for this cross-cutting concern is centrally managed in withAsync's implementation, so we account for loading and error states "for free" just by using the HOC pattern here.

However, similar to presentational and container components, HOCs are often also discarded in favor of hooks, since hooks provide similar benefits with added convenience.

Composing HOCs

Composing multiple HOCs together is a common pattern in React, which allows developers to mix and match functionalities and behaviors across components. Here's an example of how you might compose multiple HOCs:

Suppose you have two HOCs, `withLogging` and `withUser`:

```
// withLogging.js
const withLogging = (WrappedComponent) => {
  return (props) => {
    console.log("Rendered with props:", props);
    return <WrappedComponent {...props} />;
  };
};

// withUser.js
const withUser = (WrappedComponent) => {
  const user = { name: "John Doe" }; // Assume this comes from some data source
  return (props) => <WrappedComponent {...props} user={user} />;
};
```

Now, say you want to compose these two HOCs together. One way to do this is to nest them:

```
const EnhancedComponent = withLogging(withUser(MyComponent));
```

However, nested HOC calls can be difficult to read and maintain, especially as the number of HOCs increases. Imagine this in your application over time:

```
const EnhancedComponent = withErrorHandler(
  withLoadingSpinner(
    withAuthentication(
      withAuthorization(
        withPagination(
          withDataFetching(
            withLogging(withUser(withTheme(withIntl(withRouting(MyComponent)))))
          )
        )
      )
    )
  )
);
```

Yuck! A better approach is to create a utility function that composes multiple HOCs together into a single HOC. Such a utility function might look like this:

```
// compose.js
const compose =
  (...hocs) =>
  (WrappedComponent) =>
    hocs.reduceRight((acc, hoc) => hoc(acc), WrappedComponent);
```

```
// Usage:
const EnhancedComponent = compose(withLogging, withUser)(MyComponent);
```

In this `compose` function, `reduceRight` is used to apply each HOC from right to left to the `WrappedComponent`. This way, you can list your HOCs in a flat list, which is easier to read and maintain. The `compose` function is a common utility in functional programming, and libraries like Redux provide their own `compose` utility function for this purpose.

To revisit our previous yucky example with our new `compose` utility, it would look more like this:

```
const EnhancedComponent = compose(
  withErrorHandler,
  withLoadingSpinner,
  withAuthentication,
  withAuthorization,
  withPagination,
  withDataFetching,
  withLogging,
  withUser,
  withTheme,
  withIntl,
  withRouting
)(MyComponent);
```

Isn't that better? Less indentation, more readability, and easier maintenance. Each HOC in the chain wraps the component produced by the previous HOC, adding its own behavior to the mix. This way, you can build up complex components from simpler components and HOCs, each focused on a single concern. This makes your code more modular, easier to understand, and easier to test.

HOCs versus hooks

Since the introduction of hooks, HOCs have become less popular. Hooks provide a more convenient way to add functionality to components, and they also solve some of the problems that HOCs have. For example, HOCs can cause issues with ref forwarding, and they can also cause unnecessary rerenders when used incorrectly. Table 5-1 shows a little bit of a detailed comparison between the two.

Table 5-1. Comparison of HOCs versus hooks

Feature	HOCs	Hooks
Code reuse	Excellent for sharing logic across multiple components.	Ideal for extracting and sharing logic within a component or across similar components.
Rendering logic	Can control rendering of wrapped component.	Do not affect rendering directly, but can be used within functional components to manage side effects related to rendering.

Feature	HOCs	Hooks
Prop manipulation	Can inject and manipulate props, providing additional data or functions.	Cannot inject or manipulate props directly.
State management	Can manage and manipulate state outside of the wrapped component.	Designed to manage local state within functional components.
Lifecycle methods	Can encapsulate lifecycle logic related to the wrapped component.	`useEffect` and other hooks can handle lifecycle events within functional components.
Ease of composition	Can be composed together, but may result in "wrapper hell" if not managed well.	Easily composable and can be used alongside other hooks without adding layers of components.
Ease of testing	Testing can be more complex due to additional wrapper components.	Generally easier to test as they can be isolated easier than HOCs.
Type safety	With TypeScript, can be tricky to type correctly, especially with deeply nested HOCs.	Better type inference and easier to type with TypeScript.

Table 5-1 provides a side-by-side comparison of HOCs and hooks, showcasing their respective strengths and use cases. While HOCs are still a useful pattern, hooks are generally preferred for most use cases due to their simplicity and ease of use.

From this table, we can observe that HOCs and hooks are pivotal in React for sharing logic across components, yet they cater to slightly different use cases. HOCs excel in sharing logic across multiple components and are particularly adept at controlling the rendering of the wrapped component and manipulating props, providing additional data or functions to components. They can manage state outside of the wrapped component and encapsulate lifecycle logic related to the wrapped component. However, they can lead to a "wrapper hell" if not managed well, especially when many HOCs are nested together. This nesting can also make testing more complex, and type safety with TypeScript can become tricky, especially with deeply nested HOCs.

On the other hand, hooks are ideal for extracting and sharing logic within a component or across similar components without adding extra layers of components, thus avoiding the "wrapper hell" scenario. Unlike HOCs, hooks do not affect rendering directly and cannot inject or manipulate props directly. They are designed to manage local state within functional components and handle lifecycle events using the `useEffect` Hook, among others. Hooks promote ease of composition, and are generally easier to test as they can be isolated easier than HOCs. Moreover, when used with TypeScript, hooks provide better type inference and are easier to type, thus potentially reducing bugs related to type errors.

While both HOCs and hooks provide mechanisms to reuse logic, hooks offer a more direct and less complicated approach to managing state, lifecycle events, and other React features within functional components. On the flip side, HOCs provide a more structured way to inject behavior into components, which can be beneficial in larger codebases or in codebases that have not yet adopted hooks. Each has its own set of advantages, and the choice between using HOCs or hooks would largely depend on the specific requirements of your project and the team's familiarity with these patterns.

Can we think of any React HOCs that we use fairly frequently? Yes, we can! React.memo is one that we just covered in this chapter and is indeed an HOC! Let's look at another one: React.forwardRef. This is an HOC that forwards a ref to a child component. Let's look at an example:

```
const FancyInput = React.forwardRef((props, ref) => (
  <input type="text" ref={ref} {...props} />
));

const App = () => {
  const inputRef = useRef(null);

  useEffect(() => {
    inputRef.current.focus();
  }, []);

  return (
    <div>
      <FancyInput ref={inputRef} />
    </div>
  );
};
```

In this example, we're using React.forwardRef to forward a ref to the FancyInput component. This allows us to access the input element's focus method in the parent component. This is a common pattern in React, and it's a great example of how HOCs can be used to solve problems that are difficult to solve with regular components.

Render Props

Since we've already talked about JSX expressions, a common pattern is to have props that are functions that receive component-scoped state as arguments to facilitate code reuse. Here's a simple example:

```
<WindowSize
  render={({ width, height }) => (
    <div>
      Your window is {width}x{height}px
    </div>
  )}
/>
```

Notice how there's a prop called render that receives a function as a value. This prop even outputs some JSX markup that's actually rendered. But why? Turns out Window Size does some magic internally to compute the size of a user's window, and then calls `props.render` to return the structure we declare, making use of enclosing state to render the window size.

Let's take a look at `WindowSize` to understand this a bit more:

```
const WindowSize = (props) => {
  const [size, setSize] = useState({ width: -1, height: -1 });

  useEffect(() => {
    const handleResize = () => {
      setSize({ width: window.innerWidth, height: window.innerHeight });
    };
    window.addEventListener("resize", handleResize);
    return () => window.removeEventListener("resize", handleResize);
  }, []);

  return props.render(size);
};
```

From this example, we can see that `WindowSize` uses an event listener to store some stuff in state on every resize, but the component itself is headless: it has no opinions about what UI to present. Instead, it yields control to whatever parent is rendering it and calls the *render prop* it's supplied, effectively inverting control to its parent for the rendering job.

This helps a component that depends on the window size for rendering receive this information without duplicating the `useEffect` blocks and keeps our code a little bit more DRY (Don't Repeat Yourself). This pattern is no longer as popular and has since been effectively replaced with React Hooks.

Children as a function

Since `children` is a prop, some have preferred to drop the `render` prop name altogether and instead just use `children`. This would change the use of `WindowSize` to look like this:

```
<WindowSize>
  {(({ width, height }) => (
    <div>
      Your window is {width}x{height}px
    </div>
  )}
</WindowSize>
```

Some React authors prefer this because it's truer to the intent of the code: `WindowSize` in this case looks a bit like a React Context, and whatever we display tends to feel like children that consume this context. Still, React Hooks eliminate the need for this pattern altogether, so maybe proceed with caution.

Control Props

The Control Props pattern in React is a strategic approach to state management that expands upon the concept of controlled components. It provides a flexible mechanism for determining how state is managed within a component. To understand this, let's first understand controlled components.

Controlled components are components that do not maintain their own internal state. Instead, they receive their current value as a prop from a parent component, which is the single source of truth for their state. When the state should change, controlled components notify the parent using callback functions, typically onChange. The parent is thus responsible for managing the state and updating the value of the controlled component.

For example, a controlled `<input>` element looks like this:

```
function Form() {
  const [inputValue, setInputValue] = React.useState("");

  function handleChange(event) {
    setInputValue(event.target.value);
  }

  return <input type="text" value={inputValue} onChange={handleChange} />;
}
```

The Control Props pattern takes the principle of controlled components further by allowing a component to either be controlled externally by props or manage its own state internally, providing optional external control. A component following the Control Props pattern accepts both the state value and a function to update that state as props. This dual capability enables the parent to exert control over the child component's state if it chooses to do so, but it also allows the child component to operate independently if not controlled.

An example of the Control Props pattern is a toggle button that can either be controlled by its parent or manage its own state:

```
function Toggle({ on, onToggle }) {
  const [isOn, setIsOn] = React.useState(false);

  const handleToggle = () => {
    const nextState = on === undefined ? !isOn : on;
    if (on === undefined) {
      setIsOn(nextState);
    }
    if (onToggle) {
      onToggle(nextState);
    }
  };
```

```
    return (
      <button onClick={handleToggle}>
        {on !== undefined ? on : isOn ? "On" : "Off"}
      </button>
    );
  }
```

In the `Toggle` component, `isOn` represents the internal state, while `on` is the external control prop. The component can operate in a controlled mode if the `on` prop is provided by the parent. If not, it falls back to its internal state, `isOn`. The `onToggle` prop is a callback that allows the parent component to respond to state changes, providing the parent with the opportunity to synchronize its own state with the state of the `Toggle`.

This pattern enhances component flexibility, offering both controlled and uncontrolled modes of operation. It allows the parent to be in charge when necessary, while also letting the component retain autonomy over its own state when not explicitly controlled.

Prop Collections

We often need to bundle a whole bunch of props together. For example, when creating drag-and-drop user interfaces, there are quite a few props to manage:

onDragStart
> To tell the browser what to do when a user starts dragging an element

onDragOver
> To identify a dropzone

onDrop
> To execute some code when an element is dropped on this element

onDragEnd
> To tell the browser what to do when an element is done being dragged

Moreover, data/elements cannot be dropped in other elements by default. To allow an element to be dropped on another, we must prevent the default handling of the element. This is done by calling the `event.preventDefault` method for the `onDragOver` event for a possible dropzone.

Since these props usually go together, and since `onDragOver` usually defaults to `event => { event.preventDefault(); moreStuff(); }`, we can collect these props together and reuse them in various components, like so:

```
export const droppableProps = {
  onDragOver: (event) => {
    event.preventDefault();
```

```
  },
  onDrop: (event) => {},
};

export const draggableProps = {
  onDragStart: (event) => {},
  onDragEnd: (event) => {},
};
```

Now, if we have a React component we expect to behave like a dropzone, we can use the prop collection on it, like this:

```
<Dropzone {...droppableProps} />
```

This is the prop collection pattern, and it makes a number of props reusable. This is often quite widely used in the accessibility space to include a number of aria-* props on accessible components. One problem that's still present though is that if we write a custom onDragOver prop and override the collection, we lose the event.prevent Default call that we get out of the box using the collection.

This can cause unexpected behavior, removing the ability to drop a component on Dropzone:

```
<Dropzone
  {...droppableProps}
  onDragOver={() => {
    alert("Dragged!");
  }}
/>
```

Thankfully, we can fix this using prop getters.

Prop getters

Prop getters essentially compose prop collections with custom props and merge them. From our example, we'd like to preserve the event.preventDefault call in the droppableProps collection's onDragOver handler, while also adding a custom alert("Dragged!"); call to it. We can do this using prop getters.

First, we'll change the droppableProps collection to a prop getter:

```
export const getDroppableProps = () => {
  return {
    onDragOver: (event) => {
      event.preventDefault();
    },
    onDrop: (event) => {},
  };
};
```

At this point, nothing has changed besides where we once exported a prop collection, we now export a function that returns a prop collection. This is a prop getter. Since this is a function, it can receive arguments—like a custom onDragOver. We can compose this custom onDragOver with our default one, like so:

```
const compose =
  (...functions) =>
  (...args) =>
    functions.forEach((fn) => fn?.(...args));

export const getDroppableProps = ({
  onDragOver: replacementOnDragOver,
  ...replacementProps
}) => {
  const defaultOnDragOver = (event) => {
    event.preventDefault();
  };

  return {
    onDragOver: compose(replacementOnDragOver, defaultOnDragOver),
    onDrop: (event) => {},
    ...replacementProps,
  };
};
```

Now, we can use the prop getter like this:

```
<Dropzone
  {...getDroppableProps({
    onDragOver: () => {
      alert("Dragged!");
    },
  })}
/>
```

This custom onDragOver will compose into our default onDragOver, and both things will happen: event.preventDefault() and alert("Dragged!"). This is the prop getter pattern.

Compound Components

Sometimes, we have accordion components like this:

```
<Accordion
  items={[
    { label: "One", content: "lorem ipsum for more, see https://one.com" },
    { label: "Two", content: "lorem ipsum for more, see https://two.com" },
    { label: "Three", content: "lorem ipsum for more, see https://three.com" },
  ]}
/>
```

This component is intended to render a list similar to this, except *only one item* can be open at a given time:

- One

- Two

- Three

The inner workings of this component would look something like this:

```
export const Accordion = ({ items }) => {
  const [activeItemIndex, setActiveItemIndex] = useState(0);

  return (
    <ul>
      {items.map((item, index) => (
        <li onClick={() => setActiveItemIndex(index)} key={item.id}>
          <strong>{item.label}</strong>
          {index === activeItemIndex && i.content}
        </li>
      ))}
    </ul>
  );
};
```

But what if we wanted a custom separator between items Two and Three? What if we wanted the third link to be red or something? We'd probably resort to some type of hack like this:

```
<Accordion
  items={[
    { label: "One", content: "lorem ipsum for more, see https://one.com" },
    { label: "Two", content: "lorem ipsum for more, see https://two.com" },
    { label: "---" },
    { label: "Three", content: "lorem ipsum for more, see https://three.com" },
  ]}
/>
```

But that wouldn't look the way we want. So we'd probably do more hacks on our current hack:

```
export const Accordion = ({ items }) => {
  const [activeItemIndex, setActiveItemIndex] = useState(0);

  return (
    <ul>
      {items.map((item, index) =>
        item === "---" ? (
          <hr />
        ) : (
          <li onClick={() => setActiveItemIndex(index)} key={item.id}>
            <strong>{item.label}</strong>
```

```
        {index === activeItemIndex && i.content}
      </li>
    )
  )}
  </ul>
);
};
```

Now is that code we'd be proud of? I'm not sure. This is why we need *compound components*: they allow us to have a grouping of interconnected, distinct components that share state, but are atomically renderable, giving us more control of the element tree.

This accordion, expressed using the compound components pattern, would look like this:

```
<Accordion>
  <AccordionItem item={{ label: "One" }} />
  <AccordionItem item={{ label: "Two" }} />
  <AccordionItem item={{ label: "Three" }} />
</Accordion>
```

If we decide to explore how this pattern can be implemented in React, we might consider two ways:

- With `React.cloneElement` on the children
- With React Context

`React.cloneElement` is considered a legacy API, so let's pursue doing this with React Context. First, we'll start with a context that each part of the accordion can read from:

```
const AccordionContext = createContext({
  activeItemIndex: 0,
  setActiveItemIndex: () => 0,
});
```

Then, our `Accordion` component will just provide context to its children:

```
export const Accordion = ({ items }) => {
  const [activeItemIndex, setActiveItemIndex] = useState(0);

  return (
    <AccordionContext.Provider value={{ activeItemIndex, setActiveItemIndex }}>
      <ul>{children}</ul>
    </AccordionContext.Provider>
  );
};
```

Now, let's create discrete `AccordionItem` components that consume and respond to this context as well:

```
export const AccordionItem = ({ item, index }) => {
  // Note we're using the context here, not state!
```

```
    const { activeItemIndex, setActiveItemIndex } = useContext(AccordionContext);

    return (
      <li onClick={() => setActiveItemIndex(index)} key={item.id}>
        <strong>{item.label}</strong>
        {index === activeItemIndex && i.content}
      </li>
    );
};
```

Now that we've got multiple parts for our `Accordion` making it a compound component, our usage of the `Accordion` goes from this:

```
<Accordion
  items={[
    { label: "One", content: "lorem ipsum for more, see https://one.com" },
    { label: "Two", content: "lorem ipsum for more, see https://two.com" },
    { label: "Three", content: "lorem ipsum for more, see https://three.com" },
  ]}
/>
```

to this:

```
<Accordion>
  {items.map((item, index) => (
    <AccordionItem key={item.id} item={item} index={index} />
  ))}
</Accordion>
```

The benefit of this is that we have far more control, while each `AccordionItem` is aware of the larger state of `Accordion`. So now, if we wanted to include a horizontal line between items `Two` and `Three`, we could break out of the `map` and go more manual if we wanted to:

```
<Accordion>
  <AccordionItem key={items[0].id} item={items[0]} index={0} />
  <AccordionItem key={items[1].id} item={items[1]} index={1} />
  <hr />
  <AccordionItem key={items[2].id} item={items[2]} index={2} />
</Accordion>
```

Or, we could do something more hybrid, like:

```
<Accordion>
  {items.slice(0, 2).map((item, index) => (
    <AccordionItem key={item.id} item={item} index={index} />
  ))}
  <hr />
  {items.slice(2).map((item, index) => (
    <AccordionItem key={item.id} item={item} index={index} />
  ))}
</Accordion>
```

This is the benefit of compound components: they invert control of rendering to the parent, while preserving contextual state awareness among children. The same approach could be used for a tab UI, where tabs are aware of the current tab state while having varying levels of element nesting.

Another benefit is that this pattern promotes separation of concerns, which helps applications scale significantly better over time.

State Reducer

The state reducer pattern in React was invented and popularized by Kent C. Dodds (*@kentcdodds*), one of the most prominent and proficient engineers and educators in the React space, and a true world-renowned expert in the field. This pattern offers a powerful way to create flexible and customizable components. Let's illustrate this concept with a real-world example: a toggle button component. This example will demonstrate how a basic toggle component can be enhanced to allow consumers to customize its state logic, disabling the toggle on certain days of the week for some business reason.

First, we start with a basic toggle component using the `useReducer` hook. The component maintains its own state, determining whether the toggle is in an `On` or `Off` position. The initial state is set to `false`, indicating the `Off` state:

```
import React, { useReducer } from "react";

function toggleReducer(state, action) {
  switch (action.type) {
    case "TOGGLE":
      return { on: !state.on };
    default:
      throw new Error(`Unhandled action type: ${action.type}`);
  }
}

function Toggle() {
  const [state, dispatch] = useReducer(toggleReducer, { on: false });

  return (
    <button onClick={() => dispatch({ type: "TOGGLE" })}>
      {state.on ? "On" : "Off"}
    </button>
  );
}
```

To implement the state reducer pattern, the `Toggle` component is modified to accept a `stateReducer` prop. This prop allows the component's internal state logic to be customized or extended. The component's `internalDispatch` function combines the internal reducer logic with the external reducer provided by the `stateReducer` prop:

```
function Toggle({ stateReducer }) {
  const [state, dispatch] = useReducer(
    (state, action) => {
      const nextState = toggleReducer(state, action);
      return stateReducer(state, { ...action, changes: nextState });
    },
    { on: false }
  );

  return (
    <button onClick={() => internalDispatch({ type: "TOGGLE" })}>
      {state.on ? "On" : "Off"}
    </button>
  );
}

Toggle.defaultProps = {
  stateReducer: (state, action) => state, // Default reducer does nothing special
};
```

From this code snippet, we can see that the stateReducer prop is used to customize the component's internal state logic. The stateReducer function is called with the current state and the action object; however, we add an extra property of metadata to the action: changes. This changes property contains the next state of the component, which is calculated by the internal reducer. This allows the external reducer to access the next state of the component and make decisions based on that.

Let's see how the Toggle component can be utilized with custom behavior based on this pattern. In the following example, the App component uses the Toggle but provides a custom stateReducer. This reducer contains logic that prevents the toggle from being turned off on Wednesdays because Wednesday in this app's location is a universal "no off" day. This illustrates how the state reducer pattern allows for flexible modification of component behavior without changing the component itself:

```
function App() {
  const customReducer = (state, action) => {
    // Custom logic: prevent toggle off on Wednesdays
    if (new Date().getDay() === 3 && !changes.on) {
      return state;
    }
    return action.changes;
  };

  return <Toggle stateReducer={customReducer} />;
}
```

With this example, we see the power of the state reducer pattern in creating highly flexible and reusable components. By allowing external logic to integrate with the internal state management of a component, we can cater to a wide range of behaviors and use cases, enhancing both the utility and versatility of the component.

Whew! What a chapter! Let's wrap things up and summarize what we learned.

Chapter Review

Throughout this chapter, we've discussed various aspects of React, including memoization, lazy loading, reducers, and state management. We've explored the advantages and potential drawbacks of different approaches to these topics and how they can impact the performance and maintainability of React applications.

We started by discussing memoization in React and its benefits for optimizing component rendering. We looked at the `React.memo` function and how it can be used to prevent unnecessary rerenders of components. We also examined some potential issues with memoization, such as stale state and the need to carefully manage dependencies.

Next, we talked about lazy loading in React and how it can be used to defer the loading of certain components or resources until they are actually needed. We looked at the `React.lazy` and `Suspense` components and how they can be used to implement lazy loading in a React application. We also discussed the trade-offs of lazy loading, such as increased complexity and potential performance issues.

We then moved on to reducers and how they can be used for state management in React. We explored the differences between `useState` and `useReducer`, and discussed the advantages of using a centralized reducer function for managing state updates.

Throughout our conversation, we used code examples from our own implementations to illustrate the concepts we discussed. We explored how these examples work under the hood and how they can impact the performance and maintainability of React applications.

Through the use of code examples and in-depth explanations, we gained a deeper understanding of these topics and how they can be applied in real-world React applications.

Review Questions

Let's ask ourselves a few questions to test our understanding of the concepts we learned in this chapter:

1. What is memoization in React, and how can it be used to optimize component rendering?

2. What are the advantages of using `useReducer` for state management in React, and how does it differ from `useState`?

3. How can lazy loading be implemented in a React application using the `React.lazy` and `Suspense` components?

4. What are some potential issues that can arise when using memoization in React, and how can they be mitigated?

5. How can the `useCallback` hook be used to memoize functions passed as props to components in React?

Up Next

In the next chapter, we'll look at React on the server side—diving into serve-side rendering, its benefits and trade-offs, hydration, frameworks, and more. See you there!

CHAPTER 6

Server-Side React

React has evolved considerably since its inception. Although it started as a client-side library, the demand for server-side rendering (SSR) has grown over time for reasons we will come to understand in this chapter. Together, we will explore server-side React and understand how it differs from client-only React, and how it can be used to level up our React applications.

As we've discussed in earlier chapters, React was initially developed by Meta to address the need for efficient and scalable UIs. In Chapter 3 we looked at how it does this through the virtual DOM, which enables developers to create and manage UI components with ease. React's client-side approach unlocked fast, responsive user experiences across the web. However, as the web continued to evolve, the limitations of client-side rendering became more apparent.

Limitations of Client-Side Rendering

user interfaces with React since it was first released as open source software in 2013. Eventually, a number of limitations with this approach started to appear. These limitations eventually led to us moving more and more concerns to the server side.

SEO

One of the significant limitations of client-side rendering is that search engine crawlers may not correctly index the content, as some of them do not execute JavaScript, or those that do execute JavaScript may not execute it as we expect.

Given the wide variety of search engine crawler implementations, along with the fact that a lot of them are proprietary and unknowable to the public, this makes client-only rendering somewhat questionable with regard to the reach of a given website or application.

That said, an article from Search Engine Land in 2015 (*https://oreil.ly/r5hF2*) described some experiments to test how various search engines work with client-only applications, and this is what they mentioned:

> We ran a series of tests that verified Google is able to execute and index JavaScript with a multitude of implementations. We also confirmed Google is able to render the entire page and read the DOM, thereby indexing dynamically generated content.

This article found that at the time of writing, Google and Bing were advanced enough to index client-only websites, but ultimately this is just one research project in an otherwise vast and unknowable proprietary ocean.

Thus, while client-only applications may work well with modern search engines, there is an inherent risk in not having a server-based counterpart. In traditional web applications, when a user or a search engine crawler requests a page, the server renders the HTML for the page and sends it back. The HTML contains all the content, links, and data, making it easy for search engine crawlers to read and index the content for search engine results since all the content of the page is nothing more than text, i.e., markup.

However, in a client-side rendered application, often built with libraries or frameworks like React, the server sends back a near-empty HTML file whose sole job is to load JavaScript from a separate JavaScript file on the same or an alternate server. The JavaScript file then downloads and executes in the browser, rendering the page content dynamically. This approach provides a smooth user experience, resembling that of a native application, but it has a downside when it comes to search engine optimization (SEO) and performance: we don't download anything useful for human readers on the first request, but instead have to do another request immediately after the page loads for the JavaScript that will power the entire site. This is known as a network waterfall.

Thus, another downside of client-only rendering is performance. Let's talk about that.

Performance

Client-side rendered applications may suffer from performance issues, especially on slow networks or less powerful devices. The need to download, parse, and execute JavaScript before rendering the content can lead to significant delays in content rendering. This "time to interactive" is a crucial metric as it directly impacts user engagement and bounce rates (bounce as in the rate at which users abandon a page). Users might leave a page if it takes too long to load, and this behavior can further negatively impact the SEO ranking of the page.

Additionally, if a device is low-powered with minimal CPU availability, client-only rendering also creates a poor user experience. This is because the device may not have enough processing power to execute the JavaScript quickly, resulting in a slow and unresponsive application. This can lead to frustrated users and a poor user experience. If we executed this JavaScript on the server and sent minimal data or markup to the client, low-power clients don't have to do much work and thus the user experience is better.

On a broader spectrum, the issues of SEO and performance in client-side rendered applications highlight the importance of adhering to web standards and best practices. They also underline the need for server-side rendering or static site generation as more reliable alternatives for delivering content in a performant and accessible manner, especially for content-heavy sites or applications.

The principle of progressive enhancement, where basic content and functionality are delivered to all browsers, while advanced features are considered as an enhancement, aligns well with these alternatives. By rendering the core content server-side, you ensure that all users and search engines have access to the fundamental content and functionality, regardless of JavaScript execution. Then, client-side JavaScript can enhance the user experience by adding interactivity, richer animations, and other advanced features for the browsers and devices that can support them. It does not make any sense to have *the entire experience* be client-side JavaScript only, as this is not the original design of the web. JavaScript's role is to *enhance* a web page, not *be* a web page.

Consider the following example:

```
import React, { useEffect, useState } from "react";

const Home = () => {
  const [data, setData] = useState([]);

  useEffect(() => {
    fetch("https://api.example.com/data")
      .then((response) => response.json())
      .then((data) => setData(data));
  }, []);

  return (
    <div>
      {data.map((item) => (
        <div key={item.id}>{item.title}</div>
      ))}
    </div>
  );
};

export default Home;
```

In this example, we are fetching data from an API and rendering it on the client side. We can tell it's the client side because we are using the useEffect hook to fetch the data, and the `useState` hook to store the data in state. The `useEffect` hook executes inside a browser (a client) only.

A serious limitation with this is that some search engine crawlers may not be able to see this content unless we implement server-side rendering. Instead, there is a risk that they see a blank screen or a fallback message, which can result in poor SEO.

Another common problem with client-only applications is network waterfalls, wherein the initial page load is blocked by the amount of JavaScript that needs to be downloaded, parsed, and executed by the browser before the website or web app becomes visible. In cases where network connectivity is a limited resource, this would render a website or application completely unresponsive for significant amounts of time.

In the example, we're initiating a data fetch request to an external API endpoint (`https://api.example.com/data`) to retrieve some data. This fetch happens *after* our initial JavaScript bundle is downloaded, parsed, and executed, and that happens only *after* the initial HTML loads. This is a network waterfall and leads to less-than-optimal performance. If we visualize it, it would look like Figure 6-1.

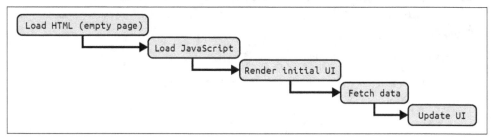

Figure 6-1. Data fetch request

Yuck. With server-side rendering, we can do better and enable our users to see useful content immediately, altering the diagram to look like this:

```
Load HTML (full UI, with data fetched on the server)
```

Indeed, the first load is already packed with information that is useful to the user because we fetched our data and rendered our component on the server. There is no waterfall here, and the user gets all their information immediately. This is the value of server-side rendering.

As of React 18, the bundle sizes of React and React DOM are 6.4 kB and 130.2 kB, respectively. These sizes are for the latest version of React at the time of writing and may vary depending on the version and configuration of React that you are using today. This means that even in production environments, our users have to download around 136 kB of JavaScript just for React alone (i.e., React + React DOM), before downloading, parsing, and executing the rest of our application's code. This can result in a slower initial page load, especially on slower devices and networks, and potentially frustrated users. Moreover, because React essentially owns the DOM and we have no user interface without React in client-only applications, our users have no choice but to wait for React and React DOM to load *first* before the rest of our application does.

In contrast, a server rendered application would stream rendered HTML to the client before any JavaScript downloads, enabling users to get meaningful content immediately. It would then load relevant JavaScript after the initial page renders, probably while the user is still orienting themselves with a user interface through a process called "hydration." More on this in the coming sections.

Initially streaming rendered HTML and then hydrating the DOM with JavaScript allows users to interact with the application sooner, resulting in a better user experience: it is immediately available to the user without them having to wait for any extras—that they may or may not even need—to load.

Security

Client-only rendering can also have security issues, especially when dealing with sensitive data. This is because all of the application's code is downloaded to the client's browser, making it vulnerable to attacks such as cross-site request forgery (CSRF).

Without getting too much into the weeds about CSRF, a common way to mitigate against it is to have control of the server that serves the website or web app to your users. If we have control of this server, we can send appropriate anti-CSRF tokens from the server as a trusted source to the client, and then the client submits the tokens via a form or similar back to the server, which can verify that the request is coming from the correct client. This is a common way to mitigate against CSRF.

While it is technically possible to serve client-only applications from a static site server we control, and mitigate against CSRF that way, it's still not the best way to serve a website in general because of the other trade-offs we've discussed so far. If we do have control of a server, then why not add SSR to it from there?

Ultimately, here's what we're saying:

- If we don't have access to the server side but work in a team where it's just `git push` frontend client-only code and then it's magically deployed somewhere, there are inherent CSRF risks here.
- If we have access to the server side and if our website or web app is still client only, we can mitigate against CSRF quite well already and the security risks around it go away.
- If we have access to the server side and if our website or web app is still client only, there's a strong argument to be made to add server-side rendering to it,

since we have access to the server, enabling the other benefits around SEO and performance that we've already covered.

Let's get a little bit practical and consider the following example:

```
import React, { useState } from "react";

const Account = () => {
  const [balance, setBalance] = useState(100);

  const handleWithdrawal = async (amount) => {
    // Assume this request goes to a server to process the withdrawal
    const response = await fetch("/withdraw", {
      method: "POST",
      headers: {
        "Content-Type": "application/json",
      },
      credentials: "include",
      body: JSON.stringify({ amount }),
    });

    if (response.ok) {
      const updatedBalance = await response.json();
      setBalance(updatedBalance);
    }
  };

  return (
    <div>
      <h1>Account Balance: {balance}</h1>
      <button onClick={() => handleWithdrawal(10)}>Withdraw $10</button>
      <button onClick={() => handleWithdrawal(50)}>Withdraw $50</button>
      <button onClick={() => handleWithdrawal(100)}>Withdraw $100</button>
    </div>
  );
};

export default Account;
```

In this code, handleWithdrawal sends a POST request to a hypothetical server-side endpoint /withdraw to process the withdrawal. A CSRF risk could occur if this endpoint does not properly validate the origin of the request and doesn't require any form of anti-CSRF token.

An attacker could create a malicious webpage that tricks a user into clicking a button, which then sends a POST request to the /withdraw endpoint on the user's behalf, possibly leading to unauthorized withdrawals from the user's account. This is because the browser automatically includes cookies in the request, which the server uses to authenticate the user. If the server does not validate the origin of the request, it could be tricked into processing the request and sending the funds to the attacker's account.

If this component is rendered on the client side, it could be vulnerable to CSRF attacks because the server and client do not have a shared common secret or contract between them. To speak poetically, the client and server don't know each other. This could allow an attacker to steal funds or manipulate the application's data.

If we used server rendering, we could mitigate these security issues by rendering the component on the server with a special secret token generated by the server, and then sending HTML containing the secret token to the client. The client would then send this token back to the server that issued it, establishing a secure bidirectional contract. This would allow the server to verify that the request is coming from the correct client that it has preauthorized and not an unknown one, which could possibly be a malicious attacker.

The Rise of Server Rendering

For these reasons, server-side rendering has emerged as an arguably superior technique for improving the performance and user experience of web applications. With server rendering, applications can be optimized for speed and accessibility, resulting in faster load times, better SEO, and improved user engagement.

Benefits of Server Rendering

Let's dive deeper into the benefits of server rendering. These should become immediately clear as we further understand the limitations of client-only rendering:

The time to first meaningful paint is faster with server rendering.
This is because the server can render the initial HTML markup and send it to the client, which can then be displayed immediately. This is in contrast to client-only rendering, where the client must wait for the JavaScript to be downloaded, parsed, and executed before the application can be rendered.

Server rendering improves the accessibility of web applications.
Users with slow internet connections or low-power devices may have a better experience if they receive fully rendered HTML instead of waiting for client-side JavaScript to load and render the page.

Server rendering can improve the SEO of web applications.
When search engine crawlers index your site, they can see the fully rendered HTML, making it easier for them to understand the content and structure of your site.

Server rendering can also improve the security of web applications.
By rendering the core content server-side, you ensure that all users and search engines have access to the fundamental content and functionality, regardless of JavaScript execution. Then, client-side JavaScript can enhance the user experi-

ence by adding interactivity, richer animations, and other advanced features for the browsers and devices that can support them.

However, server rendered HTML is static and lacks interactivity as it does not have any JavaScript initially loaded. It includes no event listeners or other dynamic functionality attached. To enable user interactions and other dynamic features, the static HTML must be "hydrated" with the necessary JavaScript code. Let's understand the concept of hydration a little better.

Hydration

Hydration is a term used to describe the process of attaching event listeners and other JavaScript functionality to static HTML that is generated on the server and sent to the client. The goal of hydration is to enable a server rendered application to become fully interactive after being loaded in the browser, providing users with a fast and smooth experience.

In a React application, hydration happens after a client downloads a server rendered React application. Then, the following steps occur:

Loading the client bundle
> While the browser is rendering the static HTML, it also downloads and parses the JavaScript bundle that contains the application's code. This bundle includes the React components and any other code that is necessary for the application's functionality.

Attaching event listener
> Once the JavaScript bundle is loaded, React "hydrates" the static HTML by attaching event listeners and other dynamic functionality to the DOM elements. This is typically done using the `hydrateRoot` function from `react-dom`, which takes the root React component and the DOM container as arguments. Hydration essentially transforms the static HTML into a fully interactive React application.

After the hydration process is complete, the application is fully interactive and can respond to user input, fetch data, and update the DOM, as necessary.

During hydration, React matches the structure of the DOM elements in the static HTML to the structure defined by the React components via JSX. It is crucial that the structure generated by the React components matches the structure of the static HTML. If there is a mismatch, React will not be able to correctly attach event listeners and will not be aware of what React element directly maps to what DOM element, which results in the application not behaving as expected.

By combining server-side rendering and hydration, developers can create web applications that load quickly and provide a smooth, interactive user experience.

Hydration Considered Harmful

While hydration is a great way to take server rendered HTML and make it interactive, some criticize hydration for being slower than necessary, often citing resumability as a superior alternative (see Figure 6-2). Let's explore this a little bit.

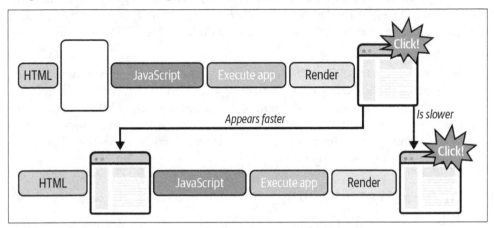

Figure 6-2. Hydration

With hydration, we render a React application on the server and then pass the rendered output to a client. However, at this point in time, nothing is interactive. From here, our browser needs to download the client bundle, attach event listeners, and effectively "rerender" the client. This is a lot of work, and sometimes presents a delay between when content appears to a user and when the user can actually use the site.

Alternatively, resumability works slightly differently, as shown in Figure 6-3.

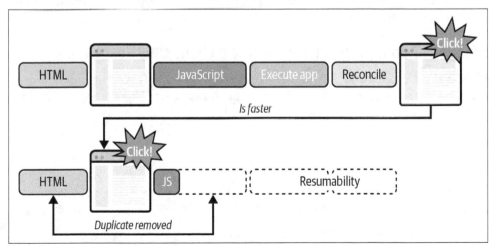

Figure 6-3. Resumability

With resumability, the entire application is rendered on the server and streamed to a browser. Along with the initial markup, all interactive behavior is serialized and also sent to the client. From there, the client already has all the information on how to become interactive on demand and thus *resume* where the server left off. It does not need to hydrate (that is, attach event listeners and render the page on the client side), but instead can deserialize the stuff the server gave it and react accordingly. Skipping the hydration step can result in a faster time to interactive (TTI) and a better user experience.

While there is measurable benefit to resumability, the engineering community questions whether the complexity of implementing it is worth the benefit. Indeed, it is a more complex approach than hydration, and it is not yet clear whether the benefits outweigh the costs: yes, time to interactive is faster by a few milliseconds, but is it worth the complexity of implementing resumability? This is a question that is still being debated in the React community.

Creating Server Rendering

If you have an existing client-only React app, you may be wondering how to add server rendering to it. Fortunately, it's relatively straightforward to add server rendering to an existing React app. One approach is to use a server rendering framework, such as Next.js or Remix. While these frameworks are indeed the best way to server rendered React applications, abstractions like this can leave the more curious of us hungry to understand the underlying mechanisms used to accomplish this.

If you're a curious person and are interested in how you would add server rendering to a client-only React app manually, or if you're interested in how frameworks do it, read on. Once again, this is stuff you'd probably not use in production, but is more for educational purposes for the curious.

Manually Adding Server Rendering to a Client-Only React App

If you've got a client-only application, this is how you'd add server rendering to it. First, you'd create a *server.js* file in the root of your project. This file will contain the code for your server:

```
// server.js

// Importing necessary modules
const express = require("express"); // Importing Express.js library
const path = require("path"); // Importing Path module to handle file paths
const React = require("react"); // Importing React library
// Importing ReactDOMServer for server-side rendering
const ReactDOMServer = require("react-dom/server");

// Importing the main App component from the src directory
```

```
const App = require("./src/App");

// Initializing an Express application
const app = express();

// Serving static files from the 'build' directory
app.use(express.static(path.join(__dirname, "build")));

// Handling all GET requests
app.get("*", (req, res) => {
  // Rendering the App component to an HTML string
  const html = ReactDOMServer.renderToString(<App />);

  // Sending an HTML response that includes the rendered App component
  res.send(`
    <!DOCTYPE html>
    <html>
      <head>
        <title>My React App</title>
      </head>
      <body>
        <!-- Injecting the rendered App component -->
        <div id="root">${html}</div>
        <!-- Linking to the main JavaScript bundle -->
        <script src="/static/js/main.js"></script>
      </body>
    </html>
  `);
});

// Starting the server on port 3000
app.listen(3000, () => {
  // Logging a message to the console once the server is running
  console.log("Server listening on port 3000");
});
```

In this example, we're using Express to create a server that serves static files from the *./build* directory and then renders our React app on the server. We're also using `ReactDOMServer` to render our React app to an HTML string and then inject it into the response sent to the client.

In this scenario, we're assuming our client-only React app has some type of `build` script that would output a client-only JavaScript bundle into a directory called *build* that we reference in the snippet. This is important for hydration. With all these pieces in order, let's go ahead and start our server:

```
node server.js
```

Running this command should start our server on port 3000 and should output `Server listening on port 3000`.

With these steps, we now have a server rendered React app. By taking this "peek under the hood" approach to server rendering, we gain a deeper understanding of how server rendering works and how it can benefit our React applications.

If we open a browser and visit *http://localhost:3000*, we should see a server rendered application. We can confirm that it is in fact server rendered by viewing the source code of this page, which should reveal actual HTML markup instead of a blank document.

For the sake of completion, this is what the HTML markup should look like:

```html
<!DOCTYPE html>
<html>
  <head>
    <title>My React App</title>
  </head>
  <body>
    <div id="root">
      <div>
        <h1>Hello, world!</h1>
        <p>This is a simple React app.</p>
      </div>
    </div>
    <script src="/static/js/main.js"></script>
  </body>
</html>
```

This is the HTML markup that is sent to the client. It contains the fully rendered HTML for our React app, which can be indexed by search engines and more efficiently accessed by users with slow or unreliable internet connections. This can result in better SEO and improved accessibility for our React app.

Hydrating

With server rendered output making it to users, hydration happens when we load our client bundle with the `<script>` tag toward the end of the file. As discussed, hydration is the process of attaching event listeners and other JavaScript functionality to static HTML that is generated on the server and sent to the client. The goal of hydration is to enable a server rendered application to become fully interactive after being loaded in the browser.

If we want to explore the hydration step of the client-side bundle of our app, it would look like this:

```js
// Import necessary libraries
import React from "react";
import { hydrateRoot } from "react-dom/client";
// Assuming App is the main component of your application
import App from "./App";
```

```
// Hydrate the app on the client side
hydrateRoot(document, <App />);
```

With server rendering and client hydration, our app is fully interactive and can respond to user input, fetch data, and update the DOM, as necessary.

Server Rendering APIs in React

In the previous section, we manually added server rendering to a client-only React app using Express and `ReactDOMServer`. Specifically, we used `ReactDOMServer.ren derToString()` to render our React app to an HTML string. This is the most basic way to add server rendering to a React app. However, there are other ways to add server rendering to React apps. Let's take a deeper look at server rendering APIs exposed by React and understand when and how to use them.

Let's consider the `renderToString` API in detail, exploring its usage, advantages, disadvantages, and when it is appropriate to use it in a React application. Specifically, let's look into:

- What it is
- How it works
- How it fits into our everyday usage of React

To start with this, let's talk about what it is.

renderToString

`renderToString` is a server-side rendering API provided by React that enables you to render a React component into an HTML string on the server. This API is synchronous and returns a fully rendered HTML string, which can then be sent to the client as a response. `renderToString` is commonly used in server rendered React applications to improve performance, SEO, and accessibility.

Usage

To use `renderToString`, you'd need to import the `renderToString` function from the `react-dom/server` package. Then, you can call the function with a React component as its argument. It will then return the fully rendered HTML as a string. Here's an example of using `renderToString` to render a simple React component:

```
import React from "react";
import { renderToString } from "react-dom/server";

function App() {
  return (
    <div>
```

```
      <h1>Hello, world!</h1>
      <p>This is a simple React app.</p>
    </div>
  );
}

const html = renderToString(<App />);
console.log(html);
```

In this example, we create a simple App component and call `renderToString` with the component as its argument. The function returns the fully rendered HTML, which can be sent to the client.

How it works

This function traverses the tree of React elements, converts them to a string representation of real DOM elements, and finally outputs a string.

It's worth recalling here that in React, `<div>` is converted to:

```
React.createElement("div", {}, "Hello, world!");
```

whose output is:

```
{
  type: "div",
  props: {},
  children: ["Hello, world!"]
}
```

We've covered this in prior chapters, but it's worth recalling here for the discussion we're about to have. Fundamentally, JSX turns into HTML with the following flow:

```
JSX -> React.createElement -> React element -> renderToString(React element) -> HTML
```

`renderToString` as an API is synchronous and blocking, meaning it cannot be interrupted or paused. If a component tree from the root is many levels deep, it can require quite a bit of processing. Since a server typically services multiple clients, `renderToString` could be called for each client unless there's some type of cache preventing this, and quickly block the event loop and overload the system.

In terms of code, `renderToString` converts this:

```
React.createElement(
  "section",
  { id: "list" },
  React.createElement("h1", {}, "This is my list!"),
  React.createElement(
    "p",
    {},
    "Isn't my list amazing? It contains amazing things!"
  ),
  React.createElement(
```

```
    "ul",
    {},
    amazingThings.map((t) => React.createElement("li", { key: t.id }, t.label))
  )
);
```

to this:

```
<section id="list">
  <h1>This is my list!</h1>
  <p>Isn't my list amazing? It contains amazing things!</p>
  <ul>
    <li>Thing 1</li>
    <li>Thing 2</li>
    <li>Thing 3</li>
  </ul>
</section>
```

Because React is declarative and React elements are declarative abstractions, a tree of them can be turned into a tree of anything else—in this case, a tree of React elements is turned into a string-representation of a tree of HTML elements.

Disadvantages

While `renderToString` offers several advantages, it also has some downsides:

Performance

One of the main disadvantages of `renderToString` is that it can be slow for large React applications. Because it is synchronous, it can block the event loop and make the server unresponsive. This can be especially problematic if you have a high-traffic application with many concurrent users.

Moreover, `renderToString` returns a fully rendered HTML string, which can be memory intensive for large applications. This can lead to increased memory usage on your server and potentially slower response times, or a panic that kills the server process under heavy load.

Lack of streaming support

`renderToString` does not support streaming, which means that the entire HTML string must be generated before it can be sent to the client. This can result in a slower time to first byte (TTFB) and a longer time for the client to start receiving the HTML. This limitation can be particularly problematic for large applications with lots of content, as the client must wait for the entire HTML string to be generated before any content can be displayed.

For larger applications or situations where the downsides of `renderToString` become problematic, React offers alternative APIs for server-side rendering, such as `renderToPipeableStream` and `renderToReadableStream`. These APIs return a Node.js stream and a browser stream, respectively, instead of a fully rendered HTML string, which can provide better performance and support for streaming. We will cover these more in the next section.

renderToPipeableStream

renderToPipeableStream is a server-side rendering API introduced in React 18. It provides a more efficient and flexible way to render large React applications to a Node.js stream. It returns a stream that can be piped to a response object. renderTo PipeableStream provides more control over how the HTML is rendered and allows for better integration with other Node.js streams.

In addition, it fully supports React's concurrent features, including Suspense, which unlocks better handling of asynchronous data fetching during server-side rendering. Because it is a stream, it is also streamable over the network, where chunks of HTML can be asynchronously and cumulatively sent to clients over the network without blocking. This leads to faster TTFB measures and generally better performance.

To rewrite our earlier server using renderToPipeableStream, we'd do the following:

```
// server.js

const express = require("express");
const path = require("path");
const React = require("react");
const ReactDOMServer = require("react-dom/server");

const App = require("./src/App");

const app = express();

app.use(express.static(path.join(__dirname, "build")));

app.get("*", (req, res) => {
  // Changes begin here
  const { pipe } = ReactDOMServer.renderToPipeableStream(<App />, {
    // When our app is ready before fetching its own data,
    onShellReady: () => {
      // Tell the client we're sending HTML
      res.setHeader("Content-Type", "text/html");
      pipe(res); // pipe the output of the React stream to the response stream
    },
  });
});

app.listen(3000, () => {
  console.log("Server listening on port 3000");
});
```

Let's dive deep into `renderToPipeableStream`, discussing its features, advantages, and use cases. We'll also provide code snippets and examples to help you better understand how to implement this API in your React applications.

How it works

Similar to `renderToString`, `renderToPipeableStream` takes a declaratively described tree of React elements and, instead of turning them into a string of HTML, turns the tree into a Node.js stream. A Node.js stream is a fundamental concept in the Node.js runtime environment that enables efficient data processing and manipulation. Streams provide a way to handle data incrementally in chunks, rather than loading the entire data set into memory at once. This approach is particularly useful when dealing with large strings or data streams that cannot fit entirely in memory or over the network.

Node.js streams.   At its core, a Node.js stream represents a flow of data between a source and a destination. It can be thought of as a pipeline through which data flows, with various operations applied to transform or process the data along the way.

Node.js streams are categorized into four types based on their nature and direction of data flow:

Readable streams
> A readable stream represents a source of data from which you can read. It emits events like `data`, `end`, and `error`. Examples of readable streams include reading data from a file, receiving data from an HTTP request, or generating data using a custom generator.
>
> React's `renderToPipeableStream` function returns a readable stream where you can read a stream of HTML and output it to a writable stream like the `res` response object from Express.

Writable streams
> A writable stream represents a destination where you can write data. It provides methods like `write()` and `end()` to send data into the stream. Writable streams emit events like `drain` when the destination can handle more data, and `error` when an error occurs during writing. Examples of writable streams include the Express `res` response object.

Duplex streams
> A duplex stream represents both a readable and writable stream simultaneously. It allows bidirectional data flow, meaning you can both read from and write to the stream. Duplex streams are commonly used for network sockets or communication channels where data needs to flow in both directions.

Transform streams

A transform stream is a special type of duplex stream that performs data transformations while data flows through it. It reads input data, processes it, and provides the processed data as output. Transform streams can be used to perform tasks such as compression, encryption, decompression, or data parsing.

One of the powerful features of Node.js streams is the ability to pipe data between streams. Piping allows you to connect the output of a readable stream directly to the input of a writable stream, creating a seamless flow of data. This greatly simplifies the process of handling data and reduces memory usage. Indeed, this is how streaming server-side rendering in React works.

Streams in Node.js also support backpressure handling. Backpressure is a problem that occurs during data handling and describes a buildup of data behind a buffer during data transfer. When the writable stream is unable to handle data quickly enough, the readable stream will pause emitting `data` events, preventing data loss. Once the writable stream is ready to consume more data, it emits a `drain` event, signaling the readable stream to resume emitting data.

Without diving too deep and digressing too much here, Node.js streams are a powerful abstraction for handling data in a scalable and memory-efficient manner. By breaking data into manageable chunks and allowing incremental processing, streams enable efficient handling of large data sets, file I/O operations, network communication, and much more.

React's renderToPipeableStream. In React, the purpose of streaming React components to a writable stream is to enhance the TTFB performance of server rendered applications. Instead of waiting for the entire HTML markup to be generated before sending it to the client, these methods enable the server to start sending chunks of the HTML response as they are ready, thus reducing the overall latency.

The `renderToPipeableStream` function is a part of React's server renderer, which is designed to support streaming rendering of a React application to a Node.js stream. It's a part of the server renderer architecture called "Fizz."

 We're about to dive super deep into React implementation details that are prone to change over time. Once again, this is for educational purposes and to satisfy the curiosity of the reader. It may not perfectly match the implementation details of React at the time of reading, but it's close enough to get a good idea of how this works at the time of writing. This stuff is probably not something you'd use in production and is nonessential to knowing how to use React, but is just for education and curiosity.

Without distracting from our context of server rendering too much, here's a simplified explanation of the flow of how server rendering works:

Creating a request

The function `renderToPipeableStream` takes as input the React elements to be rendered and an optional options object. It then creates a request object using a `createRequestImpl` function. This request object encapsulates the React elements, resources, response state, and format context.

Starting the work

After creating the request, the `startWork` function is called with the request as an argument. This function initiates the rendering process. The rendering process is asynchronous and can be paused and resumed as needed, which is where React Suspense comes in. If a component is wrapped in a Suspense boundary and it initiates some asynchronous operation (like data fetching), the rendering of that component (and possibly its siblings) can be "suspended" until the operation finishes.

While a component is suspended, it can be rendered in a "fallback" state, which is typically a loading indicator or a placeholder. Once the operation finishes, the component is "resumed" and rendered in its final state. Suspense is a powerful feature that enables React to handle asynchronous data fetching and lazy loading more effectively during server-side rendering.

The benefits are that we are able to serve the user a meaningful page immediately, and then progressively enhance it with more data as it becomes available. This is a powerful technique that can be used to improve the user experience of React applications.

Returning a pipeable stream

`renderToPipeableStream` then returns an object that includes a `pipe` method and an `abort` method. The `pipe` method is used to pipe the rendered output to a writable stream (like an HTTP response object in Node.js). The `abort` method can be used to cancel any pending I/O and put anything remaining into client-rendered mode.

Piping to a destination

When the `pipe` method is called with a destination stream, it checks if the data has already started flowing. If not, it sets `hasStartedFlowing` to `true` and calls the `startFlowing` function with the request and the destination. It also sets up handlers for the `drain`, `error`, and `close` events of the destination stream.

Handling stream events

The `drain` event handler calls `startFlowing` again to resume the flow of data when the destination stream is ready to receive more data. The `error` and `close` event handlers call the `abort` function to stop the rendering process if an error occurs in the destination stream or if the stream is closed prematurely.

Aborting the rendering
> The `abort` method on the returned object can be called with a reason to stop the rendering process. It calls the `abort` function from the `react-server` module with the request and the reason.

The actual implementation of these functions involves more complex logic to handle things like progressive rendering, error handling, and integration with the rest of the React server renderer. The code for these functions can be found in the `react-server` and `react-dom` packages of the React source code.

Features of renderToPipeableStream

`renderToPipeableStream` features include:

Streaming
> `renderToPipeableStream` returns a pipeable Node.js stream, which can be piped to a response object. This allows the server to start sending the HTML to the client before the entire page is rendered, providing a faster user experience and better performance for large applications.

Flexibility
> `renderToPipeableStream` offers more control over how the HTML is rendered. It can be easily integrated with other Node.js streams, allowing developers to customize the rendering pipeline and create more efficient server-side rendering solutions.

Suspense support
> `renderToPipeableStream` fully supports React's concurrent features, including Suspense. This allows developers to manage asynchronous data fetching and lazy loading more effectively during server-side rendering, ensuring that data-dependent components are only rendered once the necessary data is available.

How it fits

Let's take a look at some code that illustrates the benefits of this API. We have an application that displays a list of dog breeds. The list is populated by fetching data from an API endpoint. The application is rendered on the server using `renderTo PipeableStream` and then sent to the client. Let's start by looking at our dog list component:

```
// ./src/DogBreeds.jsx

const dogResource = createResource(
  fetch("https://dog.ceo/api/breeds/list/all")
```

```
    .then((r) => r.json())
    .then((r) => Object.keys(r.message))
);

function DogBreeds() {
  return (
    <ul>
      <Suspense fallback="Loading...">
        {dogResource.read().map((profile) => (
          <li key={profile}>{profile}</li>
        ))}
      </Suspense>
    </ul>
  );
}

export default DogBreeds;
```

Now, let's look at our overall App that contains the DogBreeds component:

```
// src/App.js
import React, { Suspense } from "react";

const ListOfBreeds = React.lazy(() => import("./DogBreeds"));

function App() {
  return (
    <div>
      <h1>Dog Breeds</h1>
      <Suspense fallback={<div>Loading Dog Breeds...</div>}>
        <ListOfBreeds />
      </Suspense>
    </div>
  );
}

export default App;
```

Notice, we're using React.lazy here as mentioned in prior chapters, just so we have another Suspense boundary to demonstrate how renderToPipeableStream handles Suspense. OK, let's tie this all together with an Express server:

```
// server.js
import express from "express";
import React from "react";
import { renderToPipeableStream } from "react-dom/server";
import App from "./App.jsx";

const app = express();

app.use(express.static("build"));

app.get("/", async (req, res) => {
```

```
// Define the starting HTML structure
const htmlStart = `
  <!DOCTYPE html>
  <html lang="en">
    <head>
      <meta charset="UTF-8" />
      <meta name="viewport" content="width=device-width, initial-scale=1.0" />
      <title>React Suspense with renderToPipeableStream</title>
    </head>
    <body>
      <div id="root">
`;

// Write the starting HTML to the response
res.write(htmlStart);

// Call renderToPipeableStream with the React App component
// and an options object to handle shell readiness
const { pipe } = renderToPipeableStream(<App />, {
  onShellReady: () => {
    // Pipe the rendered output to the response when the shell is ready
    pipe(res);
  },
});
});

// Start the server on port 3000 and log a message to the console
app.listen(3000, () => {
  console.log("Server is listening on port 3000");
});
```

What we're doing in this code snippet is responding to a request with a stream of HTML. We're using `renderToPipeableStream` to render our `App` component to a stream, and then piping that stream to our response object. We're also using the `onShellReady` option to pipe the stream to the response object once the shell is ready. The shell is the HTML that is rendered before the React application is hydrated, and before data dependencies wrapped in Suspense boundaries are resolved. In our case, the shell is the HTML that is rendered before the dog breeds are fetched from the API. Let's take a look at what happens when we run this code.

If we visit *http://localhost:3000*, we get a page with a heading "Dog Breeds," and our Suspense fallback "Loading Dog Breeds...." This is the shell that is rendered before the dog breeds are fetched from the API. The really cool thing is that even if we don't include React on the client side in our HTML and hydrate the page, the Suspense fallback is replaced with the actual dog breeds once they are fetched from the API. This swapping of DOM when data becomes available happens entirely from the server side, without client-side React!

Let's understand how this works in a bit more detail.

Once again, we are about to dive deep into React implementation details here that are quite likely to change over time. The point of this exercise (and this book) is not to obsess over single implementation details, but instead to understand the underlying mechanism so we can learn and reason about React better. This isn't required to *use* React, but understanding the mechanism can give us hints and practical tools to use in our day-to-day working with React. With that, let's move forward.

When we visit *http://localhost:3000*, the server responds with the HTML shell, which includes the heading "Dog Breeds" and the Suspense fallback "Loading Dog Breeds…." This HTML looks like this:

```
<!DOCTYPE html>
<html lang="en">
  <head>
    <meta charset="UTF-8" />
    <meta name="viewport" content="width=device-width, initial-scale=1.0" />
    <title>React Suspense with renderToPipeableStream</title>
  </head>
  <body>
    <div id="root">
      <div>
        <h1>User Profiles</h1>
        <!--$?--><template id="B:0"></template>
        <div>Loading user profiles...</div>
        <!--/$-->
      </div>
      <div hidden id="S:0">
        <ul>
          <!--$-->
          <li>affenpinscher</li>
          <li>african</li>
          <li>airedale</li>
          [...]
          <!--/$-->
        </ul>
      </div>
      <script>
        function $RC(a, b) {
          a = document.getElementById(a);
          b = document.getElementById(b);
          b.parentNode.removeChild(b);
          if (a) {
            a = a.previousSibling;
            var f = a.parentNode,
              c = a.nextSibling,
              e = 0;
            do {
              if (c && 8 === c.nodeType) {
                var d = c.data;
```

```
      if ("/$" === d)
        if (0 === e) break;
        else e--;
      else ("$" !== d && "$?" !== d && "$!" !== d) || e++;
    }
    d = c.nextSibling;
    f.removeChild(c);
    c = d;
  } while (c);
  for (; b.firstChild; ) f.insertBefore(b.firstChild, c);
  a.data = "$";
  a._reactRetry && a._reactRetry();
      }
    }
    $RC("B:0", "S:0");
  </script>
  </div>
 </body>
</html>
```

What we see here is quite interesting. There's a `<template>` element with a generated ID (B:0 in this case), and some HTML comments. The HTML comments are used to mark the start and end of the shell. These are markers or "holes" where resolved data will go once Suspense is resolved. `<template>` elements in HTML provide a way to construct document subtrees and hold nodes without introducing an additional wrapping level of the DOM hierarchy. They serve as lightweight containers for managing groups of nodes, improving performance by reducing the amount of work done during DOM manipulation.

There's also a `<script>` element. This `<script>` tag contains a function called `$RC` that is used to replace the shell with the actual content. The `$RC` function takes two arguments: the ID of the `<template>` element that contains the marker, and the ID of the `<div>` element that contains the fallback. The function then fills the marker with rendered UI after data is available, while removing the fallback.

It's pretty unfortunate that this function is minified, but let's try to unminify it and understand what it does. If we do, this is what we observe:

```
function reactComponentCleanup(reactMarkerId, siblingId) {
  let reactMarker = document.getElementById(reactMarkerId);
  let sibling = document.getElementById(siblingId);
  sibling.parentNode.removeChild(sibling);

  if (reactMarker) {
    reactMarker = reactMarker.previousSibling;
    let parentNode = reactMarker.parentNode,
      nextSibling = reactMarker.nextSibling,
      nestedLevel = 0;

    do {
```

```
    if (nextSibling && 8 === nextSibling.nodeType) {
      let nodeData = nextSibling.data;
      if ("/$" === nodeData) {
        if (0 === nestedLevel) {
          break;
        } else {
          nestedLevel--;
        }
      } else if ("$" !== nodeData && "$?" !== nodeData && "$!" !== nodeData) {
        nestedLevel++;
      }
    }
    let nextNode = nextSibling.nextSibling;
    parentNode.removeChild(nextSibling);
    nextSibling = nextNode;
  } while (nextSibling);

  while (sibling.firstChild) {
    parentNode.insertBefore(sibling.firstChild, nextSibling);
  }

  reactMarker.data = "$";
  reactMarker._reactRetry && reactMarker._reactRetry();
  }
}

reactComponentCleanup("B:0", "S:0");
```

Let's break this down further.

The function takes two arguments: `reactMarkerId` and `siblingId`. Effectively, the marker is a hole where rendered components will go once they're available, and the sibling is the Suspense fallback.

The function then removes the sibling element (the fallback) from the DOM using the `removeChild` method on its parent node when data is available.

If the `reactMarker` element exists, the function runs. It sets the `reactMarker` variable to the previous sibling of the current `reactMarker` element. The function also initializes the variables `parentNode`, `nextSibling`, and `nestedLevel`.

A do...while loop is used to traverse the DOM tree, starting with the `nextSibling` element. The loop continues as long as the `nextSibling` element exists. Inside the loop, the function checks whether the `nextSibling` element is a comment node (indicated by a `nodeType` value of 8):

- If the `nextSibling` element is a comment node, the function inspects its data (i.e., the text content of the comment). It checks whether the data is equal to "/$", which signifies the end of a nested structure. If the `nestedLevel` value is 0, the loop breaks, indicating that the desired end of the structure has been reached.

If the `nestedLevel` value is not 0, it means that the current "/$" comment node is part of a nested structure, and the `nestedLevel` value is decremented.

- If the comment node data is not equal to "/$", the function checks whether it is equal to "$", "$?", or "$!". These values indicate the beginning of a new nested structure. If any of these values are encountered, the `nestedLevel` value is incremented.

During each iteration of the loop, the `nextSibling` element (that is, the Suspense boundary) is removed from the DOM using the `removeChild` method on its parent node. The loop continues with the next sibling element in the DOM tree.

Once the loop has completed, the function moves all child elements of the sibling element to the location immediately before the `nextSibling` element in the DOM tree using the `insertBefore` method. This process effectively restructures the DOM around the `reactMarker` element and replaces a Suspense fallback with the component it wraps.

The function then sets the data of the `reactMarker` element to "$", which is likely used to mark the component for future processing or reference. If a `reactRetry` property exists on the `reactMarker` element and it is a function, the function invokes this method.

If some of this was difficult to follow, don't worry about it. We can summarize all of this here: essentially, this function waits for data-dependent React components to be ready, and when they are, swaps out Suspense fallbacks for the server rendered components. It uses comment nodes with specific data values to determine the structure of the components, and manipulates the DOM accordingly. Since this is inlined in our HTML from the server, we can stream data like this using `renderToPipeable Stream` and have the browser render the UI as it becomes available without even including React in the browser bundle or hydrating.

Thus, `renderToPipeableStream` gives us quite a bit more control and power compared to `renderToString` when server rendering.

renderToReadableStream

The previous API we covered, `renderToPipeableStream`, makes use of Node.js streams under the hood. However, browsers also have support for streams and browser streams slightly differ from Node.js streams. Node.js streams are primarily designed to operate in a server-side environment, where they deal with file I/O, network I/O, or any kind of end-to-end streaming. They follow a custom API defined by the Node.js environment and have been a core part of Node.js for a long time. Node.js streams have distinct classes for readable, writable, duplex, and transform streams, and utilize events like `data`, `end`, and `error` to manage stream flow and handle data.

Browser streams are designed to operate in a client-side environment within web browsers. They often deal with streaming data from network requests, media streaming, or other data-processing tasks in the browser. Browser streams follow the Streams standard defined by the WHATWG (Web Hypertext Application Technology Working Group), aiming to standardize APIs across the web. Unlike Node.js streams, browser streams use methods like `read()`, `write()`, and `pipeThrough()` to control the flow of data and then process that streamed data. They provide a more standardized and promise-based API. Here is an example of a readable stream in a browser environment:

```
const readableStream = new ReadableStream({
  start(controller) {
    controller.enqueue("Hello, ");
    controller.enqueue("world!");
    controller.close();
  },
});

const reader = readableStream.getReader();

async function readAllChunks(streamReader) {
  let result = "";
  while (true) {
    const { done, value } = await streamReader.read();
    if (done) {
      break;
    }
    result += value;
  }
  return result;
}

readAllChunks(reader).then((text) => {
  console.log(text);
});
```

While both Node.js streams and browser streams serve the purpose of handling streaming data, they operate in different environments with slightly different APIs and standards. Node.js streams are event driven and are well suited for server-side operations, whereas browser streams are promise based, aligning with modern web standards, and are tailored for client-side operations.

To support both environments, React has `renderToPipeableStream` for Node.js streams, and `renderToReadableStream` for browser streams. The `renderToReadableStream` API is similar to `renderToPipeableStream`, but it returns a readable stream for the browser instead of a Node.js-native stream.

When to Use What

`renderToString` isn't ideal because it is synchronous. This is quite problematic for a number of reasons:

Network I/O is asynchronous.
> Any data fetching we do depends on retrieving data from somewhere: a database, a web service, the filesystem, etc. These operations are often asynchronous: meaning that they start and end at discrete points in time, not at the same time. Because `renderToString` is synchronous, it cannot wait for asynchronous requests to complete and *must* send a string instantly to the browser. This means that the server cannot complete things, the client gets a shell before any data has loaded, and the client ideally picks up where the server left off after hydration. This presents performance problems by way of network waterfalls.

Servers serve multiple clients.
> If your server that calls `renderToString` is busy rendering to a string and 30 clients have sent new requests to it, those new clients will have to wait for it to finish its current work. Because `renderToString` is synchronous, it blocks until it's done. In the one-to-many relationship between servers and clients, blocking means your clients wait longer than they should.

Newer alternatives like `renderToPipeableStream` and `renderToReadableStream` are asynchronous stream-based approaches that solve for both of these problems, with `renderToReadableStream` being browser native and `renderToPipeableStream` being server native. Thus, if the question is "what's the best API to use on the server?" the answer is clearly either `renderToPipeableStream` or `renderToReadableStream`, depending on the environment.

That said, while `renderTo*Stream` appears to be a superior set of APIs, there is currently no "full user story" around these APIs at the time of writing. Many third-party libraries that are currently around will not work with them, especially considering data fetching or CSS libraries. This is because they conceptually need a "full run" on the server, then need to create data, and then rerender the application with that data to actually stream from the server. They don't support scenarios where an app hasn't finished rendering on the server yet, but needs to start partially hydrating in the browser.

This is a React problem: there are no APIs in React 18 (the latest release at the time of writing) that would allow for support of any kind of streaming or partial rehydration of third-party data. The React team has recently added a bunch of new APIs to `react-dom`, like `prefetchDNS`, `preconnect`, `preload`, etc., to address that, but those will only ship with React 19. Even with these APIs, there are still a few important APIs missing to make `renderToPipeableStream` a viable option.

The only really viable option to use `renderToPipeableStream` right now would be to prefetch all required data (or in the case of a CSS library, render the full application with `renderToString` to "prerecord" all classes that need rendering) before calling `renderToPipeableStream` in the first place—which would pretty much eliminate most of its benefits over `renderToString`, essentially making it a synchronous API again.

All things considered, these are complex topics that require a good amount of forethought, careful planning, and further consideration around which APIs to use that equally depend on your current projects and use cases. Thus, the answer is once again "it depends," or "just use a framework" and defer the decision to the broader community.

Don't Roll Your Own

Creating a custom server rendering implementation for a React application can be a challenging and time-consuming task. While React does provide some APIs for server rendering, building a custom solution from scratch can lead to various issues and inefficiencies. In this section, we'll explore the reasons why it's better to rely on established frameworks like Next.js and Remix, rather than building your own server rendering solution:

Handling edge cases and complexities
> React applications can become quite complex, and implementing server rendering requires addressing various edge cases and complexities. These can include handling asynchronous data fetching, code splitting, and managing various React lifecycle events. By using a framework like Next.js or Remix, you can avoid the need to handle these complexities yourself, as these frameworks have built-in solutions for many common edge cases.
>
> One such edge case is security. As the server processes numerous client requests, it's crucial to ensure that sensitive data from one client doesn't inadvertently leak to another. This is where frameworks like Next.js, Remix, and Gatsby can provide invaluable assistance in handling these concerns. Imagine a scenario where client A accesses the server, and their data is cached by the server. If the server accidentally serves this cached data to client B, sensitive information could be exposed.
>
> Consider the following example:
>
> ```
> // server.js
>
> // Import the express module
> const express = require("express");
>
> // Create a new express application instance
> const app = express();
> ```

```
// Declare a variable to hold cached user data
// Initially, it is null as there's no data cached yet
let cachedUserData = null;

// Define a route handler for GET requests to "/user/:userId"
// This will respond with user data for the specified user ID
app.get("/user/:userId", (req, res) => {
  // Extract the userId from the request parameters
  const { userId } = req.params;

  // Check if there's cached user data
  // If so, respond with the cached data
  if (cachedUserData) {
    return res.json(cachedUserData);
  }

  // If not, fetch user data from a database or another source
  // The fetchUserData function is assumed to be defined elsewhere
  const userData = fetchUserData(userId);

  // Update the cache with the fetched user data
  cachedUserData = userData;

  // Respond with the fetched user data
  res.json(userData);
});

// Start the server, listening on port 3000
// Log a message to the console once the server is ready
app.listen(3000, () => {
  console.log("Server listening on port 3000");
});
```

In the given code, `cachedUserData` is intended to cache the user data, but it's shared across all requests regardless of the `userId`. Every time a request is made to /user/:userId, the server checks `cachedUserData` to see if there's cached data. If there is, it returns the cached data regardless of whether the `userId` matches the `userId` of the cached data. If there isn't, it fetches the data, caches it, and returns it. This means that if two requests are made in sequence to /user/1 and /user/2, the second request would receive the data of the first user, which is a significant security issue.

A more secure caching strategy would be to cache the data in a way that's associated with the `userId` so that each user has their own cache. One way to do this would be to use an object to hold the cached data, with the `userId` as the key.

If we roll our own, the risk of human error is ever present. If we lean on frameworks built by large communities, this risk is mitigated. These frameworks are designed with security in mind and ensure that sensitive data is handled properly.

They prevent potential data leakage scenarios by using secure and isolated data-fetching methods.

Performance optimizations

Frameworks come with numerous performance optimizations out of the box. These optimizations can include automatic code splitting, server rendering, and caching. Building a custom server rendering solution might not include these optimizations by default, and implementing them can be a challenging and time-consuming task.

One such optimization Next.js makes, for example, is route-based code splitting for the pages router that was the default for Next.js 13 and earlier. Each page in this case is automatically code split into its own bundle, which is then loaded only when the page is requested. This can significantly improve performance by reducing the initial bundle size and improving the TTFB.

Developer experience and productivity

Building a custom server rendering implementation can be a complex and time-consuming endeavor. By using a framework like Next.js or Remix, developers can focus on building features and functionality for their application instead of worrying about the underlying server rendering infrastructure. This can lead to increased productivity and a better overall developer experience.

Best practices and conventions

Using a framework like Next.js or Remix can help enforce best practices and conventions in your project. These frameworks have been designed with best practices in mind, and by following their conventions, you can ensure that your application is built on a solid foundation:

```
// Example of best practices with Remix
// File: routes/posts/$postId.tsx

import { useParams } from "react-router-dom";
import { useLoaderData } from "@remix-run/react";

// Best practice: data fetching as early as possible
// Best practice: colocating data with UI
export function loader({ params }) {
  return fetchPost(params.postId);
}

function Post() {
  const { postId } = useParams();
  const post = useLoaderData();

  return (
    <div>
      <h1>{post.title}</h1>
```

```
      <div>{post.content}</div>
    </div>
  );
}

export default Post;
```

Considering the benefits and optimizations provided by established frameworks like Next.js and Remix, it becomes evident that building a custom server rendering solution for a React application is not an ideal approach. By leveraging these frameworks, you can save development time, ensure that best practices are followed, and benefit from the ongoing improvements and support provided by their respective communities.

Chapter Review

In conclusion, server-side rendering and hydration are powerful techniques that can significantly improve the performance, user experience, and SEO of web applications. React provides a rich set of APIs for server rendering, such as `renderToString` and `renderToPipeableStream`, each with its own strengths and trade-offs. By understanding these APIs and selecting the right one based on factors such as application size, server environment, and developer experience, you can optimize your React application for both server- and client-side performance.

As we've seen throughout this chapter, `renderToString` is a simple and straightforward API for server rendering that is suitable for smaller applications. However, it may not be the most efficient option for larger applications due to its synchronous nature and potential to block the event loop. On the other hand, `renderToPipeable Stream` is a more advanced and flexible API that allows for better control over the rendering process and improved integration with other Node.js streams, making it a more suitable choice for larger applications.

Review Questions

Now that you've gained a solid understanding of server-side rendering and hydration in React, it's time to test your knowledge with some review questions. If you can confidently answer these, it's a good sign that you've got a solid understanding of mechanism in React and can comfortably move forward. If you cannot, we'd suggest reading through things a little more, although this will not hurt your experience as you continue through the book.

1. What is the main advantage of using server-side rendering in a React application?

2. How does hydration work in React, and why is it important?

3. What is resumability? How does it claim to be superior to hydration?

4. What are the key benefits and weaknesses of client-only rendering?

5. What are the key differences between the `renderToReadableStream` and `renderToPipeableStream` APIs in React?

Up Next

Once you've mastered server-side rendering and hydration, you're ready to explore even more advanced topics in React development. In the next chapter, we'll dive into concurrent React. As web applications become more complex, handling asynchronous actions becomes increasingly important for creating smooth user experiences.

By learning how to leverage concurrent React, you'll be able to create highly performant, scalable, and user-friendly applications that can handle complex data interactions with ease. So, stay tuned and get ready to level up your React skills as we continue our journey into the world of concurrent React!

CHAPTER 7

Concurrent React

In the previous chapter, we delved deep into the world of server-side rendering with React. We examined the importance of server-side rendering for improving the performance and user experience of our applications, especially in the context of modern web development. We explored different server rendering APIs, such as `renderTo String` and `renderToPipeableStream`, and discussed their use cases and benefits. We also touched upon the challenges of implementing server-side rendering and how it's better to rely on established frameworks like Next.js and Remix to handle the complexities for us.

We covered the concept of hydration and its significance in connecting server-rendered markup with client-side React components, creating a seamless user experience. Additionally, we discussed the potential security issues and challenges that come with managing multiple client connections in a serverful environment, emphasizing the need for using frameworks that handle these concerns effectively.

Now, as we transition to the next concurrent React—we will build upon our understanding of all that we've learned so far. We will dive into the Fiber reconciler and learn about the concurrent features of React, as well as how efficiently it manages updates and rendering. By examining scheduling, deferring updates, and render lanes, we'll gain insights into the performance optimizations made possible by React's core architecture.

Once again, it's worth noting that Fiber itself and the things we're about to discuss are implementation details in React that are likely to change and that you don't need to know to use React effectively. However, learning the underlying mechanisms will help you better understand how React works and how to use it effectively, while also making you more knowledgeable as an engineer in general.

With that, let's embark on our journey into the fascinating world of concurrent React, as we continue to build on our expertise and discover new ways to harness the power of React for creating high-performance applications.

The Problem with Synchronous Rendering

To recap, the problem with synchronous rendering is that it blocks the main thread, which can lead to a poor user experience. This is especially true for complex applications with many components and frequent updates. In such cases, the UI can become unresponsive, resulting in a frustrating user experience.

A typical mitigation step to this problem is to batch a series of updates into one update and minimize work done on the main thread: instead of processing 10 things 10 times, batch them and process them once. We covered batching in Chapter 4, so we won't go into more detail here, but for the purposes of our discussion, it's important to understand that batching is a mitigation step to these problems, but even that has limitations, as we'll uncover in the next few paragraphs.

The problems we've been talking about, even with batching, are further compounded by the fact that by design, synchronous rendering has no sense of priority. It treats all updates equally, regardless of their visibility. For example, with sync rendering you may block the main thread with rendering work for items that the user can't see, such as tabs that aren't visible, content behind a modal, or content in a loading state. You still want those items to render if there is CPU available, but you want to prioritize rendering the thing the user can see and interact with. Before React had concurrent features, we often had situations where critical updates were blocked by less important ones, resulting in a poor user experience.

With concurrent rendering, React can prioritize updates based on their importance and urgency, ensuring that critical updates are not blocked by less important ones. This allows React to maintain a responsive UI even under heavy load, resulting in a better user experience. For example, when a user hovers over or clicks on a button, the expectation is that it immediately shows feedback for that action. If React is working on rerendering a long list of items, then the hover or active state feedback will be delayed until the entire list is rendered. With concurrent rendering, rendering tasks that are CPU bound and CPU intensive can be given a back seat to rendering tasks that are more important, such as user interactions and animations.

Moreover, with the concurrent rendering capabilities, React is able to time slice: that is, it can break up the rendering process into smaller chunks and process them incrementally. This allows React to perform work over multiple frames, and if the work needs to be interrupted, it can be.

We'll dive into all of this together starting now.

Revisiting Fiber

As covered in Chapter 4, the Fiber reconciler is the core mechanism in React that enables concurrent rendering. It was introduced in React 16 and represented a significant architectural shift from the previous stack reconciler. The primary goal of the Fiber reconciler is to improve the responsiveness and performance of React applications, particularly for large and complex UIs.

The Fiber reconciler achieves this by breaking the rendering process into smaller, more manageable units of work called Fibers. This allows React to pause, resume, and prioritize rendering tasks, making it possible to defer or schedule updates based on their importance. This improves the responsiveness of the application and ensures that critical updates are not blocked by less important tasks.

Scheduling and Deferring Updates

React's ability to schedule and defer updates is crucial for maintaining a responsive application. The Fiber reconciler enables this functionality by relying on a scheduler and a number of efficient APIs. These APIs allow React to perform work during idle periods and schedule updates at the most opportune times.

We'll dive into the scheduler in more detail in upcoming sections, but for now, consider it to be exactly what it sounds like: a system that receives updates and says, "you do this now," "you do this later," etc., using browser APIs like `setTimeout`, `Message Channel`, and others.

Consider a real-time chat application where users can send and receive messages. We will have a chat component that displays a list of messages, and a message input component where users can type and submit their messages. Additionally, the chat application receives new messages from the server in real time. In this scenario, we want to prioritize user interactions (typing and submitting messages) to maintain a responsive experience, while ensuring that incoming messages are rendered efficiently without blocking the UI.

To make this example a little more concrete, let's create some components. First, a list of messages:

```
const MessageList = ({ messages }) => (
  <ul>
    {messages.map((message, index) => (
      <li key={index}>{message}</li>
    ))}
  </ul>
);
```

Next, we have a message input component that allows users to type and submit messages:

```
const MessageInput = ({ onSubmit }) => {
  const [message, setMessage] = useState("");

  const handleSubmit = (e) => {
    e.preventDefault();
    onSubmit(message);
    setMessage("");
  };

  return (
    <form onSubmit={handleSubmit}>
      <input
        type="text"
        value={message}
        onChange={(e) => setMessage(e.target.value)}
      />
      <button type="submit">Send</button>
    </form>
  );
};
```

Finally, we have a chat component that combines the two components and handles the logic for sending and receiving messages:

```
const ChatApp = () => {
  const [messages, setMessages] = useState([]);

  useEffect(() => {
    // Connect to the server and subscribe to incoming messages
    const socket = new WebSocket("wss://your-websocket-server.com");
    socket.onmessage = (event) => {
      setMessages((prevMessages) => [...prevMessages, event.data]);
    };

    return () => {
      socket.close();
    };
  }, []);

  const sendMessage = (message) => {
    // Send the message to the server
  };

  return (
    <div>
      <MessageList messages={messages} />
      <MessageInput onSubmit={sendMessage} />
    </div>
  );
};
```

In this example, React's concurrent rendering capabilities come into play by efficiently managing the updates of both the message list and the user's interactions with the message input. When a user types or submits a message, React prioritizes the text input updates above other updates to ensure a smooth user experience.

When new messages arrive from the server and need to be rendered, they are rendered in the default/unknown render lane, which updates the DOM synchronously and instantly in a blocking manner: this would delay any user input. If we want rendering the new list of messages to be de-prioritized, we can wrap the corresponding state update in a startTransition function from the useTransition hook, like so:

```
const ChatApp = () => {
  const [messages, setMessages] = useState([]);
  const [isPending, startTransition] = useTransition();

  useEffect(() => {
    // Connect to the server and subscribe to incoming messages
    const socket = new WebSocket("wss://your-websocket-server.com");
    socket.onmessage = (event) => {
      startTransition(() => {
        setMessages((prevMessages) => [...prevMessages, event.data]);
      });
    };

    return () => {
      socket.close();
    };
  }, []);

  const sendMessage = (message) => {
    // Send the message to the server
  };

  return (
    <div>
      <MessageList messages={messages} />
      <MessageInput onSubmit={sendMessage} />
    </div>
  );
};
```

With this, we signal to React to schedule the message list updates with a lower priority and render them without blocking the UI, allowing the chat application to function efficiently, even under heavy load. Thus, user input is never interrupted, and incoming messages are rendered with a lower priority than user interactions since they are less critical to the user experience.

This example demonstrates how React's concurrent rendering capabilities can be leveraged to build responsive applications that handle complex interactions and frequent updates without compromising on performance or user experience. We will dive deeper into useTransition further in this chapter. For now, let's look a little deeper at how, exactly, React schedules updates.

Diving Deeper

In React, the process of scheduling, prioritizing, and deferring updates is essential to maintaining a responsive user interface. This process ensures that high-priority tasks are addressed promptly, while low-priority tasks can be deferred, allowing the UI to remain smooth even under heavy load. To delve deeper into this topic, we'll examine several core concepts: the scheduler, the priority levels of tasks, and the mechanisms that defer updates.

Before we proceed—let's remind ourselves one more time that the information covered here consists of implementation details and is *not requisite to using React*. However, understanding these concepts will help you better understand how React works and how to use it effectively, while also teaching you the underlying mechanism that you can apply in other engineering endeavors, improving your overall skill set. With that in mind, let's proceed.

The Scheduler

At the core of React's architecture, the scheduler is a standalone package that provides timing-related utilities, independent of the Fiber reconciler. React uses this scheduler within the reconciler. The scheduler and reconciler, through the usage of render lanes, enable tasks to cooperate by prioritizing and organizing them based on their urgency. We will dive deep into render lanes shortly. The scheduler's primary role in React today is to manage the yielding of the main thread, mainly by scheduling microtasks to ensure smooth execution.

To understand this in a little more detail, let's look at a portion of React's source code at the time of writing:

```
export function ensureRootIsScheduled(root: FiberRoot): void {
  // This function is called whenever a root receives an update. It does two
  // things 1) it ensures the root is in the root schedule, and 2) it ensures
  // there's a pending microtask to process the root schedule.
  //
  // Most of the actual scheduling logic does not happen until
  // `scheduleTaskForRootDuringMicrotask` runs.

  // Add the root to the schedule
  if (root === lastScheduledRoot || root.next !== null) {
    // Fast path. This root is already scheduled.
  } else {
    if (lastScheduledRoot === null) {
      firstScheduledRoot = lastScheduledRoot = root;
```

```
    } else {
      lastScheduledRoot.next = root;
      lastScheduledRoot = root;
    }
  }

  // Any time a root received an update, we set this to true until the next time
  // we process the schedule. If it's false, then we can quickly exit flushSync
  // without consulting the schedule.
  mightHavePendingSyncWork = true;

  // At the end of the current event, go through each of the roots and ensure
  // there's a task scheduled for each one at the correct priority.
  if (__DEV__ && ReactCurrentActQueue.current !== null) {
    // We're inside an `act` scope.
    if (!didScheduleMicrotask_act) {
      didScheduleMicrotask_act = true;
      scheduleImmediateTask(processRootScheduleInMicrotask);
    }
  } else {
    if (!didScheduleMicrotask) {
      didScheduleMicrotask = true;
      scheduleImmediateTask(processRootScheduleInMicrotask);
    }
  }

  if (!enableDeferRootSchedulingToMicrotask) {
    // While this flag is disabled, we schedule the render task immediately
    // instead of waiting for a microtask.
    // TODO: We need to land enableDeferRootSchedulingToMicrotask ASAP to
    // unblock additional features we have planned.
    scheduleTaskForRootDuringMicrotask(root, now());
  }

  if (
    __DEV__ &&
    ReactCurrentActQueue.isBatchingLegacy &&
    root.tag === LegacyRoot
  ) {
    // Special `act` case: Record whenever a legacy update is scheduled.
    ReactCurrentActQueue.didScheduleLegacyUpdate = true;
  }
}
```

The ensureRootIsScheduled function in React's codebase plays a crucial role in managing the rendering process. When a React root, represented by root: Fiber Root, receives an update, this function is called to perform two critical actions. Remember from Chapter 4: a React root is the final "swap" that happens during the commit phase to make updates.

When `ensureRootIsScheduled` is called, it confirms that the root is included in the root schedule: a list that tracks which roots need to be processed. Secondly, it ensures the existence of a pending microtask dedicated to processing this root schedule.

A microtask is a concept in JavaScript event-loop management, representing a type of task that is managed by the microtask queue. To understand microtasks, it's important to first have a basic grasp of the JavaScript event loop and the task queues associated with it:

Event loop
> The JavaScript engine uses an event loop to manage asynchronous operations. The event loop continuously checks if there's any work (like executing a callback) that needs to be done. It operates on two kinds of task queues: the task queue (macro task queue) and the microtask queue.

Task queue (macro task queue)
> This queue holds tasks such as handling events, executing `setTimeout` and `set Interval` callbacks, and performing I/O operations. Tasks in this queue are processed one at a time, and the next task is picked up only after the current one is completed.

Microtask queue
> A microtask is a smaller, more immediate task. Microtasks arise from operations like promises, `Object.observe`, and `MutationObserver`. They are stored in the microtask queue, which is different from the regular task queue.

Execution
> Microtasks are processed at the end of the current task, before the JavaScript engine picks up the next (macro) task from the task queue. After executing a task, the engine checks if there are any microtasks in the microtask queue and executes them all before moving on. This ensures that microtasks are processed quickly and in order, just after the currently executing script and before any other tasks, like rendering or handling events.

Characteristics and usage
> Microtasks have higher priority over other tasks in the task queue, meaning they are executed before moving on to the next macro task. If a microtask continuously adds more microtasks to the queue, it can lead to a situation where the task queue never gets processed. This is known as *starvation*.

In the context of React and the `ensureRootIsScheduled` function, a microtask is used to ensure that the processing of the root schedule happens promptly and with high priority, right after the current script execution and before the browser performs other tasks like rendering or handling events. This helps in maintaining smooth UI updates and efficient task management within the React framework.

The function starts by adding the root to the schedule. This involves checking if the root is either the last scheduled one or already present in the schedule. If it's not present, the function adds the root to the end of the schedule, updating the lastScheduledRoot to point to the current root. If no root was previously scheduled (lastScheduledRoot === null), the current root becomes both the first and the last in the schedule.

Next, the function sets the flag mightHavePendingSyncWork to true. This flag signals that there might be synchronous work pending, essential for the flushSync function, which we'll cover in the next section.

The function then ensures that a microtask is scheduled to process the root schedule. This is done by calling scheduleImmediateTask(processRootScheduleInMicro task). This scheduling happens both within and outside of React's act testing utility scope, indicated by __DEV__ and ReactCurrentActQueue.current.

Another significant part of this function is the conditional block checking the enable DeferRootSchedulingToMicrotask flag. If this flag is disabled, the function schedules the render task immediately instead of deferring it to a microtask. This part is marked with a TODO comment (at the time of writing), indicating future plans to enable this feature for unlocking additional functionalities.

Finally, the function includes a condition for handling legacy updates within React's act utility. This is specific to testing scenarios where updates are batched differently, and it records whenever a legacy update is scheduled.

The long and short of this is that ensureRootIsScheduled is a sophisticated function that integrates several aspects of React's scheduling and rendering logic, focusing on efficiently managing updates to React roots and ensuring smooth rendering by strategically scheduling tasks and microtasks.

From this, we understand the role of the scheduler in React: scheduling work based on the render lanes that work falls into. We get pretty deep into lanes in the next section, but for now, suffice it to say that lanes are indicative of an update's priority.

If we model the scheduler's behavior in code, it would look like this:

```
if (nextLane === Sync) {
  queueMicrotask(processNextLane);
} else {
  Scheduler.scheduleCallback(callback, processNextLane);
}
```

From this, we see that:

- If the next lane is Sync, then the scheduler queues a microtask to process the next lane immediately. Ideally, by now we understand what microtasks are and how this fits.

- If the next lane is not Sync, then the scheduler schedules a callback and processes the next lane.

Thus, the scheduler is exactly what it sounds like: a system that schedules functions to run determined by that function's lane. OK, we've been talking about lanes for a while. Let's dive in and understand them in detail!

Render Lanes

Render lanes are an essential part of React's scheduling system, which ensures efficient rendering and prioritization of tasks. A lane is a unit of work that represents a priority level and can be processed by React as part of its rendering cycle. The concept of render lanes was introduced in React 18, replacing the previous scheduling mechanism that used expiration times. Let's dive into the details of render lanes, how they work, and their underlying representation as bitmasks.

 Once again, these are implementation details in React that may change at any time. The point here is to understand the underlying mechanism that will help us in our everyday engineering work, and will also help us understand how React works and enable us to use it more effectively or fluently. It would serve us well to not get hung up on the details, but to instead stick to the mechanism and its potential for real-world application.

First off, a render lane is a lightweight abstraction that React uses to organize and prioritize updates that need to be made during the rendering process.

For example, when you call setState, that update is put into a lane. We can understand the different priorities based on the context of the updates, like so:

- If setState is called inside of a click handler, it is put into the Sync lane (highest priority) and scheduled in a microtask.
- If setState is called inside a transition from startTransition, it's put in a transition lane (lower priority) and scheduled in a microtask.

Each lane corresponds to a specific priority level, with higher-priority lanes processed before lower-priority lanes. Some examples of lanes in React are:

SyncHydrationLane
    When users click on a React app during hydration, the click event is put into this lane.

SyncLane
    When users click on a React app, the click event is put into this lane.

InputContinuousHydrationLane

> Hover events, scroll events, and other continuous events during hydration are put into this lane.

InputContinuousLane

> Same as the preceding, but for after a React app is hydrated.

DefaultLane

> Any updates from the network, timers like setTimeout, and the initial render where priority isn't inferred are put into this lane.

TransitionHydrationLane

> Any transitions from startTransition during hydration are put into this lane.

TransitionLanes *(1–15)*

> Any transitions from startTransition after hydration are put into these lanes.

RetryLanes *(1–4)*

> Any Suspense retries are put into these lanes.

It's worth noting that these lanes are indicative of React's internal implementation at the time of writing and are subject to change. To reiterate, the point of this book is to understand the *mechanism* by which React works without being too married to the exact implementation details, so the names of lanes likely don't matter too much. What matters infinitely more is our understanding of the mechanism—that is, how React uses the concept—and how we can apply it to our work.

How Render Lanes Work

When a component updates or a new component is added to the render tree, React assigns a lane to the update based on its priority using the lanes we previously discussed. As we know, the priority is determined by the type of update (e.g., user interaction, data fetching, or background task) and other factors, such as the component's visibility.

React then uses the render lanes to schedule and prioritize updates in the following manner:

1. Collect updates

> React collects all the updates that have been scheduled since the last render and assigns them to their respective lanes based on their priority.

2. Process lanes

> React processes the updates in their respective lanes, starting with the highest priority lane. Updates in the same lane are batched together and processed in a single pass.

3. Commit phase

After processing all the updates, React enters the commit phase, where it applies the changes to the DOM, runs effects, and performs other finalization tasks.

4. Repeat

The process repeats for each render, ensuring that updates are always processed in priority order, and that high-priority updates are not starved by lower-priority ones.

React takes care of assigning updates to the correct lanes based on these priorities, allowing the application to function efficiently without manual intervention.

When an update is triggered, React performs the following steps to determine its priority and assign it to the correct lane:

1. Determine the update's context

React evaluates the context in which the update was triggered. This context could be a user interaction, an internal update due to state or props changes, or even an update that's a result of a server response. The context plays a crucial role in determining the priority of the update.

2. Estimate priority based on the context

Based on the context, React estimates the priority of the update. For instance, if the update is a result of user input, it's likely to have a higher priority, while an update triggered by a noncritical background process might have a lower priority. We've already discussed the different priority levels in detail, so we won't go into more detail here.

3. Check for any priority overrides

In some cases, developers can explicitly set the priority of an update using React's `useTransition` or `useDeferredValue` hooks. If such a priority override is present, React will consider the provided priority instead of the estimated one.

4. Assign the update to the correct lane

Once the priority is determined, React assigns the update to the corresponding lane. This process is done using the bitmask we just looked at, which allows React to efficiently work with multiple lanes and ensure that updates are correctly grouped and processed.

Throughout this process, React relies on its internal heuristics and the context in which updates occur to make informed decisions about their priorities. This dynamic assignment of priorities and lanes allows React to balance responsiveness and performance, ensuring that applications function efficiently without manual intervention from developers.

Let's look into how exactly React processes updates in their respective lanes.

Processing Lanes

Once updates have been assigned to their respective lanes, React processes them in priority order. In our chat application example, React would process updates in the following order:

ImmediatePriority
> Process updates to the message input, ensuring it remains responsive and updates quickly.

UserBlockingPriority
> Process updates to the typing indicator, providing users with real-time feedback.

NormalPriority
> Process updates to the message list, displaying new messages and updates at a reasonable pace.

By processing updates in priority order, React ensures that the most important parts of the application remain responsive even under heavy load.

Commit Phase

After processing all the updates in their respective lanes, React enters the commit phase, where it applies the changes to the DOM, runs effects, and performs other finalization tasks. In our chat application example, this might include updating the message input value, showing or hiding the typing indicator, and appending new messages to the message list. React then moves on to the next render cycle, repeating the process of collecting updates, processing lanes, and committing changes.

This process, however, is exceedingly more complex than we can truly appreciate in this book: there are concepts like *entanglement*, which decides when two lanes need to be processed together, and further concepts like *rebasing*, which decides when an update needs to be rebased on top of updates that have already been processed. Rebasing is useful, for example, in cases where a transition is interrupted by a sync update before it finished, and you need to run both together.

There's also a lot to say here about flushing effects. For example, like when there is a synchronous update, React may flush effects before/after the update to ensure consistent ordering of state between sync updates.

Ultimately, this is why React exists, and the true value React adds behind the scenes as an abstraction layer: it fundamentally handles the update problems, their prioritization, and their ordering for us, while we continue to focus on our applications.

It's important to note that while React is good at estimating priorities, it's not always perfect. As a developer, you may sometimes need to override the default priority assignments using some of the APIs we've mentioned so far: useTransition and useDeferredValue to fine-tune your application's performance and responsiveness. Let's dive into these APIs in more detail.

useTransition

useTransition is a powerful React Hook that allows you to manage the priority of state updates in your components and prevent the UI from becoming unresponsive due to high-priority updates. It's particularly useful when dealing with updates that can be visually disruptive, such as loading new data or navigating between pages.

It essentially puts whatever update you wrap in its returned startTransition function into the transition lane, which is lower priority than the Sync lane as we've seen earlier, allowing you to control the timing of updates and maintain a smooth user experience, even when other higher-priority updates are competing for the main thread.

useTransition is a hook, meaning you can only use it inside function components. It returns an array containing two elements:

isPending
  A boolean indicating whether a transition is in progress. One interesting part about the way useTransition works is that the first thing it does when you call startTransition is schedule a sync setState({ isPending: false }) on this property, which means updates depending on isPending need to be fast or it defeats the purpose of useTransition.

startTransition
  A function that you can use to wrap updates that should be deferred or given a lower priority.

It's probably worth mentioning here that there is also a startTransition API that is available not as a hook, but as a regular function. The second way to start a nonurgent transition is by using the function startTransition imported directly from React. This approach doesn't give us access to the isPending flag, but it's available for places in your code when you can't use hooks, like useTransition, but still want to signal a low-priority update to React.

Simple Example

Here's a simple example that demonstrates the basic usage of useTransition:

```
import React, { useState, useTransition } from "react";

function App() {
  const [count, setCount] = useState(0);
  const [isPending, startTransition] = useTransition();
```

```
  const handleClick = () => {
    doSomethingImportant();
    startTransition(() => {
      setCount(count + 1);
    });
  };

  return (
    <div>
      <p>Count: {count}</p>
      <button onClick={handleClick}>Increment</button>
      {isPending && <p>Loading...</p>}
    </div>
  );
}

export default App;
```

In this example, we use `useTransition` to manage the priority of a state update that increments a counter. By wrapping the `setCount` update inside the `startTransition` function, we are telling React that this update can be deferred, preventing the UI from becoming unresponsive if there are other high-priority updates happening simultaneously.

Advanced Example: Navigation

`useTransition` is also useful when navigating between pages. By managing the priority of updates related to navigation, you can ensure that the user experience remains smooth and responsive, even when dealing with complex page transitions.

Consider this example where we demonstrate how to use `useTransition` for managing page transitions in a single-page application (SPA):

```
import React, { useState, useTransition } from "react";

const PageOne = () => <div>Page One</div>;
const PageTwo = () => <div>Page Two</div>;

function App() {
  const [currentPage, setCurrentPage] = useState("pageOne");
  const [isPending, startTransition] = useTransition();

  const handleNavigation = (page) => {
    startTransition(() => {
      setCurrentPage(page);
    });
  };

  const renderPage = () => {
    switch (currentPage) {
```

```
    case "pageOne":
      return <PageOne />;
    case "pageTwo":
      return <PageTwo />;
    default:
      return <div>Unknown page</div>;
  }
};

return (
  <div>
    <nav>
      <button onClick={() => handleNavigation("pageOne")}>Page One</button>
      <button onClick={() => handleNavigation("pageTwo")}>Page Two</button>
    </nav>
    {isPending && <p>Loading...</p>}
    {renderPage()}
  </div>
);
}

export default App;
```

In this example, we have two simple components representing different pages in our SPA. We use useTransition to wrap the state update that changes the current page, ensuring that the page transition is deferred if there are other high-priority updates (like user input) happening simultaneously.

In this example, you might be thinking, "Wait, shouldn't the page transition be instant though since it happens in response to a user click?" Yes, you'd be right; however, if the next page requires some data to be fetched using Suspense, then the page transition might be delayed. This is where useTransition comes in handy, as it allows you to manage the priority of updates related to navigation, ensuring that the user experience remains smooth and responsive, even when dealing with complex page transitions. It's worth noting that if the next page data fetching happens in an effect, then startTranstion won't wait for the data in the effect to be fetched; however, when you suspend inside of a transition, React will tie the isPending state to the data fetch and the rendering of that data when it comes back.

In this case, the isPending state will be true while the page transition is in progress, allowing us to immediately show a loading indicator to the user in response to their button click. Once the transition is complete, the isPending state will be false, and the new page will be rendered.

Diving Deeper

With the background knowledge of React's Fiber architecture, the React scheduler, priority levels, and the render lanes mechanism, we can now delve into the inner workings of the `useTransition` hook.

The `useTransition` hook works by creating a transition and assigning a specific priority level to the updates made within that transition. When an update is wrapped in a transition, React ensures that the update gets scheduled and rendered based on the assigned priority level.

Here's an overview of the steps involved in using the `useTransition` hook:

1. Import and invoke the `useTransition` hook within a functional component.

2. The hook returns an array with two elements: the first is the `isPending` state, and the second is the `startTransition` function.

3. Use the `startTransition` function to wrap any state update or component rendering that you want to control the timing of.

4. The `isPending` state provides an indicator of whether the transition is still in progress or has completed.

5. React ensures that updates wrapped in a transition are treated with the appropriate priority level. This is achieved by using the scheduler and render lanes mechanism to assign and manage the updates.

By using `useTransition`, we can effectively control the timing of updates and maintain a smooth user experience, even when other higher-priority updates are competing for the main thread.

useDeferredValue

`useDeferredValue` is a React Hook that allows for the deferral of certain UI updates to a later time, especially useful in scenarios where the application is dealing with a heavy load or computationally intensive tasks, thereby aiding in managing update prioritization and promoting smoother transitions and an improved user experience.

During the initial render, the returned deferred value is the same as the supplied value. In subsequent updates, `useDeferredValue` helps maintain a smooth user experience by keeping the old value for a longer duration before updating to the new value, particularly in scenarios with computationally intensive operations. This does not entail multiple rerenders with old and new values, but a controlled update to the new value. This mechanism is akin to a `stale-while-revalidate` strategy, holding on to stale values to keep the UI responsive while awaiting new values.

Looking through React's commit history, we see that the first implementation of use DeferredValue looked something like this:

```
function useDeferredValue(value) {
  const [newValue, setNewValue] = useState(value); // only stores initial value
  useEffect(() => {
    // update the returned value in a transition whenever it changes,
    // "deferring" it
    startTransition(() => {
      setNewValue(value);
    });
  }, [value]);

  return newValue;
}
```

Let's chat a bit about what this code is doing. Initially, it sets up a state (newValue) with the initial value passed to it. The function then utilizes the useEffect hook to observe changes in this value. When a change is detected, the startTransition function is invoked, which is crucial for deferring the update.

Within startTransition, the state is updated to the new value using setNewValue. The use of startTransition signifies to React that this update is not urgent, allowing React to prioritize other, more critical updates first. This is more or less exactly how useDeferredValue works today and should be helpful for our mental model of it.

useDeferredValue is a part of React's concurrent features that enables interruptibility by allowing certain state updates to be deferred.

When a component rerenders with a deferred value, React keeps showing the old value for a certain period, allowing high-priority updates to be processed before low-priority ones. This breaks up the rendering work into smaller chunks, which can be spread out over time, improving responsiveness and ensuring that high-priority updates (like user interactions) are not delayed by lower-priority updates, hence boosting positive user experience.

Purpose of useDeferredValue

The primary purpose of useDeferredValue is to allow you to defer the rendering of less critical updates. This is particularly useful when you want to prioritize more important updates, such as user interactions, over less critical ones, such as displaying updated data from the server.

By using useDeferredValue, you can provide a smoother user experience and ensure that your application remains responsive even under heavy load or when dealing with complex operations.

To use `useDeferredValue`, you will need to import it from the React package and pass a value to be deferred as its argument. The hook will then return a deferred version of the value that can be used in your component.

Here's an example of how to use `useDeferredValue` in a simple application:

```
import React, { memo useState, useDeferredValue } from "react";

function App() {
  const [searchValue, setSearchValue] = useState("");
  const deferredSearchValue = useDeferredValue(searchValue);

  return (
    <div>
      <input
        type="text"
        value={searchValue}
        onChange={(event) => setSearchValue(event.target.value)}
      />
      <SearchResults searchValue={deferredSearchValue} />
    </div>
  );
}

const SearchResults = memo(({ searchValue }) => {
  // Perform the search and render the results
})
```

In this example, we have a search input and a `SearchResults` component that displays the results. We use `useDeferredValue` to defer the rendering of the search results, allowing the application to prioritize user input and remain responsive even when rendering the list of results is expensive. Let's understand this in a little more detail:

1. We use `memo` on the component to make sure it doesn't unnecessarily update, as we've discussed in prior chapters.

2. When it updates, it causes performance problems because it's expensive to render.

3. When we give it a deferred prop, `deferredSearchValue`, since the prop itself is updated after more urgent rendering work, so is the component. Thus, the component only rerenders when there's no more urgent work to be done, like updating the text input field.

One might ask here, "Why not just debounce or throttle `searchValue`?"

Great question. Let's contrast those here:

Debouncing

 Involves a pause before updating the list, waiting for the user to finish typing, such as a delay of one second

Throttling

 Updates the list at regular intervals, say, no more than once per second

While these methods can be effective in certain situations, `useDeferredValue` emerges as a more tailored solution for rendering optimization since it adapts seamlessly to the performance capabilities of the user's device and isn't some arbitrary delay.

The key difference with `useDeferredValue` lies in its dynamic approach to delays. It eliminates the need for setting a fixed delay time. On a high-performance device, such as a powerful laptop, the delay in rerendering is almost imperceptible, occurring almost instantaneously. Conversely, on slower devices, the rendering delay adjusts accordingly, causing the list to update with a slight lag in response to the input, proportional to the device's speed.

Moreover, `useDeferredValue` has a significant advantage in its ability to interrupt deferred rerenders. In scenarios where React is processing a substantial list, and the user enters a new keystroke, React can pause the rerendering, respond to the new input, and then resume the rendering process in the background. This is a contrast to debouncing and throttling, which, despite delaying updates, can still lead to a disjointed experience as they block interactivity during rendering.

That said, debouncing and throttling are still useful in scenarios not directly related to rendering. For instance, they can be effective in reducing the frequency of network requests. These techniques can also be used in conjunction with `useDeferredValue` for a comprehensive optimization strategy.

Based on all of this, we see several advantages to using `useDeferredValue` in React applications:

Improved responsiveness

 In the example, when the user types into the search box, the input field updates immediately and the results are deferred. If the user quickly types five characters in a row, the input field updates immediately five times, and the `searchResults` are only rendered once, after the user stops typing. For characters 1–4, the rendering of `SearchResults` is interrupted by the new values.

Declarative prioritization

 `useDeferredValue` provides a simple and declarative way to manage the prioritization of updates in your application. By encapsulating the logic for deferring updates within the hook, you can keep your component code clean and focused on the essential aspects of your app.

Better resource utilization

By deferring less critical updates, `useDeferredValue` allows your application to make better use of available resources. This can help reduce the likelihood of performance bottlenecks and improve the overall performance of your application.

When to Use useDeferredValue

`useDeferredValue` is most useful in situations where your application needs to prioritize certain updates over others. Some common scenarios where you might consider using `useDeferredValue` include:

- Searching or filtering large data sets
- Rendering complex visualizations or animations
- Updating data from a server in the background
- Handling computationally expensive operations that could impact user interactions

Let's take a look at an example where `useDeferredValue` can be particularly useful. Imagine we have a large list of items that we want to filter based on user input. Filtering a large list can be computationally expensive, so using `useDeferredValue` can help keep the application responsive:

```
import React, { memo, useState, useMemo, useDeferredValue } from "react";

function App() {
  const [filter, setFilter] = useState("");
  const deferredFilter = useDeferredValue(filter);

  const items = useMemo(() => generateLargeListOfItems(), []);
  const filteredItems = useMemo(() => {
    return items.filter((item) => item.includes(deferredFilter));
  }, [items, deferredFilter]);

  return (
    <div>
      <input
        type="text"
        value={filter}
        onChange={(event) => setFilter(event.target.value)}
      />
      <ItemList items={filteredItems} />
    </div>
  );
}

const ItemList = memo(({ items }) => {
  // Render the list of items
```

```
  });

  function generateLargeListOfItems() {
    // Generate a large list of items for the example
  }
```

In this example, we use `useDeferredValue` to defer the rendering of the filtered list. As the user types in the filter input, the deferred value updates less frequently, allowing the application to prioritize the user input and remain responsive.

The `useMemo` hooks are used to memoize the items and `filteredItems` arrays, preventing unnecessary rerendering and recalculations. This further improves the performance of the application.

When Not to Use useDeferredValue

While `useDeferredValue` can be beneficial in certain scenarios, it's important to recognize the trade-offs. Namely, by deferring updates, there's a possibility that the data displayed to the user might be slightly out-of-date. While this is usually acceptable for less critical updates, it's important to consider the implications of displaying stale data to users.

A good question to ask yourself when deciding whether to use `useDeferredValue` or not is, "Is this update user input?"

React is called React for a reason: it enables our web applications to react to things. Anything that causes a user to expect a reaction ought not be deferred. Everything else should be.

While the usage of `useDeferredValue` can greatly enhance your application's responsiveness under load, it should not be seen as a magic bullet. Always remember that the best way to improve performance is to write efficient code and avoid unnecessary computations.

Problems with Concurrent Rendering

Concurrent rendering, while allowing for performant and responsive user interactions, presents new problems for developers to consider. The main problem is that it's difficult to reason about the order in which updates will be processed, which can lead to unexpected behavior and bugs.

One such bug is called *tearing*, where the UI becomes inconsistent due to updates being processed out of order. This can happen when a component depends on some value that is updated while it's still rendering, causing applications to be rendered with inconsistent data. Let's dive into this a little bit.

Tearing

Tearing is a bug that occurs when a component depends on some state that is updated while the application is still rendering. To understand this, let's contrast synchronous rendering with concurrent rendering.

In a synchronous world, React would walk down a tree of components and render them one by one, from top to bottom. This ensures that the state of the application is consistent throughout the rendering process, as each component is rendered with the latest state.

Consider this example:

```
import { useState, useSyncExternalStore, useTransition } from "react";

// External state
let count = 0;
setInterval(() => count++, 1);

export default function App() {
  const [name, setName] = useState("");
  const [isPending, startTransition] = useTransition();

  const updateName = (newVal) => {
    startTransition(() => {
      setName(newVal);
    });
  };

  return (
    <div>
      <input value={name} onChange={(e) => updateName(e.target.value)} />
      {isPending && <div>Loading...</div>}
      <ul>
        <li>
          <ExpensiveComponent />
        </li>
        <li>
          <ExpensiveComponent />
        </li>
        <li>
          <ExpensiveComponent />
        </li>
        <li>
          <ExpensiveComponent />
        </li>
        <li>
          <ExpensiveComponent />
        </li>
      </ul>
    </div>
  );
```

```
  }

  const ExpensiveComponent = () => {
    const now = performance.now();

    while (performance.now() - now < 100) {
      // Do nothing, just wait.
    }

    return <>Expensive count is {count}</>;
  };
```

At the very top of our app, we have `count`: a variable that we set globally and keep updating via `setInterval` outside of the React render cycle so that we can simulate a tearing bug by having it update while the application is rendering. Since rendering is concurrent and interruptible, it's possible for the `ExpensiveComponent` to be rendered with different values for `count`, resulting in inconsistent data being displayed to the user, or tearing.

We expect to see inconsistent values for `count` rendered inside `ExpensiveComponent` as React "stops" rendering on user input to prioritize a more urgent update, like updating the text input field, thereby leaving a stale value of `count` in the `Expensive Component`, but only sometimes.

Our example renders a text input field and a list of five `ExpensiveComponents`. These components are not memoized intentionally to illustrate a point here, as they cause performance problems and we need these performance problems, to identify tearing for the purposes of understanding it. In the real world, you'll want to wrap `Expensive Component` in `React.memo`. Here, we're intentionally avoiding this to demonstrate tearing—which you'll want to avoid in your application.

`ExpensiveComponent` takes a long time to render, simulating a computationally expensive operation. The `ExpensiveComponent` also displays the current value of the `count` variable, which is incremented every millisecond and read from an external store, in this case the global namespace.

If we run this example, we'll see that for the five instances of `ExpensiveComponent` that we render, after typing a few keystrokes in the `input`, the `ExpensiveComponents` will render with different values for `count`.

This is because the `ExpensiveComponent` is rendered five times, and each time it's rendered, the value of `count` is different. Since React is rendering the components concurrently, it's possible for the `ExpensiveComponent` to be rendered with different values for `count`, resulting in inconsistent data displayed to the user.

This is called tearing, and it's a bug that can occur when a component depends on some state that is updated while the application is still rendering. In this case, the

ExpensiveComponent depends on the count variable, which is updated while the component is still rendering, causing the application to be rendered with inconsistent data. With tearing, we see the following output for the five instances of ExpensiveComponent:

- Expensive count is 568
- Expensive count is 568
- Expensive count is 569
- Expensive count is 569
- Expensive count is 570

This makes sense because earlier instances of the component are rendered, the updated count value is flushed/committed to the DOM, and lower instances continue to be rendered and yielded (flushed, updated) with newer values of count.

This isn't a huge deal because React will eventually render the consistent state. The bigger issue is when you have something like:

```
<UserDetails id={user.id} />
```

With this code, if the user is deleted from the global store between renders, this will throw a sudden error that can surprise a user. This is why tearing is a problem.

To solve this problem of tearing, React exposes a hook called useSyncExternalStore. Let's dive into this hook.

useSyncExternalStore

useSyncExternalStore is a React Hook that allows you to synchronize external state with the internal state of your application. It's particularly useful when dealing with computationally expensive operations that might cause tearing if not handled properly. The "sync" in useSyncExternalStore has a double meaning. It's "synchronize," but it's also "synchronous": it forces a synchronous update when the store changes.

The useSyncExternalStore hook has the following signature:

```
const value = useSyncExternalStore(store.subscribe, store.getSnapshot);
```

store.subscribe

A function that receives a callback function as its first and only argument. Inside this function, you can subscribe to changes in the external store and call the callback function whenever the store changes. The callback can be considered a call to prompt React to rerender the component with the new value. The expected return of this function is a cleanup function that unsubscribes from the store.

A typical `subscribe` function looks like this:

```
const store = {
  subscribe(rerender) {
    const newData = getNewData().then(rerender);
    return () => {
      // unsubscribe somehow
    };
  },
};
```

A simple use case for this would be subscribing to browser events, such as `resize` or `scroll` events, and updating the component when these events occur, like this:

```
const store = {
  subscribe(rerenderImmediately) {
    window.addEventListener("resize", rerenderImmediately);
    return () => {
      window.removeEventListener("resize", rerenderImmediately);
    };
  },
};
```

Now, our React components would rerender whenever the browser window is resized. However, how does it get the new value? That's where the second argument to `useSyncExternalStore` comes in.

`store.getSnapshot`
A function that returns the current value of the external store. This function is called whenever the component is rendered, and the returned value is used to update the component's internal state. This function is called synchronously, so it should not perform any asynchronous operations or have any side effects. Moreover, this function ensures the state at render time is consistent across multiple instances of the component.

To follow our window resize example, this is how we would get the current window size:

```
const store = {
  subscribe(immediatelyRerenderSynchronously) {
    window.addEventListener("resize",
      immediatelyRerenderSynchronously);
    return () => {
      window.removeEventListener("resize",
        immediatelyRerenderSynchronously);
    };
  },
  getSnapshot() {
    return {
      width: window.innerWidth,
      height: window.innerHeight,
```

```
      };
    },
  };
```

The object with `{ width, height }` is the snapshot of the current state of the window, and it's what `useSyncExternalStore` will return. We can then use this object in our component with confidence that its state will always be consistent across concurrent renders.

How can we have this confidence? It's because the `immediatelyRerenderSynchro nously` function forces a synchronous rerender and does not allow React to defer it. This is the key to solving tearing.

Now, let's take a look at how we can use `useSyncExternalStore` to solve the tearing problem in our previous example. If we recall, we saw a list of `ExpensiveComponents` that rendered with different values for `count` due to tearing. Let's see how we can fix this using `useSyncExternalStore`.

For starters, we don't want to subscribe to the store and have React rerender when updates happen; but instead we want consistent state when rerenders happen due to user input. So our `subscribe` function will be empty, but to get consistent state, we'll use the `getSnapshot` function to get the current value of `count` and return it:

```
const store = {
  subscribe() {},
  getSnapshot() {
    return count;
  },
};
```

This is what our previous example will look like with `useSyncExternalStore`:

```
import { useState, useSyncExternalStore, useTransition } from "react";

let count = 0;
setInterval(() => count++, 1);

export default function App() {
  const [name, setName] = useState("");
  const [, startTransition] = useTransition();

  const updateName = (newVal) => {
    startTransition(() => {
      setName(newVal);
    });
  };

  return (
    <div>
      <input value={name} onChange={(e) => updateName(e.target.value)} />
      <ul>
```

```
        <li>
          <ExpensiveComponent />
        </li>
        <li>
          <ExpensiveComponent />
        </li>
        <li>
          <ExpensiveComponent />
        </li>
        <li>
          <ExpensiveComponent />
        </li>
        <li>
          <ExpensiveComponent />
        </li>
      </ul>
    </div>
  );
}

const ExpensiveComponent = () => {
  // Instead of reading count globally,
  // we'll use the hook to ensure consistent state
  const consistentCount = useSyncExternalStore(
    () => {},
    () => count
  );

  const now = performance.now();
  while (performance.now() - now < 100) {
    // Do nothing
  }

  return <>Expensive count is {consistentCount}</>;
};
```

Now, if we run this example, we will see that the `ExpensiveComponents` render with the same value for `count`, preventing tearing from occurring. This is because the `useSyncExternalStore` hook ensures that the state at render time is consistent across multiple instances of the component.

We don't use a `subscribe` function because its purpose is to tell React when to rerender with the latest state, but in our case we just want state to be consistent across renders. We use the `getSnapshot` function to get the current value of `count` and return it, ensuring that the state at render time is consistent across multiple instances of the component.

This is how we can use `useSyncExternalStore` to solve the tearing problem in our previous example, ensuring that the state at render time is consistent across multiple instances of the component.

OK, this ensures that when the text input changes and ExpensiveComponent reren-ders, it will have the same value of count as the other instances of ExpensiveCompo-nent, preventing tearing—but what if we wanted to update count inside ExpensiveComponent at the same interval that we update count outside of Expensive Component?

We just create a store for this that follows the same update rules:

```
import { useState, useSyncExternalStore, useTransition } from "react";

let count = 0;
setInterval(() => count++, 1);

const store = {
  subscribe(forceSyncRerender) {
    // Whenever count changes,
    forceSyncRerender();
  },
  getSnapshot() {
    return count;
  },
};

export default function App() {
  const [name, setName] = useState("");
  const [, startTransition] = useTransition();

  const updateName = (newVal) => {
    startTransition(() => {
      setName(newVal);
    });
  };

  return (
    <div>
      <input value={name} onChange={(e) => updateName(e.target.value)} />
      <ul>
        <li>
          <ExpensiveComponent />
        </li>
        <li>
          <ExpensiveComponent />
        </li>
        <li>
          <ExpensiveComponent />
        </li>
        <li>
          <ExpensiveComponent />
        </li>
        <li>
          <ExpensiveComponent />
```

```
          </li>
        </ul>
      </div>
    );
  }

  const ExpensiveComponent = () => {
    // Instead of reading count globally,
    // we'll use the hook to ensure consistent state
    const consistentCount = useSyncExternalStore(
      store.subscribe,
      store.getSnapshot
    );

    const now = performance.now();
    while (performance.now() - now < 100) {
      // Do nothing
    }

    return <>Expensive count is {consistentCount}</>;
  };
```

Now, whenever `count` changes, `ExpensiveComponent` will rerender with the new value of `count`, and we'll see the same value for `count` across all instances of `ExpensiveComponent`. The change detection logic itself can be as simple or as complex as you want it to be, but the key is that we understand the mechanisms of how `useSyncExternalStore` does its main things, which are:

- Ensuring consistent state across concurrent renders
- Forcing a synchronous rerender when the store changes

Now that we understand how `useSyncExternalStore` works and solves the tearing problem, we have a solid grasp not only of concurrent rendering in React but also of how to solve some of the problems that come with it. This is a great place to be in as a React developer.

This was quite a deep dive, but we're nearly done. Let's review.

Chapter Review

This comprehensive conversation focused on the deep exploration of concurrent React, touching on multiple aspects, including the Fiber Reconciler, scheduling, deferring updates, render lanes, and new hooks, such as `useTransition` and `useDeferredValue`.

We began by discussing the Fiber reconciler, the heart of React's concurrent rendering engine. It's the algorithm behind the framework's ability to break work into smaller chunks and manage the execution priority, allowing React to be "interruptible" and support concurrent rendering. This contributes significantly to the ability of React to handle complex, high-performance applications smoothly, ensuring user interactions remain responsive even during heavy computation.

Then we moved on to the concept of scheduling and deferring updates, which essentially allows React to prioritize certain state updates over others. React can defer lower-priority updates in favor of higher-priority ones, thus maintaining a smooth user experience even under heavy load. An example illustrated a chat application where incoming message updates were intelligently scheduled and rendered without blocking the user interface.

The discussion then moved to render lanes, a central concept in React's concurrent features. Render lanes are a mechanism that React uses to assign priority to updates and effectively manage their execution. It's the secret behind how React decides which updates are urgent and need to be processed immediately and which ones can be deferred until later. The detailed explanation mentioned how these render lanes use bitmasking to efficiently handle multiple priorities.

We then delved into the new hooks introduced for concurrent operations in React, `useTransition` and `useDeferredValue`. These hooks are designed to handle transitions and provide smoother user experiences, particularly for operations that take a considerable amount of time.

The `useTransition` hook was first discussed, which allows React to transition between states in a way that ensures a responsive user interface even if the new state takes a while to prepare. In other words, it allows for delaying an update to the next render cycle if the component is currently rendering.

We also discussed the `useDeferredValue` hook, which defers the update of less critical parts of a component, thus preventing janky user experience. It essentially allows React to "hold on" to the previous value for a little longer if the new value is taking too much time.

Finally, we dove into issues with concurrency, including tearing, and explored how `useSyncExternalStore` can help keep state consistent across multiple concurrent renders.

Throughout the conversation, the recurring theme was understanding the "what" and "why" behind React's strategies for managing complex, dynamic applications with heavy computation, and how developers can utilize these strategies to deliver a smooth, responsive user experience.

Review Questions

Let's ask ourselves a few questions to test our understanding of the concepts in this chapter:

1. What is the Fiber reconciler in React, and how does it contribute to the handling of complex, high-performance applications?

2. Explain the concept of scheduling and deferring updates in React. How does it help in maintaining a smooth user experience even under heavy load?

3. What are render lanes in React, and how do they manage the execution of updates? Can you describe how render lanes use bitmasking to handle multiple priorities?

4. What is the purpose of the `useTransition` and `useDeferredValue` hooks in React? Describe a situation where each hook would be beneficial.

5. When might it be inappropriate to use `useDeferredValue`? What are some of the trade-offs involved with using these hooks?

Up Next

Now that you have a deep understanding of the concurrent features of React and its inner workings, you are well equipped to harness its full potential in building high-performance applications. In Chapter 8, we will explore various popular frameworks built on top of React, such as Next.js and Remix, which further streamline the development process by providing best practices, conventions, and additional features.

These frameworks are designed to help you build complex applications with ease, taking care of many common concerns, such as server rendering, routing, and code splitting. By leveraging the power of these frameworks, you can focus on building your application's features and functionality while ensuring optimal performance and user experience.

Stay tuned for an in-depth exploration of these powerful frameworks, and learn how to build scalable, performant, and feature-rich applications using React and its ecosystem.

CHAPTER 8

Frameworks

In our journey through React thus far, we have uncovered an extensive range of features and principles that contribute to its power and versatility. The previous chapter delved into the fascinating world of asynchronous React, which empowers us with tools like `useTransition` and `useDeferredValue` to create highly responsive and user-friendly interfaces. We explored how these tools utilize the sophisticated scheduling and prioritization mechanisms of React, made possible by the Fiber reconciler, to achieve optimal performance. The understanding of these asynchronous patterns is critical as we venture into the realm of React frameworks in this chapter.

React by itself is incredibly powerful, but as applications grow in complexity, we often find ourselves repeating similar patterns or needing more streamlined solutions for common challenges. This is where frameworks come in. React frameworks are software libraries or toolkits built on top of React, providing additional abstractions to handle common tasks more efficiently and enforce best practices.

Why We Need a Framework

While React provides the building blocks to create interactive user interfaces, it leaves many important architectural decisions up to the developers. React is unopinionated in this regard, giving developers the flexibility to structure their applications in the way they see fit. However, as applications scale, this freedom can turn into a burden. You might find yourself reinventing the wheel, dealing with common challenges such as routing, data fetching, and server-side rendering again and again.

This is where React frameworks come in. They provide a predefined structure and solutions to common problems, allowing developers to focus on what's unique about their application, rather than getting bogged down with boilerplate code. This can significantly accelerate the development process and improve the quality of the code-base by adhering to best practices enforced by the framework.

To fully understand this, let's try to write our own minimal framework. In order to do this, we need to identify a few key features that we get from frameworks that we do not get as easily from plain React. For the sake of brevity, we'll identify three key features along these lines that we get from frameworks . It's worth noting that frameworks do far more, but this subset will help us form the basis of a great discussion:

- Server rendering
- Routing
- Data fetching

Let's take a preexisting imaginary React application and incrementally add these features to understand what frameworks do for us. The React app we're "framework-ifying" has the following structure:

```
- index.js
- List.js
- Detail.js
- dist/
  - clientBundle.js
```

Here's what each file looks like:

```
// index.js

import React from "react";
import { createRoot } from "react-dom/client";
import Router from "./Router";

const root = createRoot(document);

const params = new URLSearchParams();
const thingId = params.get("id");

root.render(
  window.location.pathname === "/" ? <List /> : <Detail thingId={thingId} />
);

// List.js

export const List = () => {
  const [things, setThings] = useState([]);
  const [requestState, setRequestState] = useState("initial");
  const [error, setError] = useState(null);

  useEffect(() => {
    setRequestState("loading");
    fetch("https://api.com/get-list")
```

```
            .then((r) => r.json())
            .then(setThings)
            .then(() => {
              setRequestState("success");
            })
            .catch((e) => {
              setRequestState("error");
              setError(e);
            });
      }, []);

      return (
        <div>
          <ul>
            {things.map((thing) => (
              <li key={thing.id}>{thing.label}</li>
            ))}
          </ul>
        </div>
      );
    };

    // Detail.js

    export const Detail = ({ thingId }) => {
      const [thing, setThing] = useState([]);
      const [requestState, setRequestState] = useState("initial");
      const [error, setError] = useState(null);

      useEffect(() => {
        setRequestState("loading");
        fetch("https://api.com/get-thing/" + thingId)
          .then((r) => r.json())
          .then(setThings)
          .then(() => {
            setRequestState("success");
          })
          .catch((e) => {
            setRequestState("error");
            setError(e);
          });
      }, []);

      return (
        <div>
          <h1>The thing!</h1>
          {thing}
        </div>
      );
    };
```

There are a few issues with this that affect all client-only rendered React applications:

We ship an empty page to a user with only code to load, then parse and execute JavaScript.
A user downloads a blank page until JavaScript kicks in, and then they get our app. If the user is a search engine, they may see nothing. If the search engine crawler does not support JavaScript, the search engine will not index our website.

We start fetching data too late.
Our app falls prey to a user-experience curse called *network waterfalls*: a phenomenon that occurs when network requests happen in succession and slow down applications. Our application has to make multiple requests to a server for basic functionality. For instance, it executes like so:

- Download, parse, and execute JavaScript.
- Render and commit React components.
- `useEffect` starts fetching data.
- Render and commit spinners, etc.
- `useEffect` finishes fetching data.
- Render and commit data. All of this can be avoided if we serve a page with data straight to the browser: if we send HTML markup as covered in Chapter 7 on server-side React.

Our router is purely client based.
If a browser requests *https://our-app.com/detail?thingId=24*, the server responds with a 404 page because there is no such file on the server. A common hack used to remedy this is to render an HTML file when a 404 is encountered that loads JavaScript and has the client-side router take over. This hack doesn't work for search engines or environments where JavaScript support is limited.

Frameworks help resolve all these issues and more. Let's explore how exactly they do this.

Server Rendering

To start with, frameworks usually give us server rendering out of the box. To add server rendering to this application, we need a server. We can write one ourselves using a package like Express.js. We would then deploy this server and we're in business. Let's explore the code that would power such a server.

Before we do, please be aware that we're using `renderToString` merely for simplicity and to illustrate the underlying mechanisms behind how frameworks implement these features. In a real production use case, it's almost always better to rely on more powerful asynchronous APIs for server rendering like `renderToPipeableStream`, as covered in Chapter 6.

With that out of the way, let's do this:

```javascript
// ./server.js

import express from "express";
import { renderToString } from "react-dom/server"; // Covered in Chapter 6

import { List } from "./List";
import { Detail } from "./Detail";

const app = express();

app.use(express.static("./dist")); // Get static files like client JS, etc.

const createLayout = (children) => `<html lang="en">
<head>
  <title>My page</title>
</head>
<body>
  ${children}
  <script src="/clientBundle.js"></script>
</body>
<html>`;

app.get("/", (req, res) => {
  res.setHeader("Content-Type", "text/html");
  res.end(createLayout(renderToString(<List />)));
});

app.get("/detail", (req, res) => {
  res.setHeader("Content-Type", "text/html");
  res.end(
    createLayout(renderToString(<Detail thingId={req.params.thingId} />))
  );
});

app.listen(3000, () => {
  console.info("App is listening!");
});
```

This code is all we need to add server rendering to our application. Notice how `index.js` on the client side has its own client router, and how we essentially just added another one for the server. Frameworks ship *isomorphic routers*, which are routers that work on both the client and the server.

Routing

While this server is *OK*, it doesn't scale well: for each route we add, we'll have to manually add more `req.get` calls. Let's make this a little more scalable. We can solve this in a number of ways, like with a configuration object that maps routes to components, or with filesystem-based routing. For the sake of education (and frankly, fun) let's explore *filesystem-based routing*. This is where the reasoning for and mechanism behind the conventions and opinions of frameworks like Next.js become more clear. When we enforce a convention such that all pages must go in a *./pages* directory and all filenames in this directory become router paths, then our server can rely on the convention as an assumption and become more scalable.

Let's illustrate this with an example. First, we'll augment our directory structure. The new directory structure looks like this:

```
- index.js
- pages/
  - list.js
  - detail.js
- dist/
  - clientBundle.js
```

Now, we can assume that everything in `pages` becomes a route. Let's update our server to match this:

```
// ./server.js

import express from "express";
import { join } from "path";
import { renderToString } from "react-dom/server"; // Covered in Chapter 6

const app = express();

app.use(express.static("./dist")); // Get static files like client JS, etc.

const createLayout = (children) => `<html lang="en">
<head>
  <title>My page</title>
</head>
<body>
  ${children}
  <script src="/clientBundle.js"></script>
</body>
<html>`;

app.get("/:route", async (req, res) => {
  // Import the route's component from the pages directory
  const exportedStuff = await import(
    join(process.cwd(), "pages", req.params.route)
  );
```

```
  // We can no longer have named exports because we need predictability
  // so we opt for default exports instead.
  // `.default` is standardized and therefore we can rely on it.
  const Page = exportedStuff.default;

  // We can infer props from the query string maybe?
  const props = req.query;

  res.setHeader("Content-Type", "text/html");
  res.end(createLayout(renderToString(<Page {...props} />)));
});

app.listen(3000, () => {
  console.info("App is listening!");
});
```

Now, our server scales far better because of the new *./pages* directory convention we've adopted! Great! However, we're now forced to have each page's component be a default export since our approach is more general and there would otherwise be no way to predict what name to import. This is one of the trade-offs of working with frameworks. In this case, the trade-off seems to be worth it.

Data Fetching

Great! We're 2 for 3. We've got server rendering and filesystem-based routing, but we're still suffering from network waterfalls. Let's fix the data fetching story. To start with, we'll update our components to receive initial data through props. For simplicity, we'll deal with just the List component and leave the Detail component for you to do as homework:

```
// ./pages/list.jsx
// Note the default export for filesystem-based routing.

export default function List({ initialThings } /* <- adding initial prop */) {
  const [things, setThings] = useState(initialThings);
  const [requestState, setRequestState] = useState("initial");
  const [error, setError] = useState(null);

  // This can still run to fetch data if we need it to.
  useEffect(() => {
    if (initialThings) return;
    setRequestState("loading");
    fetch("https://api.com/get-list")
      .then((r) => r.json())
      .then(setThings)
      .then(() => {
        setRequestState("success");
      })
      .catch((e) => {
        setRequestState("error");
        setError(e);
```

```
      });
    }, [initialThings]);

    return (
      <div>
        <ul>
          {things.map((thing) => (
            <li key={thing.id}>{thing.label}</li>
          ))}
        </ul>
      </div>
    );
  }
```

Great. Now that we've added an initial prop, we need some way to fetch the data this page needs on the server, and then pass it to the component before rendering it. Let's explore how we can do that. Ideally, what we want to do is this:

```
// ./server.js

import express from "express";
import { join } from "path";
import { renderToString } from "react-dom/server"; // Covered in Chapter 6

const app = express();

app.use(express.static("./dist")); // Get static files like client JS, etc.

const createLayout = (children) => `<html lang="en">
<head>
  <title>My page</title>
</head>
<body>
  ${children}
  <script src="/clientBundle.js"></script>
</body>
<html>`;

app.get("/:route", async (req, res) => {
  const exportedStuff = await import(
    join(process.cwd(), "pages", req.params.route)
  );

  const Page = exportedStuff.default;

  // Get component's data
  const data = await exportedStuff.getData();
  const props = req.query;

  res.setHeader("Content-Type", "text/html");

  // Pass props and data
```

```
    res.end(createLayout(renderToString(<Page {...props} {...data.props} />)));
});

app.listen(3000, () => {
  console.info("App is listening!");
});
```

This means we'll need to export a fetcher function called `getData` from any page components that need data! Let's adjust the list to do this:

```jsx
// ./pages/list.jsx

// We'll call this on the server and pass these props to the component
export const getData = async () => {
  return {
    props: {
      initialThings: await fetch("https://api.com/get-list").then((r) =>
        r.json()
      ),
    },
  };
};

export default function List({ initialThings } /* <- adding initial prop */) {
  const [things, setThings] = useState(initialThings);
  const [requestState, setRequestState] = useState("initial");
  const [error, setError] = useState(null);

  // This can still run to fetch data if we need it to.
  useEffect(() => {
    if (initialThings) return;
    setRequestState("loading");
    getData()
      .then(setThings)
      .then(() => {
        setRequestState("success");
      })
      .catch((e) => {
        setRequestState("error");
        setError(e);
      });
  }, [initialThings]);

  return (
    <div>
      <ul>
        {things.map((thing) => (
          <li key={thing.id}>{thing.label}</li>
        ))}
      </ul>
    </div>
  );
}
```

Done! Now we're:

- Fetching data as early as possible on the server for each route per file
- Rendering a full page as an HTML string
- Sending this to a client

We've successfully added and understood the three features we've identified from various frameworks and implemented a basic version of them. By doing this, we've learned and now understand the underlying mechanism by which frameworks do what they do. Specifically, we learned how frameworks:

- Give us server rendering
- Have isomorphic routing, influenced by the filesystem
- Fetch data through exported functions

If you've used Next.js versions before 13, the reasoning for its various patterns should become abundantly clear at this point, specifically patterns around:

- The *./pages* directory
- All page exports are default exports
- `getServerSideProps` and `getStaticProps`

Now that we understand the mechanism behind frameworks at the code level and the reasons for some of their conventions, let's zoom out and summarize the benefits of using a framework.

Benefits of Using a Framework

The benefits of using a framework include:

Structure and consistency
Frameworks enforce a certain structure and pattern to organize the codebase. This leads to consistency, making it easier for new developers to understand the flow of the application. It also enables us to focus on our products and features without worrying about the minutiae of how to structure our code.

Best practices
Frameworks often come with baked-in best practices that developers are encouraged to follow. This can lead to better code quality and fewer bugs. For example, frameworks might encourage you to fetch data early—i.e., on the server—rather than waiting for the client to fetch it. This can lead to better performance and user experience.

Abstractions

Frameworks provide higher-level abstractions to handle common tasks such as routing, data fetching, server rendering, and more. This can make your code cleaner, more readable, and easier to maintain, while leaning on the broader community to ensure the quality of these abstractions. An example of this is the `useRouter` hook provided by Next.js, which makes it easy to access the router in your components.

Performance optimizations

Many frameworks come with out-of-the-box optimizations such as code splitting, server-side rendering, and static site generation. These can significantly improve the performance of your application. For example, Next.js automatically code-splits your application and preloads the code for the next page when the user hovers over a link, leading to faster page transitions.

Community and ecosystem

Popular frameworks have a large community and a rich ecosystem of plug-ins and libraries. This means you can often find a solution or get help quickly if you run into a problem.

Trade-Offs of Using a Framework

While frameworks come with many advantages, they are not without their trade-offs. Understanding these can help you make an informed decision about whether to use a framework and which one to choose:

Learning curve

Every framework comes with its own set of concepts, APIs, and conventions that you need to learn. If you're new to React, trying to learn a framework at the same time can be overwhelming but is still recommended. If you're already familiar with React, you'll need to invest time in learning the framework's specific features and APIs.

Flexibility versus convention

While the enforced structure and conventions of a framework can be a boon, they can also be constraining. If your application has unique requirements that don't fit into the framework's model, you might find yourself fighting against the framework rather than being helped by it. There are some cases where you're building for a specific user group with fast internet and a modern browser, and you don't need server-side rendering or data fetching. In these cases, a framework might be overkill.

Dependency and commitment

Choosing a framework is a commitment. You're tying your application to the fate of the framework. If the framework stops being maintained or if it takes a direction that doesn't align with your needs, you may face difficult decisions about whether to undertake a costly migration to a different framework or to maintain the existing framework code yourself.

Abstraction overhead

While abstractions can simplify development by hiding complexity, they can also create "magic" that makes it difficult to understand what's happening under the hood. This can make debugging and performance tuning challenging. Furthermore, every abstraction comes with some overhead, which might impact performance. An example of this is server actions in Next.js, where the `"use server"` directive somehow magically makes the action run on the server. This is a great abstraction, but it can be difficult to understand how it works.

Now that we understand why we might want to use a React framework, and the benefits and trade-offs involved, we can delve into specific frameworks in the React ecosystem. In the upcoming sections of this chapter, we'll explore some of the popular choices, such as Next.js and Remix. Each framework offers unique features and advantages, and understanding them will equip you with the knowledge to choose the right tool for your specific needs.

Popular React Frameworks

Let's explore some of the popular React frameworks and discuss their features, advantages, and trade-offs. We'll start with a brief overview of each framework, followed by a detailed comparison of their features and performance. We'll also discuss some of the factors to consider when choosing a framework for your project.

Remix

Remix is a powerful modern web framework that leverages React and the features of the web platform. Let's get started with some practical examples to understand how it works.

A basic Remix application

First, we'll set up a basic Remix application. You can install Remix using npm:

```
npm create remix@2.2.0
```

This will create a new Remix project in your current directory. Let's look around and see what's inside. To start with, we've got an *app* directory with *entry.client.tsx* and *entry.server.tsx*. We've also got a *root.tsx* in this directory.

Off the bat, we can immediately see that Remix supports client and server entry points out of the box. Moreover, the *root.tsx* contains a shared layout component that is rendered on every page. This is a great example of how Remix provides a predefined structure to help you get started quickly.

Server rendering

Remix provides server rendering out of the box through its *entry.server.tsx*. The file is generated for us, but let's understand it a little bit. Here's what it looks like:

```
import { PassThrough } from "node:stream";

import type { AppLoadContext, EntryContext } from "@remix-run/node";
import { createReadableStreamFromReadable } from "@remix-run/node";
import { RemixServer } from "@remix-run/react";
import isbot from "isbot";
import { renderToPipeableStream } from "react-dom/server";

const ABORT_DELAY = 5_000;

export default function handleRequest(
  request: Request,
  responseStatusCode: number,
  responseHeaders: Headers,
  remixContext: EntryContext,
  loadContext: AppLoadContext
) {
  return isbot(request.headers.get("user-agent"))
    ? handleBotRequest(
        request,
        responseStatusCode,
        responseHeaders,
        remixContext
      )
    : handleBrowserRequest(
        request,
        responseStatusCode,
        responseHeaders,
        remixContext
      );
}

function handleBotRequest(
  request: Request,
  responseStatusCode: number,
  responseHeaders: Headers,
  remixContext: EntryContext
) {
  return new Promise((resolve, reject) => {
    let shellRendered = false;
    const { pipe, abort } = renderToPipeableStream(
```

```
      <RemixServer
        context={remixContext}
        url={request.url}
        abortDelay={ABORT_DELAY}
      />,
      {
        onAllReady() {
          shellRendered = true;
          const body = new PassThrough();
          const stream = createReadableStreamFromReadable(body);

          responseHeaders.set("Content-Type", "text/html");

          resolve(
            new Response(stream, {
              headers: responseHeaders,
              status: responseStatusCode,
            })
          );

          pipe(body);
        },
        onShellError(error: unknown) {
          reject(error);
        },
        onError(error: unknown) {
          responseStatusCode = 500;
          // Log streaming rendering errors from inside the shell.  Don't log
          // errors encountered during initial shell rendering since they'll
          // reject and get logged in handleDocumentRequest.
          if (shellRendered) {
            console.error(error);
          }
        },
      }
    );

    setTimeout(abort, ABORT_DELAY);
  });
}

function handleBrowserRequest(
  request: Request,
  responseStatusCode: number,
  responseHeaders: Headers,
  remixContext: EntryContext
) {
  return new Promise((resolve, reject) => {
    let shellRendered = false;
    const { pipe, abort } = renderToPipeableStream(
      <RemixServer
        context={remixContext}
```

```
        url={request.url}
        abortDelay={ABORT_DELAY}
      />,
      {
        onShellReady() {
          shellRendered = true;
          const body = new PassThrough();
          const stream = createReadableStreamFromReadable(body);

          responseHeaders.set("Content-Type", "text/html");

          resolve(
            new Response(stream, {
              headers: responseHeaders,
              status: responseStatusCode,
            })
          );

          pipe(body);
        },
        onShellError(error: unknown) {
          reject(error);
        },
        onError(error: unknown) {
          responseStatusCode = 500;
          // Log streaming rendering errors from inside the shell.  Don't log
          // errors encountered during initial shell rendering since they'll
          // reject and get logged in handleDocumentRequest.
          if (shellRendered) {
            console.error(error);
          }
        },
      }
    );

    setTimeout(abort, ABORT_DELAY);
  });
}
```

The great thing about Remix is that this file is used internally, but is exposed here for us to customize. If we delete this file, Remix will defer to its internal default implementation of the same file. This is a nice escape hatch that allows us to customize the server rendering behavior if we need to, while not locking us into the framework's "magic."

This file is defining how HTTP responses should be generated and handled in our Remix application, particularly concerning how requests are managed differently for bots and regular browsers. Remix is a framework for building modern React applications, and this file is a part of the server-side logic of a Remix app.

Initially, the file imports necessary modules and types from various libraries, such as the `node:stream`, `@remix-run/node`, `@remix-run/react`, `isbot`, and `react-dom/server`. It defines a constant `ABORT_DELAY` with a value of 5,000 milliseconds, which is used as a timeout period for rendering operations.

The file exports a default function `handleRequest` that takes several arguments, including the HTTP request, response status code, response headers, and contexts for Remix and the application's load process. Inside `handleRequest`, it checks the user-agent of the incoming request to determine if it's coming from a bot using the `isbot` library. Depending on whether the request is from a bot or a browser, it delegates the handling to either `handleBotRequest` or `handleBrowserRequest` functions, respectively.

This helps with SEO and performance. For example, if a request comes from a bot, it's important to ensure that the response contains the rendered HTML content of the page, which is what `handleBotRequest` does. On the other hand, if the request comes from a regular browser, it's important to ensure that the response contains the rendered HTML content of the page along with the necessary JavaScript code to hydrate the page, which is what `handleBrowserRequest` does. It's pretty cool that Remix handles this for us automatically.

Both `handleBotRequest` and `handleBrowserRequest` functions are fairly similar in structure but have different handlers for when the rendering shell is ready or encounters an error. They return a promise that resolves to an HTTP response. They initiate a rendering operation to a pipeable stream with `renderToPipeableStream`, passing in a `RemixServer` component along with the necessary context and URL from the request. They define a timeout to abort the rendering operation if it takes longer than `ABORT_DELAY`.

In the event handlers for the rendering operation, they create a `PassThrough` stream and a readable stream from it. They set the `Content-Type` header to `text/html` for the response. They resolve the promise with a new `Response` object that encapsulates the stream, response headers, and status code. In case of errors during rendering, they either reject the promise or log the error to the console, depending on the rendering stage where the error occurred.

This file essentially ensures that the HTTP responses are correctly generated and returned, with different rendering logic applied based on whether the request comes from a bot or a regular browser, which is crucial for SEO and performance considerations in modern web applications.

If we have no customizations to make, we can simply delete this file, and Remix will handle the server rendering for us. Let's keep it for now and explore how Remix handles routes.

Routing

In Remix, each route is represented by a file in the *routes* directory. If we create *./routes/cheese.tsx*, whose default export is:

```
export default function CheesePage() {
    return <h1>This might sound cheesy, but I think you're really grate!</h1>;
}
```

and then run the local development server with `npm run dev`, we'll see a page with a funny heading. Once again, we see how Remix provides a predefined structure to help you get started quickly, and the value of default exports in this convention is similar to our own implementation of filesystem-based routing earlier. When combined with the shared layout component in *./app/root.tsx* and both the server and client entry points, this forms the basis of most websites. However, we're still missing one crucial component for a modern web application: data fetching. Let's look at how Remix handles this.

Data fetching

The Remix data fetching story at the time of writing involves the use of functions called *loaders*. When you export an async function called `loader` that returns some value, this value becomes available to your page component through the `useLoaderData` hook. Let's see how this works with an example.

To go back to our cheese page, let's say we want to fetch a list of cheeses from an API and display them on the page. We can do this by exporting a `loader` function from *./routes/cheese.tsx*:

```
// Get some utils
import { json } from "@remix-run/node";
import { useLoaderData } from "@remix-run/react";

// The loader
export async function loader() {
  const data = await fetch("https://api.com/get-cheeses");
  return json(await data.json());
}

export default function CheesePage() {
  const cheeses = useLoaderData();
  return (
    <div>
      <h1>This might sound cheesy, but I think you're really grate!</h1>
      <ul>
        {cheeses.map((cheese) => (
          <li key={cheese.id}>{cheese.name}</li>
        ))}
      </ul>
    </div>
```

```
  );
}
```

With this, we see a recurrence in our own earlier implementation of data fetching. We can see how the Remix `loader` function is similar to our own `getData` function. We can also see how the `useLoaderData` hook is similar to our own `initialThings` prop. Ideally, at this time we're able to glean the common patterns and underlying mechanisms behind how frameworks implement these features.

So far, we've covered:

- Server rendering
- Routing
- Data fetching

But there's one more Remix feature that we haven't covered yet: forms and server actions, or mutations—that is, mutating data on the server, like creating, updating, or deleting data. Let's explore this next.

Mutating data

Remix was responsible for bringing the web back to its fundamentals, leaning heavily on native web platform conventions and behavior. This is best seen around data mutations and Remix's usage of forms. Let's explore this with an example, extending our previous cheese example: let's make the cheese list mutable. To do so, let's start by updating our *./routes/cheese.tsx* file:

```
// Get some utils
import { json } from "@remix-run/node";
import { useLoaderData } from "@remix-run/react";

// The loader
export async function loader() {
  const data = await fetch("https://api.com/get-cheeses");
  return json(await data.json());
}

export default function CheesePage() {
  const cheeses = useLoaderData();
  return (
    <div>
      <h1>This might sound cheesy, but I think you're really grate!</h1>
      <ul>
        {cheeses.map((cheese) => (
          <li key={cheese.id}>{cheese.name}</li>
        ))}
      </ul>
      <form action="/cheese" method="post">
        <input type="text" name="cheese" />
```

```
          <button type="submit">Add Cheese</button>
        </form>
      </div>
    );
  }
```

Notice we've added a new form element to the page. This form has an action of /cheese and a method of post. This is a standard HTML form that will submit a POST request to the /cheese route. Moreover, the input has a name attribute and no useState or onChange handler: Remix lets the browser manage the state and behavior of the form. This is a great example of how Remix leans on the web platform to provide a great developer experience, and doesn't try to reinvent the wheel having React manage everything.

Given that the form's action property is /cheese and we're already in the *./routes/cheese.tsx* file, we can assume that the form will submit to the same route. When this route is accessed with a POST method, we know that the form has been submitted. When this route is accessed with the GET method by default, we know that the form has not been submitted and we instead show the initial UI.

Let's update our *./routes/cheese.tsx* file to handle this:

```
// Get some utils
import { json, ActionFunctionArgs, redirect } from "@remix-run/node";
import { useLoaderData } from "@remix-run/react";

// The loader
export async function loader() {
  const data = await fetch("https://api.com/get-cheeses");
  return json(await data.json());
}

// The form action
export async function action({ params, request }: ActionFunctionArgs) {
  const formData = await request.formData();

  await fetch("https://api.com/add-cheese", {
    method: "POST",
    body: JSON.stringify({
      name: formData.get("cheese"),
    }),
  });

  return redirect("/cheese"); // Come back to this page, but with GET this time.
}

export default function CheesePage() {
  const cheeses = useLoaderData();
  return (
    <div>
      <h1>This might sound cheesy, but I think you're really grate!</h1>
```

```
      <ul>
        {cheeses.map((cheese) => (
          <li key={cheese.id}>{cheese.name}</li>
        ))}
      </ul>
      <form action="/cheese" method="post">
        <input type="text" name="cheese" />
        <button type="submit">Add Cheese</button>
      </form>
    </div>
  );
}
```

Notice how we've added a new `action` function that takes a `params` and `request` argument. The `params` argument is an object that contains the parameters of the route. The `request` argument is an object that contains the request object. We can use this to get the form data from the request and then use it to make a request to our API to add a new cheese.

We then return a redirect to the same route, but this time with a `GET` method. This will cause the page to be reloaded, and the `loader` function will be called again to fetch the updated list of cheeses.

This is how Remix fully leans on the web platform to enable JavaScript to be used where it's needed, and to let the browser handle the rest. If this page was visited without JavaScript, it would just work because it leans on the web platform. If the page does use JavaScript, Remix progressively enhances the experience by adding interactivity and a better user experience.

So far, we've covered how Remix:

- Provides server rendering
- Handles routing
- Handles data fetching
- Handles data mutations

At this point, we should be seeing strong parallels between our own implementation of these features and Remix's implementation. This is a great sign that we're understanding the underlying mechanisms behind how frameworks implement these features.

Now let's consider Next.js and how it does very similar things to isolate the commonalities behind the way these features are implemented.

Next.js

Next.js, a popular React framework by Vercel, is well-known for its rich features and simplicity in creating server-side rendered (SSR) and static websites. It follows the convention over configuration principle, reducing the amount of boilerplate and decision-making necessary to start a project. With the release of Next.js 13, a significant addition has been the introduction of the Next.js App Router.

Let's walk through a basic Next.js application to understand how it works. To start, let's run the following command to create a new Next.js project:

```
npm create next-app@14
```

This will ask us some questions, but ultimately we'll arrive at a basic Next.js project. Let's look around and see what's inside. To start with, we've got an *app* directory with *page.tsx*, *layout.tsx*, *error.tsx*, and *loading.tsx*.

One thing we immediately notice is that Next.js does not expose server configuration like Remix does, but instead hides away a large number of complexities with the intention of "getting out of the way" and letting developers focus on building their applications. This is a great example of how different frameworks have different philosophies and approaches to solving the same problems.

Let's explore Next.js in the context of the three key features we identified earlier: server rendering, routing, and data fetching.

Server rendering

Next.js not only provides server rendering but is also server-first. Every page and component in Next.js is a server component. We dive quite deep into server components in Chapter 9, but for now, suffice it to say that server components are components rendered exclusively on the server. This level of understanding is fine for now, as the focus is on Next.js, not server components. For server components, Chapter 9 should be sufficient.

What does this mean in the context of Next.js, though? In essence, we are to operate on the basis that all the code we write executes on the server exclusively unless otherwise specified by adding a `"use client"` directive to the top of a given route or component. Without this directive, all code is assumed to be server code.

However, Next.js also is static-first: at build time, the server components are rendered to as much static content as possible and then deployed. This combination of server-first and static-first is what makes Next.js so powerful and prioritizes performance pretty significantly, with static content being arguably the fastest to reach users as there's no runtime or server-side processing required; it's just text (HTML). The next step from static is server rendered content, which can be highly optimized and cached, but still requires a server to render the content. The final step is client-rendered content through hydration for interactive portions of the page.

With this approach, Next.js lends itself well to have smaller JavaScript bundles shipped to users, with the bulk of the content being some mix of static and server rendered markup. The level of granularity with which not just pages but components can be rendered on the server is a powerful feature of Next.js, enabling some very powerful data fetching and rendering patterns. Before we get to those patterns, let's explore how Next.js handles routing.

Routing

What we see in our new Next.js project is an *app* directory with *layout.tsx* and *page.tsx*. Next.js follows this pattern: the path your users see in their browser, the URL of your page, is the name of the directory where *app* is equivalent to the root (/), and every directory under it becomes a subpath.

To understand this, let's create a directory *cheese* and add a *page.tsx* file to it. When a directory under *./app* has a *page.tsx* file, that directory becomes a route. Let's add some content to *./app/cheese/page.tsx*:

```
export default function CheesePage() {
  return <h1>This might sound cheesy, but I think you're really grate!</h1>;
}
```

Now, if we run the development server and navigate to */cheese*, we'll see a page with a funny heading. It's worth noting here that Next.js also has a concept of shared layouts, similar to Remix, where you can define a layout component in *./app/layout.tsx* and it will be rendered on every page. Then, *./app/cheese/layout.tsx* will be rendered on every page under the */cheese* route. Layouts are typically portions of routes that are shared across multiple pages, such as a header or footer, or other fixed elements.

Great, this is how Next.js handles routing. It's sort of similar to Remix and our own implementation of filesystem-based routing, but with a slight difference that it's not a single file that becomes a page but instead an entire directory, and that the actual page is expected to called *page.tsx* all the time. Besides this, it's pretty similar.

Let's talk about data fetching.

Data fetching

Because every component is a server component, every component in Next.js is capable of being asynchronous and thus, `await`-ing data. Let's try to fetch cheeses like we did in our previous Remix example, but this time in Next.js:

```
export default async function CheesePage() {
  const cheeses = await fetch("https://api.com/get-cheeses").then((r) =>
    r.json()
  );
```

```
    return (
      <div>
        <h1>This might sound cheesy, but I think you're really grate!</h1>
        <ul>
          {cheeses.map((cheese) => (
            <li key={cheese.id}>{cheese.name}</li>
          ))}
        </ul>
      </div>
    );
}
```

If you're reading that and are impressed—yes. This syntax is what React engineers have hoped for for years, and is quite natural to reason about. This is possible because `CheesePage` here is a server component: it is not included in the client bundle and is instead rendered on the server. This means that we can `await` data and render it directly to the page.

Since all components are server components, we can further increase the granularity and not fetch at the page level, but at the component level too if we want to. Consider breaking this page into smaller components where `CheeseList` is reusable and is used in this page, but may be used elsewhere too.

Our page would become this:

```
import { CheeseList } from "./CheeseList";

export default function CheesePage() {
  return (
    <div>
      <h1>This might sound cheesy, but I think you're really grate!</h1>
      <CheeseList />
    </div>
  );
}
```

and our `CheeseList` component would be this:

```
export async function CheeseList() {
  const cheeses = await fetch("https://api.com/get-cheeses").then((r) =>
    r.json()
  );
  return (
    <ul>
      {cheeses.map((cheese) => (
        <li key={cheese.id}>{cheese.name}</li>
      ))}
    </ul>
  );
}
```

The true power of this approach is that we can fetch data at the component level, and then render it to the page. We don't export a function from the page level like `loader`, `getData`, `getServerSideProps`, `getStaticProps`, or anything like that. Instead, we just fetch data at the component level and render it to the page.

What happens to this data? Next.js uses it to statically generate the first load of our page when we deploy, and server renders it on subsequent loads. Next.js also has a number of caching and deduplication mechanisms that ensure data integrity and performance.

Finally, let's round out the comparison by exploring how Next.js handles data mutations.

Mutating data

Next.js has a concept of *server actions*, which are functions that run on the server. These are functions that are called when a form is submitted, a user clicks a button, or a user navigates to a page. They are functions that run on the server, and are not included in the client bundle.

Let's look at adding a cheese to the list like we did in our Remix example. To do this, we'll add a form to our page:

```
import { CheeseList } from "./CheeseList";

import { redirect } from "next/navigation";
import { revalidatePath } from "next/cache";

export default function CheesePage() {
  return (
    <div>
      <h1>This might sound cheesy, but I think you're really grate!</h1>
      <CheeseList />
      <form
        action={async (formData) => {
          "use server";
          await fetch("https://api.com/add-cheese", {
            method: "POST",
            body: JSON.stringify({
              name: formData.get("cheese"),
            }),
          });
          revalidatePath("/cheese");
          return redirect("/cheese");
        }}
        method="post"
      >
        <input type="text" name="cheese" />
        <button type="submit">Add Cheese</button>
      </form>
```

```
      </div>
    );
  }
```

We're using a standard-ish HTML form here similar to Remix, except the `action` attribute is a function this time. This function is a server action, and it is called when the form is submitted. This function is not included in the client bundle and is instead run on the server. This is enforced by the `"use server"` directive at the top.

We could move this function wherever we want, including into the body of the server component, like so:

```
import { redirect } from "next/navigation";
import { revalidatePath } from "next/cache";

export default function CheesePage() {
  async function addCheese(formData) {
    "use server";
    await fetch("https://api.com/add-cheese", {
      method: "POST",
      body: JSON.stringify({
        name: formData.get("cheese"),
      }),
    });

    revalidatePath("/cheese");
    return redirect("/cheese");
  }

  return (
    <div>
      <h1>This might sound cheesy, but I think you're really grate!</h1>
      <CheeseList />
      <form action={addCheese} method="post">
        <input type="text" name="cheese" />
        <button type="submit">Add Cheese</button>
      </form>
    </div>
  );
}
```

or even into a separate module, like so:

```
import { addCheeseAction } from "./addCheeseAction";

export default function CheesePage() {
  return (
    <div>
      <h1>This might sound cheesy, but I think you're really grate!</h1>
      <CheeseList />
      <form action={addCheese} method="post">
        <input type="text" name="cheese" />
        <button type="submit">Add Cheese</button>
```

```
        </form>
      </div>
    );
  }
```

In this case, `addCheeseAction` would be in its own file and read like so:

```
"use server";

import { redirect } from "next/navigation";
import { revalidatePath } from "next/cache";

export async function addCheeseAction(formData) {
  await fetch("https://api.com/add-cheese", {
    method: "POST",
    body: JSON.stringify({
      name: formData.get("cheese"),
    }),
  });

  revalidatePath("/cheese");
  return redirect("/cheese");
}
```

There's an inherent problem here though, because unlike Remix where all components are client components, server components do not support interactivity at all since they are not included in the client bundle and never loaded by the browser; thus, `onClick` handlers never actually make it to users. To solve this problem, Next.js has a concept of client components, which are included in the client bundle and are loaded by the browser. These components are not server components, and thus cannot be asynchronous or have server actions.

Let's explore adding a cheese, but this time with a mix of server and client components. This will also help us react to the form submission by immediately providing feedback with a spinner or similar. To do this, we'll create a new component, *./app/AddCheeseForm.tsx*:

```
"use client";
import { addCheeseAction } from "./addCheeseAction";

export function AddCheeseForm() {
  return (
    <form action={addCheeseAction} method="post">
      <input type="text" name="cheese" />
      <button type="submit">Add Cheese</button>
    </form>
  );
}
```

Now that it's a client component, we can do interactive things—like respond to form state changes. Let's update our AddCheeseForm to do that:

```
"use client";
import { addCheeseAction } from "./addCheeseAction";
import { useFormStatus } from "react-dom";

export function AddCheeseForm() {
  const { pending } = useFormStatus();

  return (
    <form action={addCheeseAction} method="post">
      <input disabled={pending} type="text" name="cheese" />
      <button type="submit" disabled={pending}>
        {pending ? "Loading..." : "Add Cheese"}
      </button>
    </form>
  );
}
```

Because our AddCheeseForm is a client component, we can use the useFormStatus to get the status of the form. This is a hook provided by React. This hook returns an object with a pending property that is true when the form is submitting, and false when the form is not submitting. We can use this to disable the form while it's submitting, and to show a loading indicator.

Now, we can use this form in our page, which is a server component, like so:

```
import { CheeseList } from "./CheeseList";
import { AddCheeseForm } from "./AddCheeseForm";

export default function CheesePage() {
  return (
    <div>
      <h1>This might sound cheesy, but I think you're really grate!</h1>
      <CheeseList />
      <AddCheeseForm />
    </div>
  );
}
```

As a result, we've got a mix of server and client components. The CheesePage and CheeseList are server components, and the AddCheeseForm is a client component. Both components are reusable and can be used elsewhere in our application. There are some rules and considerations around client and server components, but we'll explore those in Chapter 9.

For now, if we zoom out we can see that Next.js solves similar problems as Remix and our own implementation of filesystem-based routing, data fetching, and data mutations. It does so in a slightly different way, but the underlying mechanisms are somewhat similar.

Ideally, by exploring both of these frameworks, we're able to understand why we would reach for frameworks, the problems they solve, and how they solve them for our benefit.

Let's wrap up by talking about how to choose a framework.

Choosing a Framework

Deciding which React framework to use for your project can be a challenging decision, as each offers a distinct set of features, advantages, and trade-offs. In this section, we will attempt to provide some insight into what makes popular React frameworks a viable option for developers today, and discuss factors such as learning curve, flexibility, and performance, which can guide you in choosing the most suitable framework for your specific needs.

It's worth noting that one framework is not inherently better or worse than another. Each framework has its own set of strengths and weaknesses, and the best framework for your project will depend on your specific requirements and preferences.

Understanding Your Project Needs

Before we dive into the details of each framework, it's important to understand your project's specific needs. Here are some critical questions to consider:

- What is the scope of your project? Is it a small personal project, a medium-sized application with several features, or a large-scale, complex application?
- What are the main functionalities and features you want to include in your project?
- Do you require server-side rendering (SSR), site generation (SSG), or a combination of both?
- Are you building a content-heavy site like a blog or ecommerce site that might benefit from excellent SEO?
- Is real-time data or highly dynamic content a critical part of your application?
- How much flexibility do you require in terms of customization and control over the build process?
- How important are the performance and speed of your application?
- What is your proficiency level with React and general web development concepts?
- Who are your target users? Enterprise folks sitting at desks with fast internet? Or the general public with a wide range of devices and internet speeds?

Understanding the answers to these questions will give you a clearer picture of what you need from a framework.

Next.js

Let's explore some of these parameters in the context of Next.js:

Learning curve
> Next.js uses the bleeding edge of React under the hood, often making use of canary releases of React. This means that Next.js is often ahead of the curve and can be a bit more challenging to learn. However, the Next.js team does a great job of documenting the framework and providing clear guides for various features, which can help you get started quickly.

Flexibility
> Next.js is designed with flexibility in mind between static and server rendered content. It also supports entirely client-side applications, though this is not its primary use case. Next.js also provides a rich ecosystem of plug-ins and integrations, which can significantly speed up the development process.

Performance
> Next.js aggressively prioritizes performance, with a focus on static generation and server-side rendering, as well as caching. Next.js ships with four distinct purpose-driven caches at the time of writing, each tailored to provide the best performance for a number of use cases. This performance, though, can come at a cost of friction around the boundaries between client/server and the decision-making around when to use which.

It is also worth noting that some members of the team that builds React work at Vercel, where Next.js is developed, which suggests an extremely tight feedback loop of development between Next.js and React.

Remix

Compared to Next.js, Remix is a newer entry to the React framework scene, created around 10 years earlier. It's built by the creators of React Router and emphasizes web fundamentals, making fewer assumptions and providing a lot of flexibility:

Learning curve
> Remix might have a slightly flatter learning curve because it relies more heavily on web fundamentals and uses React the way many have learned it before the heavier emphasis on server components.

Intuitiveness
> Remix often gets out of the way and allows the fundamentals of the web platform to shine through. This can be a bit of a double-edged sword: on one hand, it's

great because it's intuitive and familiar, but on the other hand, it can be a bit frustrating because it's not as "magical" as other frameworks.

Performance

Remix's unique approach to routing and data loading makes it efficient and performant. Since data fetching is tied to routes, only the necessary data for a specific route is fetched, reducing the overall data requirement. Plus, its optimistic UI updates and progressive enhancement strategies improve the user experience.

Trade-Offs

Choosing a framework does not come without trade-offs, the meat of which revolve around the continuum of convenience versus control. All frameworks remove a lot of the brainwork and decision-making around our applications by conventionalizing things. For example, frameworks by default have answers for questions like:

- How do we do routing?
- Where do static assets go?
- Should we server render?
- Where do we fetch data?

Given that frameworks so heavily conventionalize these topics and more, this takes control away from us, the developers. In exchange, we get quite a bit of convenience to charge forward and work on the more central aspects of our applications, like the business logic itself.

Most, if not all, trade-offs around frameworks revolve around this continuum.

So, how to choose the right framework? It all comes down to your project needs and personal preference:

- If you need a somewhat flexible full stack framework, Next.js might be a better fit since it lets you choose between static, server-side, or entirely client-only application.
- If you prefer a serverful, progressively enhanced approach with a strong adherence to web fundamentals, Remix could be your best bet.

In any case, it's a good idea to try one out for a smaller project or a part of your application. This will give you a better understanding of how they work and which one feels most comfortable to work with.

Developer Experience

Both frameworks offer world-class developer experience, with a focus on productivity and ease of use. They both provide a rich set of features and tools to help developers build high-quality applications, as we've seen previously in this chapter.

Build performance becomes increasingly critical as a project grows in complexity and size. Both Next.js and Remix have made optimizations to improve the build time.

Next.js uses static generation by default, which means pages are prerendered at build time. This can lead to faster page loads, but also longer build times, especially for sites with a large number of pages.

To address this, Next.js introduced Incremental Static Regeneration (ISR), allowing developers to regenerate static pages after they have been built, without a full rebuild. This feature can significantly improve build times for large, dynamic sites.

Remix, on the other hand, has a unique take on build performance. It opts for a server-first architecture, which means that pages are rendered on demand by the server, and the HTML is sent down to the client.

Runtime Performance

Both Next.js and Remix are designed with performance in mind and offer several optimizations to deliver fast, responsive applications.

Next.js comes with several built-in performance optimizations. It supports automatic code splitting, which ensures that only the necessary code is loaded for each page. It also has a built-in Image component that optimizes image loading for better performance.

The hybrid SSG/SSR model in Next.js allows developers to choose the optimal data fetching strategy for each page, balancing performance and freshness. Pages that don't require fresh data can be prerendered at build time, resulting in faster page loads. For pages that require fresh data, server-side rendering or ISR can be used.

Next.js also provides automatic static optimization for pages without blocking data requirements, ensuring they are served as static HTML files, leading to faster time to first byte (TTFB).

Finally, Next.js takes full advantage of React Server Components where possible, allowing it to send less JavaScript to the client, resulting in faster page loads and other overhead.

Remix takes a slightly different approach to performance. Instead of prerendering pages, it opts for server rendering, streaming down just the HTML that the client needs. This can result in faster TTFB, especially for dynamic content.

One of the key features of Remix is its robust caching strategy. It leverages the browser's native fetch and cache APIs, allowing developers to specify caching strategies for different resources. This leads to faster page loads and a more resilient application.

Both Next.js and Remix offer compelling benefits for large-scale, complex projects. They both excel in developer experience, build performance, and runtime performance. Next.js might be a better choice if you prefer a mature ecosystem with extensive resources and plug-ins, a hybrid SSG/SSR model, and innovative features like ISR. On the other hand, Remix could be more suitable if you prefer a server rendered approach with instant deploys, a strong emphasis on embracing web platform features like fetch and cache APIs, and advanced React concepts like Suspense and Server Components.

The most suitable framework for your specific project needs would ultimately depend on your team's expertise, your project requirements, and your preference for certain architectural patterns. Regardless of the choice, both Next.js and Remix are solid foundations for building high-quality, performant React applications.

Chapter Review

Over the course of this chapter, we've delved deep into the concept of React frameworks. This chapter allowed us to explore the underlying principles, the reasoning, and the practical implications of using frameworks.

The discussion began by recapping concurrent React and its implications for efficient rendering and user interactivity. We then moved on to explore the "why" and the "what" of React frameworks: why they are necessary, what benefits they offer, and what trade-offs they entail.

We did this by implementing our own basic framework, which allowed us to understand the underlying mechanisms and concepts behind React frameworks. We then explored the concept of filesystem-based routing, which is a common feature in many React frameworks. We also looked at data fetching and how it can be implemented in a framework.

Next, we dived into a comparison between different frameworks, focusing primarily on Next.js and Remix. Each framework offers its unique set of features and advantages, and the choice often comes down to the specific needs of the project. We explored how these frameworks solve for server rendering, routing, data fetching, and data mutations, and how they compare to our own implementation of these features.

Through this, we gleaned an understanding of the mechanism through the commonalities between our own implementation and the frameworks. We also explored the trade-offs involved in using frameworks, and how they can be mitigated by understanding the underlying mechanisms.

Finally, we discussed how to choose a framework, and explored some of the trade-offs involved in this decision. We also looked at the developer experience and runtime performance of frameworks and considered what might be the best for our projects.

Review Questions

As we wrap up this chapter, here are some questions to help you review the concepts we've covered:

- What are the primary reasons for using a React framework like Next.js or Remix, and what benefits do they offer?
- What are some of the trade-offs or downsides that come with using a React framework?
- What are some common problems solved by frameworks?
- How do these frameworks solve them?

Up Next

In this chapter, we briefly mentioned React Server Components and began to scratch their surface in a crude manner. In the next chapter, we'll intensify our focus on React Server Components and dive a little bit deeper: understanding their value proposition and how they work by writing a minimal server that renders and serves React Server Components.

In addition, we'll examine why React Server Components require a new generation of build tooling, like bundlers, routers, and more. Ultimately, we will come away with an improved understanding of React Server Components and their underlying mechanism in what is sure to be an informative and educational deep dive.

CHAPTER 9

React Server Components

In the previous chapter, we dove into the world of React frameworks, particularly focusing on Next.js and Remix. We explored the reasons why you might choose to use a framework in the first place, including the benefits of abstraction, the conventions that speed up development, the comprehensive solutions they offer for common problems, and their overall impact on enhancing productivity.

We delved into the details of Remix and Next.js, demonstrating the common approaches each framework takes to solve similar problems by implementing our own bare-bones framework, and teased Next.js' server-first direction, fully embracing React Server Components (RSCs).

Speaking of RSCs, they are an interesting trend in the React ecosystem designed to improve the performance, efficiency, and user experience of React applications. This advanced application architecture combines the best aspects of server rendered multipage apps (MPAs) and client-rendered SPAs, delivering a seamless user experience without compromising on performance or maintainability. In this chapter, we will discuss the core concepts, benefits, and underlying mental models and mechanisms around which RSCs work. For the latest information, always visit react.dev.

RSCs introduce a new type of component that "runs" on the server and is otherwise excluded from the client-side JavaScript bundle. These components can run during build time, allowing you to read from the filesystem, fetch static content, or access your data layer. By passing data as props from server components to interactive client components in the browser, RSCs maintain a highly efficient and performant application.

How then do server components work? Let's dive a little deeper into what server components are to understand this with a little more fidelity.

As just described, a server component is a special type of component that is executed on the server alone. To understand this better, let's remember that a React component is nothing more than a function that returns a React element:

```
const Component = () => <div>hi!</div>;
```

In this snippet, Component is a function that returns <div>hi!</div>. Of course, <div>hi!</div> returns another React element since < in React is an alias for React.createElement. We covered this in Chapter 2 on JSX. In case you're drawing blanks here, now's a good time to quickly refresh that information and come back. Ultimately, all components return React elements, which is virtual DOM.

Server components are no different. If Component is executed either on the server or the client, it returns vDOM. In Chapter 3, we saw how React elements are just JavaScript objects that have the following schema:

```
{
  $$typeOf: Symbol("react.element"),
  type: () => ({
    $$typeOf: Symbol("react.element"),
    type: "div",
    props: {
      children: [
        {
          $$typeOf: Symbol("react.element"),
          props: {
            children: "hi!"
          },
        },
      ],
    },
  }),
}
```

Invoking our Component function in both client and server environments will return a React element, as shown.

With server components, they are *only* invoked (or called) on the server, and the resulting JavaScript object representing an element is sent over the network to a client. Of course, client components are the regular React components we're used to.

Benefits

Understanding this, we start to see some of the benefits of server components:

- They execute only on the server side, on machines whose computational power *we* control. This leads to more predictable performance, as we don't do computations on unpredictable client devices.

- They execute in our secure server environments, so we can do secure operations in server components without worrying about leaking tokens and other secure information.

- Server components can be asynchronous since we can wait for them to complete executing on our servers before we share them with clients over the network.

This is the true power of server components. Going forward, let's explore how server components interplay with server-side rendering.

Server Rendering

We've covered server rendering at length in prior chapters, so we won't go too far into its details here. Instead, we'll focus specifically on the interplay between server components and server rendering.

Essentially, server components and server rendering can be thought of as two separate independent processes where one process solely takes care of rendering components on the server and generating a tree of React elements, and another process—the server renderer—further takes this tree of React elements and converts it into markup that can be streamed to clients over the network.

If we consider these two processes, one to render components to React elements, and another to render React elements to HTML strings or streams, we start understanding how these two concepts fit together. Let's call the first process the *RSCs renderer* that turns server components into a tree of React elements, and the second process the *server renderer* that turns the React elements into a stream of HTML.

With this understanding, the interplay between server components and server rendering can be understood as follows:

1. On the server, a tree of JSX is turned into a tree of elements.

   This tree of JSX:

   ```
   <div>
     <h1>hi!</h1>
     <p>I like React!</p>
   </div>
   ```

   Becomes this tree of elements:

   ```
   {
     $$typeOf: Symbol("react.element"),
     type: "div",
     props: {
       children: [
         {
           $$typeOf: Symbol("react.element"),
           type: "h1",
   ```

```
            props: {
              children: "hi!"
            }
          },
          {
            $$typeOf: Symbol("react.element"),
            type: "p",
            props: {
              children: "I like React!"
            }
          },
        ],
      },
    }
```

2. On the server, this tree of elements is then further serialized into a string or stream.

3. This is sent to a client as a big stringified JSON object.

4. React on the client side can read this parsed JSON and render it as usual.

If we illustrate this as code from the server side, it would look something like this:

```
// server.js
const express = require("express");
const path = require("path");
const React = require("react");
const ReactDOMServer = require("react-dom/server");
const App = require("./src/App");

const app = express();

app.use(express.static(path.join(__dirname, "build")));

app.get("*", async (req, res) => {
  // This is the secret sauce
  const rscTree = await turnServerComponentsIntoTreeOfElements(<App />);
  // This is the secret sauce

  // Render the awaited server components to a string
  const html = ReactDOMServer.renderToString(rscTree);

  // Send it
  res.send(`
    <!DOCTYPE html>
    <html>
      <head>
        <title>My React App</title>
      </head>
      <body>
        <div id="root">${html}</div>
        <script src="/static/js/main.js"></script>
```

```
      </body>
    </html>
  `);
});

app.listen(3000, () => {
  console.log("Server listening on port 3000");
});
```

This server code snippet is taken directly from Chapter 6 where we discussed server-side React, except we've added a step to process server components before passing them to the server-side renderer—the second process in our example.

Logically, this is exactly how server components and server-side rendering fit together: they are complementary processes.

Again, it's worth noting that we're using `renderToString` just for illustrative purposes and—as mentioned in Chapter 6—it's almost always better to lean on a more asynchronous, interruptible API like `renderToPipeableStream` or similar for the vast majority of use cases.

Now that we understand the interplay between server rendering and server components, let's dive a little bit deeper into this magical `turnServerComponentsIntoTreeOfElements` function we invoked in the previous code snippet. What is it doing? How does it turn server components into a tree of elements? Is it a React renderer? Let's find out.

Under the Hood

The short and potentially oversimplified answer is yes, `turnServerComponentsIntoTreeOfElements` is a kind of React renderer. It recursively goes into a React tree, starting from a high level like `<App />`, and recursively calls each component to get the React element (the plain JavaScript object) it returns.

Let's lay out a reference implementation of this and then discuss what it does:

```
async function turnServerComponentsIntoTreeOfElements(jsx) {
  if (
    typeof jsx === "string" ||
    typeof jsx === "number" ||
    typeof jsx === "boolean" ||
    jsx == null
  ) {
    // Don't need to do anything special with these types.
    return jsx;
  }
  if (Array.isArray(jsx)) {
    // Process each item in an array.
    return await Promise.all(jsx.map(renderJSXToClientJSX(child)));
  }
```

```
      // If we're dealing with an object
      if (jsx != null && typeof jsx === "object") {
        // If the object is a React element,
        if (jsx.$$typeof === Symbol.for("react.element")) {
          // `{ type }` is a string for built-in components.
          if (typeof jsx.type === "string") {
            // This is a built-in component like <div />.
            // Go over its props to make sure they can be turned into JSON.
            return {
              ...jsx,
              props: await renderJSXToClientJSX(jsx.props),
            };
          }
          if (typeof jsx.type === "function") {
            // This is a custom React component (like <Footer />).
            // Call its function, and repeat the procedure for the JSX it returns.
            const Component = jsx.type;
            const props = jsx.props;
            const returnedJsx = await Component(props);
            return await renderJSXToClientJSX(returnedJsx);
          }
          throw new Error("Not implemented.");
        } else {
          // This is an arbitrary object (props, or something inside them).
          // It's an object, but not a React element (we handled that case above).
          // Go over every value and process any JSX in it.
          return Object.fromEntries(
            await Promise.all(
              Object.entries(jsx).map(async ([propName, value]) => [
                propName,
                await renderJSXToClientJSX(value),
              ])
            )
          );
        }
      }
      throw new Error("Not implemented");
    }
```

While this snippet can look a little scary, let's be clear: it's just a big if/else tree that returns things based on its arguments. Let's go branch by branch and understand what happens, starting with its input argument jsx.

For the first branch, if we consider a React element like this:

```
<div>hi!</div>
```

The child "hi!" is just a string. If we pass this string to our server component renderer, we want to return the string as is. The idea is to return types of things that React on the client side and on the server side can understand. React can understand

and render strings, numbers, and booleans on the client and on the server side, so we'll leave them as is.

Next up, if we've got an array, let's map over it and recursively process each element through our function. Arrays can be a bunch of children, like this:

```
[
  <div>hi</div>,
  <h1>hello</h1>,
  <span>love u</span>,
  (props) => <p id={props.id}>lorem ipsum</p>,
];
```

Fragments, for example, represent children as arrays. So similarly, let's just process them by recursively calling our function on each child and move on.

Next is where it gets really interesting: we process objects. Let's keep in mind that all React elements are objects, but not all objects are React elements. How do we know an object is a React element? It has a $$typeOf property with a symbol value—specifically Symbol.for('react.element'). Therefore, we check if the object has this key/value pair, and if it does, we process it as a React element. We do it in this section from the snippet:

```
if (jsx.$$typeof === Symbol.for("react.element")) {
  if (typeof jsx.type === "string") {
    // This is a component like <div />.
    // Go over its props to make sure they can be turned into JSON.
    return {
      ...jsx,
      props: await renderJSXToClientJSX(jsx.props),
    };
  }
  if (typeof jsx.type === "function") {
    // This is a custom React component (like <Footer />).
    // Call its function, and repeat the procedure for the JSX it returns.
    const Component = jsx.type;
    const props = jsx.props;
    const returnedJsx = await Component(props);
    return renderJSXToClientJSX(returnedJsx);
  }
  throw new Error("Not implemented.");
} else {
  // This is an arbitrary object (props, or something inside of them).
  // Go over every value and process any JSX in it.
  return Object.fromEntries(
    await Promise.all(
      Object.entries(jsx).map(async ([propName, value]) => [
        propName,
        await renderJSXToClientJSX(value),
      ])
    )
```

```
  );
}
```

Nested within the truthy branch of the `if` statement, we do another check: is the `jsx.type` a `"string"` or a `"function"`? We do this because React elements can have both as a type. Strings are used for built-in DOM elements like `"div"`, `"span"`, etc. Functions are used for custom components like `<Footer />`. If it's a string, we know it's a built-in DOM element, so we can just return it as is, but recursively call our function on its props—since its props can have children that are concurrent React components. If it's a function, we know it's a custom component, so we call it with its props and recursively call our function on the JSX it returns until it finally returns a string, number, boolean, array of those types, or a React element with a string type, which would fall into the other branch.

Notice the `await` before we call the function component? Since this is executed on the server side, we can `await` the function component in case it's a server component! This is the magic of server components: we can `await` them on the server side, and they'll return a React element that we can then pass to `renderToString` or `renderTo PipeableStream` to render it to a string or a stream of strings that we can send to the client. Indeed, this is what our function is doing: it's just `awaiting` all the `async` things recursively to produce a tree of elements (a JavaScript object) with all of its data dependencies resolved.

Finally, if the object is not a React element, we know it's just a regular object, so we recursively call our function on each value in the object and return the result. The object is usually just props, so in the `else` branch, we're just recursively calling our function on each prop value and return the result, effectively unwrapping any components that might be passed as props using patterns like render props, as discussed in Chapter 5.

That's it! That's our little minimal RSCs renderer. It's not perfect, but it's a good start. We can use it to render our server components to React elements that we can then send to clients.

Once we have that, we just pass it to `renderToString` or `renderToPipeableStream`, or even serialize it and send it directly to a browser, and React on the client side will be able to render it because it's literally just a tree of React elements that React can understand. There is, however, one more challenge to doing this that we need to address: serialization.

Serialization

Things get a little tricky when we try to serialize React elements. Serializing React elements is a fundamental aspect of ensuring that your application is rendered correctly and efficiently during the initial load, because the same rendered output from the server needs to match the client for React to correctly reconcile and diff things. When your application is being rendered on the server, the React elements created need to be turned into HTML strings that can be sent to the browser. This process of turning React elements into strings is referred to as *serialization*.

In a typical React application, React elements are objects in memory. They're created by invoking `React.createElement` or using JSX syntax. These elements represent the intended rendering of a component, but they are not yet actual DOM elements. They're more like instructions for how the DOM should look:

```
const element = <h1>Hello, world</h1>;
```

When rendering on the server using a function like `ReactDOMServer.renderTo String`, these React elements are serialized into HTML strings. This serialization process traverses the React element tree, generates the corresponding HTML for each element, and concatenates it all into a single HTML string:

```
const htmlString = ReactDOMServer.renderToString(element);
// htmlString will be '<h1>Hello, world</h1>'
```

This HTML string can then be sent to the client, where it will be used as the initial markup for the page. Once the JavaScript bundle is loaded on the client, React will "hydrate" the DOM, attaching event handlers and filling in any dynamic content.

The serialization step is crucial for several reasons. First, it allows the server to send a complete, ready-to-display HTML page to the client as quickly as possible. This improves the perceived load time of the page, as users can start interacting with the content sooner.

Furthermore, serializing React elements into an HTML string allows for a consistent and predictable initial render, irrespective of the environment. The HTML produced is static and will look the same whether rendered on the server or the client. This consistency is essential for ensuring a smooth user experience, as it prevents any flickering or layout shifts that might occur if the initial render were different from the final render.

Lastly, serialization facilitates the process of hydration on the client side. When the JavaScript bundle loads on the client, React needs to attach event handlers and fill in any dynamic content. Having a serialized HTML string as the initial markup ensures that React has a solid base to work from, making the rehydration process more efficient and reliable.

Even though we need to serialize components to strings, we can't just use `JSON.stringify` because React elements are not regular JavaScript objects. They're objects with a special `$$typeof` property that React uses to identify them, and the value of these properties is a symbol. Symbols cannot be serialized and sent over the network, so we need to do something else.

This isn't actually that difficult thanks to built-in support from JavaScript runtimes, including the browser and Node.js where our server lives. This built-in support comes to us in the form of JSON.stringify and JSON.parse. These functions recursively either serialize or deserialize JSON objects, which React elements are. Their API is as follows:

```
JSON.stringify(object, replacer);
JSON.parse(object, replacer);
```

where replacer is a function that receives a key and a value, and can return a replacement value if certain conditions are met. In our case, we want to replace the value of $$typeof with a serializable type, like a string. Here's how we'd do that:

```
JSON.stringify(jsxTree, (key, value) => {
  if (key === "$$typeof") {
    return "react.element"; // <- a string!!
  }

  return value; // <- return all other values as is
});
```

That's it! We're done. To deserialize this on the client side, we do the opposite:

```
JSON.parse(serializedJsxTree, (key, value) => {
  if (key === "$$typeof") {
    return Symbol.for("react.element"); // <- a symbol!!
  }

  return value; // <- return all other values as is
});
```

And that's it! We can now serialize and deserialize React elements. We can now render server components on the server and send them to clients. This handles our first load; however, we still need to handle updates and navigation. Let's tackle navigation first and deal with updates later.

Navigation

If we have a link in our RSCs-enabled app, something like:

```
<a href="/blog">Blog</a>
```

clicking on this would do a full-page navigation, which would cause the browser to make a request to the server, which would then render the page and send it back to the browser. This is how we used to do things in PHP-land so many years ago, and it comes with certain friction and a feeling of slowness. We can do better: with RSCs, we can implement soft navigation, where state is persisted between route transitions. We do this by sending the server the URL we want to navigate to, and the server sends us back the JSX tree for that page. Then, React in the browser rerenders the entire page with the new JSX tree, and we have a new page without a full-page refresh. This is exactly what we're going to do.

To do that, we need to tweak our client-side code a little bit. We need to add an event listener to all links in our app that prevents the default behavior of the link, and instead sends a request to the server for the new page. We can do that like so:

```
window.addEventListener("click", (event) => {
  if (event.target.tagName !== "A") {
    return;
  }

  event.preventDefault();
  navigate(event.target.href);
});
```

We're adding the event listener to the window because of performance: we don't want to add an event listener to every single link in our app, which could be a large number of event listeners that could slow things down. Instead, we add one event listener to the window and check if the target of the click is a link. This is called *event delegation*.

If the user does click on an A element, we then prevent the default behavior of the link, and instead call a navigate function that we'll define in a second. This function will send a request to the server for the new page, and then we'll have React render it on the client.

Let's define the navigate function:

```
async function navigate(url) {
  const response = await fetch(url, { headers: { "jsx-only": true } });
  const jsxTree = await response.json();
  const element = JSON.parse(jsxTree, (key, value) => {
    if (key === "$$typeof") {
      return Symbol.for("react.element");
    }

    return value;
  });
  root.render(element);
}
```

What we're doing here is pretty straightforward: we're sending a request to the server for the new page, deserializing the response into a React element, and then rendering that element into the root of our app. This will cause React to rerender the page with the new JSX tree, and we'll have a new page without a full-page refresh. But what is root? To understand that, we need to look at our full client-side JavaScript file:

```
import { hydrateRoot } from "react-dom/client";
import { deserialize } from "./serializer.js";
import App from "./App";
```

```
const root = hydrateRoot(document, <App />); // <- this is root

window.addEventListener("click", (event) => {
  if (event.target.tagName !== "a") {
    return;
  }

  event.preventDefault();
  navigate(event.target.href);
});

async function navigate(url) {
  const response = await fetch(url);
  const jsxTree = await response.json();
  const element = deserialize(jsxTree);
  root.render(element);
}
```

We get a root from React when we initially hydrate the page, and we can use that root to render new elements into it. This is how React works under the hood, and we're just using the same API that React uses internally. This is a good thing because it means we're not doing anything special or hacky, we're just using React's public API.

Finally, we need to have our server respond with just the JSX tree object for the next page when given a `jsx-only` header instead of responding with a full HTML string. We can do that like so:

```
app.get("*", async (req, res) => {
  const jsxTree = await turnServerComponentsIntoTreeOfElements(<App />);

  // This is the secret sauce
  if (req.headers["jsx-only"]) {
    res.end(
      JSON.stringify(jsxTree, (key, value) => {
        if (key === "$$typeof") {
          return "react.element";
        }

        return value;
      })
    );
  } else {
    const html = ReactDOMServer.renderToString(jsxTree);

    res.send(`
      <!DOCTYPE html>
      <html>
        <head>
          <title>My React App</title>
        </head>
        <body>
          <div id="root">${html}</div>
```

```
          <script src="/static/js/main.js"></script>
        </body>
      </html>
    `);
  }
});
```

Notice how when the header is present, we're not sending JSON but just a string? This is because we need to `JSON.parse` this on the client side, and `JSON.parse` expects a string, not a JSON object. This is just a quirk of the API, but it's not too bad.

Now, we have a way to navigate to new pages without a full-page refresh. We can now handle navigation in our RSCs-enabled app. All anchor link navigations happen smoothly and fluently without a full-page refresh. But what about updates? How do we handle updates? Let's tackle that next.

Making Updates

While there are a ton of positives to RSCs, there are also some limitations to be aware of, namely the added mental overhead of having to think about two different types of components (server and client). This is because not all components can be server components.

For example, consider this simple counter component that increments the counter value by 1 when a user clicks the + button:

```
function Counter() {
  const [count, setCount] = useState(0);
  return (
    <div>
      <h1>Hello friends, look at my nice counter!</h1>
      <p>About me: I like pie! Sign my guest book!</p>
      <p>Count: {count}</p>
      <button onClick={() => setCount(count + 1)}>+</button>
    </div>
  );
}
```

This component can never be a server component for two reasons:

- It uses `useState`, which is a client-side-only API. This means that the server doesn't know what the initial value of `count` is, so it can't render the initial HTML. This is a problem because the server needs to render the initial HTML before the client can take over and render the interactive UI.

  In a serverful environment, the concept of "state" is shared among multiple clients. However, in React, prior to the introduction of RSCs, state was localized to the current application. This difference poses a risk. It could lead to the leakage of state between multiple clients, potentially exposing sensitive information. Due to this discrepancy and the associated security risks, RSCs do not support the use of useState on the server side. This is because server-side state is fundamentally different from client-side state.

Moreover, the dispatcher (setState) function from useState would need to be serialized to be sent over the network to the client, and functions are not serializable, so this would be impossible.

- It uses onClick, which is a client-side-only API. This is because servers aren't interactive: you can't click on a running process in a server, so onClick in server components is a bit of an impossible state. Moreover, all props for server components are supposed to be serializable because the server needs to be able to serialize the props and send them to the client, and functions are not serializable.

Therefore, what used to be a simple counter now needs to be broken apart into a server part and a client part *if* we want to harness the power of server components, like so:

```
// Server Component
function ServerCounter() {
  return (
    <div>
      <h1>Hello friends, look at my nice counter!</h1>
      <p>
        About me: I like to count things and I'm a counter and sometimes I count
        things but other times I enjoy playing the Cello and one time at band
        camp I counted to 1000 and a pirate appeared
      </p>
      <InteractiveClientPart />
    </div>
  );
}

// Client Component
"use client";
function InteractiveClientPart() {
  const [count, setCount] = useState(0);
  return (
    <div>
      <p>Count: {count}</p>
      <button onClick={() => setCount(count + 1)}>+</button>
    </div>
  );
}
```

This is a bit of a contrived example, but it illustrates the point that you can't just take any React component and turn it into a server component. You need to think about what parts of your component are server renderable and what parts are client renderable. This introduces a bit of friction where even though in this example it's pretty obvious what parts are server renderable and what parts are client renderable, in a real-world application at scale, it may not be so obvious.

The outcome of this, though, is largely rewarding because what we just did was factor out a tiny portion of our counter application that is intended to be interactive, and *only* this portion of our app will actually make it to our users as part of a JavaScript bundle; the rest will not. As a consequence, we ship drastically smaller JavaScript bundles over the network, which means faster load times and better performance for our users both in terms of CPU, with less work needing to be done to parse and execute the JavaScript, and in terms of network, with less data needing to be downloaded.

This is why we want to render *as much as we can safely* on the server to leave the code out of client-side bundles.

Under the hood

The extra mental overhead aside, let's talk about how React delineates and works with server components and client components separately under the hood. This is important to understand because it will help us understand how to make updates to our application.

Client components are designated as such by adding a `"use client"` directive at the top of a file containing a client component. RSCs require next-generation tooling to differentiate server and client components based on the use of such directives.

Through the use of a next-generation bundler or bundler configuration, bundlers are able to produce separate module graphs for React apps: a server graph and a client graph. The server graph is never rolled into a bundle since it's never served to users, but all files that start with the `"use client"` directive are rolled into either one client bundle or multiple bundles per component that can be lazy loaded. This implementation detail is dependent on the frameworks that are built on top of RSCs.

So conceptually, we've got a server graph that executes on the server, and one or more client bundles that are downloaded and executed when they're required on the client. But how does React know when to import and execute client components? To understand this, we'll have to consider a typical React tree. Let's do this using our counter example.

In Figure 9-1, we visualize the tree of components for our counter application where orange components are rendered on the server, and green ones on the client. Since the root of the tree is a server component, the entire tree is rendered on the server. However, the `InteractiveClientPart` component is a client component, so it's not rendered on the server. Instead, the server renders a placeholder for the client component, which is a reference to the specific module that the client bundler produced.

This module reference essentially says, "when you get to this point in the tree, it's time to use this specific module."

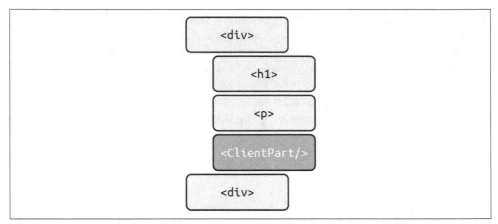

Figure 9-1. A component tree showing client and server components

The module isn't necessarily always only lazy loaded, but can be loaded from the initial bundle as well, since bundlers add a whole bunch of modules in the bundles we ship to users. It could literally be `getModuleFromBundleAtPosition([0,4])` or something similar. The point is that the server sends a reference to the right client module, and React on the client side fills in the gap.

When this happens, React will replace the module reference with the actual module from the client bundle. This is a bit of a simplification, but it should give us a good enough understanding of the mechanism. The client component is then rendered on the client, and the client component can then be interacted with as usual. This is why RSCs require a next-generation bundler: they need to be able to produce separate module graphs for server and client components.

In practice, this means that in the case of our counter example, the server would render the following tree:

```
{
  $$typeof: Symbol(react.element),
  type: "div",
  props: {
    children: [
      {
        $$typeof: Symbol(react.element),
        type: "h1",
        props: {
          children: "Hello friends, look at my nice counter!"
        }
      },
      {
```

```
      $$typeof: Symbol(react.element),
      type: "p",
      props: {
        children: "About me: I like to count things"
      }
    },
    {
      // The ClientPart element placeholder with a module reference
      // Pay attention to this: it's a module reference!
      $$typeof: Symbol(react.element),
      type: {
        $$typeof: Symbol(react.module.reference),
        name: "default",
        filename: "./src/ClientPart.js",
        moduleId: "client-part-1234"
      },
      props: {
        children: [
          // ...other server components and client module references
          {
            $$typeof: Symbol(react.element),
            type: {
              $$typeof: Symbol(react.module.reference),
              name: "default",
              filename: "./src/AnotherClientComponent.js"
            },
            props: {
              children: [],
            }
          },
          {
            $$typeof: Symbol(react.element),
            type: "div",
            props: {
              children: "I am a server component"
            }
          }
        ]
      }
    }
  ]
}
}
```

This tree would be sent to the client side, and as React renders it and encounters the module reference, React would intelligently replace the module reference with the actual module from the client bundle. This is how React knows when to import and execute client components.

Thus, we can see that the bundler is able to still render an entire tree on the server, and only leave "holes" to be filled in on the client while rendering even the children of client components recursively on the server, producing a full tree. The client then fills any holes necessary by downloading and executing client bundles.

Server components can also be wrapped into Suspense boundaries, with frameworks doing the requisite work to stream them down to users from the server side as they become "ready": that is, as any data they require is fetched and any other operations needed are completed asynchronously.

OK, hopefully now we understand how client components are split from server components, enabling updates in RSCs-oriented applications. Client components marked with `"use client"` can contain localized state and event handlers like `onClick` without issue.

Given that we've now closed the loop with client components and understand how server components are executed on the server and how client components are included in client bundles, we need to discuss some nuance around these topics.

Nuance

There's a common misconception that server components execute only on the server and client components execute only on the client. This isn't true. Server components do indeed execute only on the server and output objects representing React elements, but client components do not execute exclusively on the client.

To understand this deeper, let's discuss what "components execute" even means. When we say "components execute," we mean that the function that represents the component is called. For example, let's say we have a component like this:

```
function MyComponent() {
  return <div>hello world</div>;
}
```

When we say "MyComponent executes," we mean that the function `MyComponent` is called with its props and returns a React element—which is a plain JavaScript object that looks like this:

```
{
  $$typeof: Symbol(react.element),
  type: "div",
  props: {
    children: "hello world"
  }
}
```

This is what we mean when we say "components execute."

During server rendering, client components execute on the server and output objects representing React elements. These elements are then serialized into a string of HTML and sent to the client where the browser renders the HTML markup. Thus, client components also execute on the server, return some objects representing React elements, and then the server serializes them into HTML and sends them to the client.

To get a more accurate representation of this, we can make the following true statements:

- Server components execute on the server, output objects representing React elements.
- Client components execute on the server, output objects representing React elements.
- A big object representing all React elements from both client and server components exists on the server.
- This is turned into a string and sent to the client.
- From this point, server components are never executed on the client.
- Client components are executed exclusively on the client.

With this perspective, the execution boundaries of both server and client components become more clear. We may be splitting hairs here, but it's worth adding more detail to fully understand and appreciate the interplay between both types of components.

Rules of Server Components

Now that we understand how server components work under the hood, let's discuss some rules that we need to follow when working with server components, or more broadly, things to keep in mind when working with server components.

Serializability Is King

With server components, all props must be serializable. This is because the server needs to be able to serialize the props and send them to the client, as we've discussed earlier. Therefore, props cannot be functions or other nonserializable values in server components. This makes the render props pattern we discussed in Chapter 5 effectively obsolete.

At this point, based on our understanding of how RSCs are rendered on the server and then sent to the client on soft navigation, we should understand why this rule exists. Let's say we have a server component like this:

```
function ServerComponent() {
  return <ClientComponent onClick={() => alert("hi")} />;
}
```

This would cause an error. We could, however, work around this by encapsulating the onClick prop inside the ClientComponent.

No Effectful Hooks

The server is a vastly different environment from the client. It's not interactive, it doesn't have a DOM, and it doesn't have a window. Therefore, hooks that are effectful are not supported in server components.

Some frameworks, like Next.js, have lint rules that completely ban all hooks in server components, but this is not entirely necessary. RSCs can use hooks that do not depend on state, effects, or browser-only APIs. For example, the useRef hook is perfectly fine to use in server components because it doesn't depend on state, effects, or browser-only APIs. However, this may not be all bad, since it biases us toward more safely working with components.

State Is Not State

State in server components is not the same as state in client components. This is because server components are rendered on the server, and client components are rendered on the client. This means that state in server components may be shared between clients since server-client relationships are broadcast-style relationships instead of unicast (one client, one state), and thus the risks of leaking state between clients is high.

Combined with the hooks rule, this means that any components that require state via useState or useReducer or similar are best suited to be client components.

Client Components Cannot Import Server Components

Client components cannot import server components. This is because server components are executed only on the server, but client components are executed on both, including on browsers.

This means that if we have a client component like this:

```
"use client";
import { ServerComponent } from "./ServerComponent";

function ClientComponent() {
  return (
    <div>
      <h1>Hey everyone, check out my great server component!</h1>
      <ServerComponent />
    </div>
  );
}
```

it would cause an error because the client component is trying to import a server component. This is impossible because, since server components execute only on the server, the server component we're importing here may further import things that are not available in the client runtime environment, like Node.js APIs. This would cause errors on the client.

For all we know, the server component could look like this:

```
import { readFile } from "node:fs/promises";

export async function ServerComponent() {
  const content = await readFile("./some-file.txt", "utf-8");
  return <div>{content}</div>;
}
```

When we try to run this on the client side because a client component imported it, we'd get an error because the readFile function and the "node:fs/promises" module are not available in the browser. This is why client components cannot import server components.

However, client components can *compose* server components via props. For example, we could rewrite our client component to look like this:

```
"use client";

function ClientComponent({ children }) {
  return (
    <div>
      <h1>Hey everyone, check out my great server component!</h1>
      {children}
    </div>
  );
}
```

and then in whatever parent server component contains this client component, we could do this:

```
import { ServerComponent } from "./ServerComponent";

async function TheParentOfBothComponents() {
  return (
    <ClientComponent>
      <ServerComponent />
    </ClientComponent>
  );
}
```

This would work because there's no explicit import of a server component from a client component, but the parent server component is passing a server component as a prop to the client component. The only reason the imports are forbidden is to prevent the possibility of including server components in the client bundle, and bundlers only pay attention to import statements, not prop composition.

Client Components Are Not Bad

It's worth noting that up until server components were introduced, client components were the only type of component we had in React. This means that all of our existing components are client components, and that's OK. Client components are not bad, and they're not going away. They're still the bread and butter of React applications, and they're still the most common type of component we'll be writing.

We mention that here because there has been some confusion around this topic, and server components have been perceived by some as a superior replacement for client components. This is not true. Server components are a new type of component that we can use in addition to client components, but they're not a replacement for client components.

Server Actions

Server components are a powerful new feature in React, but they're not the only new feature. RSCs also work in tandem with a new directive "use server" that marks server-side functions that can be called from client-side code. We call these functions *server actions*.

Any async function can have "use server" as the first line of its body to signal to React and to the bundler that this function can be called from client-side code, but must only execute on the server. When calling a server action on the client, it will make a network request to the server that includes a serialized copy of any arguments passed. If the server action returns a value, that value will be serialized and returned to the client.

Instead of individually marking functions with "use server", you can also add the directive to the top of a file to mark all exports within that file as server actions that can be used anywhere, including imported in client code.

Forms and Mutations

In Chapter 8, we discussed how Next.js and Remix handle forms and mutations. React is adding (or has added) first-class primitives for these as well. Consider this form:

```
// App.js

async function requestUsername(formData) {
  'use server';
  const username = formData.get('username');
```

```
  // ...
}

export default App() {
  <form action={requestUsername}>
    <input type="text" name="username" />
    <button type="submit">Request</button>
  </form>
}
```

In this example, requestUsername is a server action passed to a <form>. When a user submits this form, there is a network request to the server function requestUser name. When calling a server action in a form, React will supply the form's FormData as the first argument to the server action.

By passing a server action to the form action, React can progressively enhance the form. This means that forms can be submitted before the JavaScript bundle is loaded.

Outside of Forms

It's worth noting that server actions are exposed server endpoints and can be called anywhere in client code.

When using a server action outside of a form, we can call the server action in a transition, which allows us to display a loading indicator, show optimistic state updates, and handle unexpected errors. Here's an example of a server action outside of a form:

```
"use client";

import incrementLike from "./actions";
import { useState, useTransition } from "react";

function LikeButton() {
  const [isPending, startTransition] = useTransition();
  const [likeCount, setLikeCount] = useState(0);

  const incrementLink = async () => {
    "use server";
    return likeCount + 1;
  };

  const onClick = () => {
    startTransition(async () => {
      // To read a server action return value, we await the promise returned.
      const currentCount = await incrementLike();
      setLikeCount(currentCount);
    });
  };

  return (
    <>
```

```
      <p>Total Likes: {likeCount}</p>
      <button onClick={onClick} disabled={isPending}>
        Like
      </button>;
    </>
  );
}
```

Thus, we can see that server actions are a powerful new feature in React that allow us to call server-side functions from client-side code. This really is intended only to be used in libraries or frameworks, as working with these directives in vanilla React is a bit cumbersome and requires quite a bit of work wiring things up. However, it's a powerful feature that enables a lot of interesting use cases.

The Future of React Server Components

RSCs are expected to evolve and improve over time. The React team is actively working on refining the implementation, addressing potential issues, and expanding the feature set. Some areas of ongoing development include:

Better bundler integration
> The React team is partnering with bundler developers to ensure better support for RSCs in bundlers like Webpack, Rollup, and others. This will make it easier to build RSCs-compatible frameworks and applications.

Ecosystem support
> As RSCs gain traction, more tools, libraries, and frameworks will likely emerge to support and extend this new application architecture. This will enable developers to more easily adopt RSCs in their projects and benefit from their performance and efficiency improvements.

RSCs represent a significant advancement in the React ecosystem, offering improved performance, simplified data fetching, and a better user experience. As RSCs continue to evolve and gain adoption, they're expected to become an essential tool for building modern, efficient, and user-friendly React applications. With this comprehensive understanding of RSCs, you are now well-equipped to explore and experiment with this cutting-edge experimental feature in your own projects.

Chapter Review

In this chapter, we exclusively focused on React Server Components (RSCs), a significant advancement in the React ecosystem aimed at enhancing the performance, efficiency, and user experience of React applications. RSCs represent an innovative application architecture that combines the best attributes of server-rendered multipage apps (MPAs) and client-rendered single-page apps (SPAs). This approach delivers a seamless user experience without compromising on performance or maintainability. We delved into the core concepts, benefits, and the underlying mental models and mechanisms of RSCs. A key highlight was the introduction of a new type of component that operates on the server, excluded from the client-side JavaScript bundle, and can run during build time. This advancement leads to a more efficient and effective application structure.

It's worth noting that, at the time of writing, RSCs are a hot topic in the React and web engineering space, and some of the details we covered may have changed. As always, we recommend having a look at react.dev and React's various community channels for the latest information.

Review Questions

1. What is the main value of React server components?
2. Can client components import server components? Why or why not?
3. What are some trade-offs between server components and traditional client-only React apps?
4. What are module references and how does React process them during reconciliation?
5. How do server actions make React apps more accessible?

Up Next

In the following chapter, we are going to take a slightly different path. We've spent most of our journey so far deeply embedded in the world of React, exploring its intricate inner workings, innovative strategies for state management, asynchronous rendering capabilities, and finally, its powerful frameworks. Now, we're going to take a step back and broaden our perspective.

We're going to venture beyond React, diving into the world of alternative UI libraries and frameworks that have grown alongside and sometimes in response to React's dominance. These alternatives have not only adopted some of React's best features, but have also introduced unique innovations of their own, giving us exciting new paradigms and possibilities in UI development.

In the forthcoming exploration, we will be delving into the workings and philosophies of some of these other UI libraries, such as Vue, Angular, Solid, Qwik, and Svelte. We will look at their unique strategies for managing state, handling side effects, and how they compare to React in terms of performance and developer experience. Each alternative comes with its own set of pros and cons, which might make it a better fit for certain types of projects or developer preferences:

Vue

Vue offers a progressive framework that is incrementally adoptable, meaning you can start small and gradually adopt more of Vue's features as you need them. Vue is renowned for its elegant API and focus on developer experience. It introduces a reactivity model that's simple yet powerful, driven by its core concept of reactive dependencies tracked during render.

Angular

Angular is a complete, opinionated framework with a steeper learning curve, but offers robust solutions out of the box. Its dependency injection system and declarative templates offer a different approach to application structure and state management compared to React.

Solid

Solid is another contender that is gaining attention in the JavaScript community. It promises fine-grained reactivity with a programming model similar to React, but with a focus on faster, more efficient rendering. How Solid tracks dependencies could be a breath of fresh air for developers looking for more efficiency at runtime.

The Qwik framework

Qwik introduces an interesting approach by focusing on optimal loading performance with "predictable" prefetching. It brings a unique perspective to how we can structure and deliver our JavaScript for optimal user experience.

Svelte

Svelte has been turning heads by compiling components at build time into imperative code that directly manipulates the DOM, leading to faster initial load times and smooth updates. Its reactivity model, marked by reactive statements, offers an intriguing contrast to the virtual DOM diffing strategy adopted by React.

While exploring these frameworks and libraries, we'll keep our knowledge of React as a touchstone. This will not only help us understand the other libraries better but also deepen our understanding of React by offering points of comparison and contrast.

Get ready to uncover the unique ways these alternate UI libraries approach reactivity, state management, side effects, and more. By studying these alternatives, we can glean insights that might inform our approach to problem-solving, regardless of the library or framework we choose to use. It's a big, diverse world of JavaScript out there, and we're about to dive in headfirst.

Buckle up! The journey is about to get even more exciting.

CHAPTER 10

React Alternatives

In the previous chapter, we covered the emerging topic of React Server Components (RSCs) in depth. We explored how they work, when to use them, and why they require powerful tools such as next-generation bundlers, routers, and more. We further differentiated between server components and server rendering, and even implemented a bare-bones RSCs renderer from scratch in order to understand the underlying mechanism for ourselves.

As we transition into exploring alternatives to React, this understanding of the role and function of frameworks and server components will provide valuable context. Each library we'll discuss in this chapter also ships with its associated frameworks, and many of the principles and trade-offs we've covered in React will apply to these ecosystems as well.

As we pivot our attention from React and its ecosystem, let's delve into some popular alternatives in the frontend development ecosystem: Vue.js, Angular, Svelte, Solid, and Qwik. Each library and framework introduces its own reactivity model and ways of thinking about UI development. Understanding these different models can broaden our perspective and give us more tools to solve problems in our projects.

Vue.js

Vue.js is a popular JavaScript framework for building user interfaces. Developed by Evan You, an ex-Google engineer who worked on AngularJS projects, Vue.js seeks to extract the good parts of Angular, but in a lighter, more maintainable, and less opinionated package.

One of Vue's most distinctive features is the unobtrusive reactivity system. Component state consists of reactive JavaScript objects. When you modify them, the view updates. It makes state management simple and intuitive, but it's also important to understand how it works to avoid some common gotchas.

In Vue's reactivity model, it intercepts the reading and writing of object properties. Vue 2 used getter/setters exclusively due to browser support limitations, but in Vue 3, proxies are used for reactive objects and getter/setters are used for refs. From the Vue docs, here's some pseudocode that illustrates how they work:

```
function reactive(obj) {
  return new Proxy(obj, {
    get(target, key) {
      track(target, key)
      return target[key]
    },
    set(target, key, value) {
      target[key] = value
      trigger(target, key)
    }
  })
}

function ref(value) {
  const refObject = {
    get value() {
      track(refObject, 'value')
      return value
    },
    set value(newValue) {
      value = newValue
      trigger(refObject, 'value')
    }
  }
  return refObject
}
```

This is somewhat oversimplified, but here we demonstrate a simplistic reactive system utilizing proxies. The `reactive` function takes an object and returns a proxy of that object, which intercepts `get` and `set` operations. On a `get` operation, it calls the `track` function and returns the requested property. On a `set` operation, it updates the value and calls the `trigger` function.

The `ref` function, on the other hand, encapsulates a value within an object and provides reactive `get` and `set` operations for that value, similar to the proxy but with a different structure, ensuring that the `track` and `trigger` functions are called appropriately during access or modification.

This is a very simple example of a reactive system, but it demonstrates the basic principles of Vue's reactivity model. This reactivity model can even be used to update the DOM. We can implement simple "reactive rendering" like this:

```
import { ref, watchEffect } from "vue";

const count = ref(0);

watchEffect(() => {
  document.body.innerHTML = `count is: ${count.value}`;
});

// updates the DOM
count.value++;
```

In fact, this is pretty close to how a Vue component keeps the state and the DOM in sync—each component instance creates a reactive effect to render and update the DOM. Of course, Vue components use much more efficient ways to update the DOM than `innerHTML`, but this should be enough to give you a basic idea of how it works.

The `ref()`, `computed()`, and `watchEffect()` APIs are all part of Vue's Composition API.

Signals

Quite a few other frameworks have introduced reactivity primitives similar to `refs` from Vue's Composition API, under the term "signals" that we'll discuss in this chapter.

Fundamentally, signals are the same kind of reactivity primitive as Vue `refs`. It's a value container that provides dependency tracking on access, and side-effect triggering on mutation. This reactivity-primitive-based paradigm isn't a particularly new concept in the frontend world: it dates back to implementations like Knockout observables and Meteor Tracker from more than a decade ago. Vue Options API and the React state management library MobX are also based on the same principles but hide the primitives behind object properties.

Although not a necessary trait for something to qualify as signals, today the concept is often discussed alongside the rendering model where updates are performed through fine-grained subscriptions. Due to the use of virtual DOM, Vue currently relies on compilers to achieve similar optimizations. However, Vue is also exploring a new Solid-inspired compilation strategy (Vapor Mode) that does not rely on virtual DOM and takes more advantage of Vue's built-in reactivity system.

Simplicity

Vue's biggest strength is its simplicity. It's incredibly easy to get started with Vue: you can simply include the Vue library in your HTML file in a `<script>` tag and start writing Vue components. Vue also provides a CLI tool for scaffolding new projects, which can be a great way to get started with a more complex application.

While we've only scratched the surface of Vue.js here, it's clear that Vue's combination of a powerful reactivity system, a template-based syntax, and a well-structured component model make it a compelling option for many developers.

Angular

Angular, developed and maintained by Google, is another well-known player in the world of JavaScript frameworks. Angular is a complete, opinionated framework, providing its own solutions for a wide range of frontend concerns, from rendering and state management to routing and form handling.

Angular introduces a different reactivity model than React. Instead of a virtual DOM diffing and reconciliation process, Angular uses a system known as change detection.

In Angular, every component gets a change detector responsible for checking the component's view for changes using a library called Zone.js. Before we proceed, let's talk about this in a little bit more detail.

Change Detection

Change detection is the process through which Angular checks to see whether your application state has changed, and if any DOM needs to be updated. At a high level, Angular walks your components from top to bottom, looking for changes. Angular runs its change detection mechanism periodically so that changes to the data model are reflected in an application's view. Change detection can be triggered either manually or through an asynchronous event.

Change detection is highly optimized and performant, but it can still cause slowdowns if the application runs it too frequently. This change detection system is a powerful and flexible tool, and Angular provides several strategies out of the box for fine-tuning its behavior to optimize performance for different scenarios.

Angular also uses a template syntax, like Vue, but it provides even more powerful directives and constructs for manipulating the DOM, such as `*ngIf` for conditionally rendering elements and `*ngFor` for rendering lists. This is different from React, which uses JSX with in-place JavaScript expressions to render dynamic data.

Signals

Angular is undergoing some fundamental changes by foregoing dirty-checking and introducing its own implementation of a reactivity primitive. The Angular Signal API looks like this:

```
const count = signal(0);

count(); // access the value
```

```
count.set(1); // set new value
count.update((v) => v + 1); // update based on previous value

// mutate deep objects with same identity
const state = signal({ count: 0 });
state.mutate((o) => {
  o.count++;
});
```

Compared to Vue refs, Angular's getter-based API style provides some interesting trade-offs when used in Vue components:

- () is slightly less verbose than .value, but updating the value is more verbose.
- There is no ref-unwrapping: accessing values always requires (). This makes value access consistent everywhere. This also means you can pass raw signals down as component props.

Angular is something of a Swiss Army knife, providing a wide range of tools for building complex applications. Its opinionated nature can be both a strength, in terms of the consistency and structure it brings to a codebase, and a limitation, in terms of flexibility and the learning curve for developers new to the framework.

Svelte

Svelte is a radical new approach to building user interfaces. Unlike traditional frameworks, Svelte is a compiler that transforms your declarative components into efficient imperative code that surgically updates the DOM. As a result, you're able to write high-performance, reactive web applications with less code.

Svelte's reactivity model is incredibly simple, yet powerful. Reactive statements in Svelte are written with a simple syntax that's reminiscent of spreadsheet formulas. Here's a basic Svelte component:

```
<script>
let count = 0;

function increment() {
    count += 1;
}
</script>

<div>{count}</div>
<button on:click={increment}>
  Click me
</button>
```

In this example, the {count} syntax in the markup will automatically update whenever the count variable changes. This is similar to React's JSX, but with one key difference: in Svelte, this reactivity is automatic. You don't need to call a setter function or use any special API to update the DOM; you just assign to the variable, and Svelte takes care of the rest.

Svelte also offers a reactive statement syntax that allows you to compute values based on your reactive data:

```
<script>
let count = 0;
let doubleCount = 0;

$: doubleCount = count * 2;

function increment() {
    count += 1;
}
</script>

<div>{doubleCount}</div>
<button on:click={increment}>
  Click me
</button>
```

In this example, `doubleCount` will automatically be updated whenever `count` changes. This is reminiscent of computed properties in Vue, but with an arguably simpler syntax.

The compiler approach taken by Svelte has several advantages. It typically results in faster runtime performance because there's no virtual DOM diffing and patching step. Instead, Svelte generates code that updates the DOM directly.

However, this approach also comes with trade-offs. The compiler-centric nature of Svelte means that some dynamic capabilities offered by virtual DOM-based frameworks, like dynamic component types, can be more cumbersome or verbose to express. Also, because the Svelte ecosystem is smaller and younger than those of React, Vue, and Angular, there may be fewer resources, libraries, and community solutions available.

Runes

Runes are symbols that influence the Svelte compiler. Whereas Svelte today uses `let`, `=`, the `export` keyword, and the `$:` label to mean specific things, runes use *function syntax* to achieve the same things and more.

For example, to declare a piece of reactive state, we can use the `$state` rune:

```
<script>
-   let count = 0;
+   let count = $state(0);
```

```
        function increment() {
            count += 1;
        }
    </script>

    <button on:click={increment}>
        clicks: {count}
    </button>
```

As applications grow in complexity, figuring out which values are reactive and which aren't can get tricky. And the current heuristic only works for `let` declarations at the top level of a component, which can cause confusion. Having code behave one way inside *.svelte* files and another way inside *.js* can make it hard to refactor code, for example, if you need to turn something into a store so that you can use it in multiple places.

With runes, reactivity extends beyond the boundaries of your *.svelte* files. Suppose we wanted to encapsulate our counter logic in a way that could be reused between components. Today, you would use a custom store in a *.js* or *.ts* file:

```
import { writable } from "svelte/store";

export function createCounter() {
    const { subscribe, update } = writable(0);

    return {
        subscribe,
        increment: () => update((n) => n + 1),
    };
}
```

Because this implements the *store contract*—the returned value has a `subscribe` method—we can reference the store value by prefixing the store name with $:

```
<script>
+    import { createCounter } from './counter.js';
+
+    const counter = createCounter();
-    let count = 0;
-
-    function increment() {
-        count += 1;
-    }
</script>

-<button on:click={increment}>
-    clicks: {count}
+<button on:click={counter.increment}>
+    clicks: {$counter}
</button>
```

This works, but it's pretty weird! The store API can get rather unwieldy when you start doing more complex things. With runes, things get much simpler:

```
-import { writable } from 'svelte/store';

export function createCounter() {
-    const { subscribe, update } = writable(0);
+    let count = $state(0);

    return {
-        subscribe,
-        increment: () => update((n) => n + 1)
+        get count() { return count },
+        increment: () => count += 1
    };
}
<script>
    import { createCounter } from './counter.js';

    const counter = createCounter();
</script>

<button on:click={counter.increment}>
-    clicks: {$counter}
+    clicks: {counter.count}
</button>
```

Note that we're using a `get` property in the returned object, so that `counter.count` always refers to the current value rather than the value at the time the function was called.

Runtime reactivity

Today, Svelte uses *compile-time reactivity*. This means that if you have some code that uses the $: label to rerun automatically when dependencies change, those dependencies are determined when Svelte compiles your component:

```
<script>
    export let width;
    export let height;

    // the compiler knows it should recalculate `area`
    // when either `width` or `height` change...
    $: area = width * height;

    // ...and that it should log the value of `area`
    // when _it_ changes
    $: console.log(area);
</script>
```

This works well…until it doesn't. Suppose we refactored the code as follows:

```
// @errors: 7006 2304
const multiplyByHeight = (width) => width * height;
$: area = multiplyByHeight(width);
```

Because the `$: area = ...` declaration can only see `width`, it won't be recalculated when `height` changes. As a result, code is hard to refactor, and understanding the intricacies of when Svelte chooses to update which values can become rather tricky beyond a certain level of complexity.

Svelte 5 introduces the `$derived` and `$effect` runes, which instead determine the dependencies of their expressions when they are evaluated:

```
<script>
    let { width, height } = $props(); // instead of `export let`

    const area = $derived(width * height);

    $effect(() => {
        console.log(area);
    });
</script>
```

As with `$state`, `$derived` and `$effect` can also be used in your *.js* and *.ts* files.

Signal boost

Like every other framework, Svelte has come to the realization that Knockout was right all along.

Svelte 5's reactivity is powered by *signals*, which are essentially what Knockout was doing in 2010. More recently, signals have been popularized by Solid (more on this later) and adopted by a multitude of other frameworks. In Svelte 5, signals are an under-the-hood implementation detail rather than something you interact with directly.

Solid

Solid is a declarative JavaScript library for building user interfaces. It's similar to React in that it provides a component model base, but Solid is based on reactive primitives. Instead of using a virtual DOM, Solid uses a fine-grained reactivity system to automatically track dependencies and update the DOM directly, which can result in more efficient updates.

Here's an example of a simple Solid component:

```
import { createSignal } from "solid-js";

function Component() {
  const [count, setCount] = createSignal(0);
```

```
    return (
      <>
        <div>{count()}</div>
        <button onClick={() => setCount(count() + 1)}>Increment</button>
      </>
    );
}
```

In this example, `createSignal` creates a reactive primitive, similar to `useState` in React. The key difference is that `count` is a function that returns the current value and implicitly registers the dependency for the reactive context. When `setCount` is called, it triggers an update for any part of the UI that depends on `count` without reinvoking the function components.

To contrast this with React, in React the component, `Component` in this case, would be reinvoked, including all of the logic inside its block. Thus, the `count` value itself is not reactive. In Solid, the `Component` function is never reinvoked, but the `count` value itself is reactive and changes whenever `setCount` is called. This is called fine-grained reactivity, and it is directly opposite to React's coarse-grained reactivity.

Solid's fine-grained reactivity system means that it can minimize unnecessary updates and avoid the need for a diffing step, resulting in very high performance. However, because it's a relatively new and less widely used library, it may not have as many resources and community solutions available as some of the more established options.

Solid's `createSignal()` API design emphasizes read/write segregation. Signals are exposed as a read-only getter and a separate setter:

```
const [count, setCount] = createSignal(0);

count(); // access the value
setCount(1); // update the value
```

Notice how the `count` signal can be passed down without the setter. This ensures that the state can never be mutated unless the setter is also explicitly exposed.

Solid reinvigorated the discussion around signals, and the concept has been adopted by many other frameworks and libraries as we've seen previously. Everything we've previously mentioned about signals comes from the work of Ryan Carniato, the author of Solid, who somehow single-handedly managed to change the entire front-end ecosystem by bringing back a concept from 2010.

Qwik

Qwik is a unique framework designed to optimize the loading of web pages and prioritize user interaction and responsiveness. Unlike traditional frameworks, it views web pages as a collection of components that can be independently loaded over the network and interacted with on demand. This approach significantly reduces the initial load time of the page, enhancing the overall user experience.

Web applications and sites built with Qwik ship with exceedingly small and constant initial amounts of JavaScript (~1 kB). The amount of initial JavaScript loaded by a Qwik site is constant, as it is the Qwik loader. This is why Qwik is known in some circles as "the O(1) framework," meaning it has a constant load time regardless of the size of the application.

Initially, Qwik loads a bare minimum amount of JavaScript, but then loads components and other behaviors as they are needed. This approach allows Qwik to prioritize the loading of the most important components first, resulting in a faster initial load time and a more responsive user experience.

An essential feature of Qwik is resumability. We covered resumability crudely in our chapter on server-side React (Chapter 6), but to recap: resumability is a process through which a server rendered snapshot of the initial state of the page is sent to the client. As the user opens the page, they interact with this static snapshot until they need more interactivity. Then, various behaviors load on demand as users continue. This mechanism provides an instant interaction opportunity for the user, a characteristic that is not prevalent in many other frameworks.

Resumability is far superior to hydration (also covered in Chapter 6) because it does not require rendering components twice. It also avoids the "uncanny valley" of user interfaces where a website is not interactive for a period of time after the initial server rendered markup has made it to the browser and before the JavaScript has loaded and hydrated the page. Qwik is instant on.

When comparing Qwik to other popular frameworks such as React, Vue, Svelte, or Solid, several differences emerge. While React and Vue also adopt a component-based approach, if we're not careful and intentional about code splitting, we can send the entire JavaScript bundle for the application to the client up front, sometimes getting into the megabyte zone. This process can lead to longer initial load times, especially for large applications. On the other hand, Qwik only loads the components and event handlers as they are needed, resulting in faster initial load times and a more responsive user experience. Qwik is also clever about prefetching, and does so for lazy-loaded elements such that everything is prefetched on initial load but only parsed and executed on demand.

Qwik, like Svelte and Solid, focuses on performance, but achieves this in different ways. Svelte compiles the components to highly efficient imperative code that manipulates the DOM directly, while Solid uses a reactive fine-grained reactivity model for its components. While also using reactive primitives, Qwik focuses on optimizing component loading and making sure the most important ones are available as soon as possible.

In terms of developer experience, Qwik offers a simple and intuitive API that makes it easy to define and work with components. Qwik components are nearly identical to React components in terms of syntax and structure, since they are also expressed with JSX (or TSX). This similarity makes it easy for developers to get started with Qwik, especially if they're already familiar with React.

Moreover, Qwik has interoperability with React, allowing developers to use React components in Qwik applications via a `qwikify` utility. This interoperability is a significant advantage for developers who want to use Qwik but also want to take advantage of the rich ecosystem of React libraries and tools.

Qwik presents a novel approach to modern web development with its component-based and event-driven architecture. Its focus on resumability and prioritized loading sets it apart from other frameworks like React, Vue, Svelte, and Solid. While each of these tools has its strengths and use cases, Qwik's unique features make it an exciting addition to the landscape of web development frameworks. It could be the right choice for developers and teams looking for a performant, user-centric, and efficient way to build their web applications.

The only drawback of Qwik is that it is still fairly new and does not have quite as mature of an ecosystem as React, Vue, or Angular. However, it is gaining traction and has a growing community of developers and contributors. As Qwik continues to evolve, it will be interesting to see how it compares to other frameworks and how it can be used to build even more powerful applications.

Common Patterns

All of these technologies—React, Angular, Qwik, Solid, and Svelte—are solutions for creating rich, interactive user interfaces for the web. Though they vary in their philosophies, methodologies, and implementation details, they share several commonalities that reflect their shared purpose.

Component-Based Architecture

One of the primary commonalities among these frameworks and libraries is the adoption of a component-based architecture. In a component-based architecture, UIs are broken down into individual pieces, or components, each of which is responsible for a specific part of the user interface.

Components encapsulate their own state and logic, and they can be composed together to build complex UIs. This modularity promotes code reuse, separation of concerns, and improved maintainability. In each of these frameworks, components can be functional, and they can often be composed, extended, or decorated to create more complex components.

Declarative Syntax

React, Angular, Qwik, Solid, and Svelte all employ a declarative syntax for defining UIs. In a declarative approach, developers specify what the UI should look like for a given state, and the framework takes care of updating the UI to match that state. This abstracts away the imperative DOM manipulations that can make UI development tedious and error prone.

All these technologies provide their own flavor of a templating language for writing declarative UIs. React, Qwik, and Solid use JSX; Angular uses its own HTML-based template syntax; and Svelte has its HTML-inspired language.

Updates

All these libraries and frameworks provide a mechanism to respond to updates in the application state and alter the UI accordingly. React and Vue use a virtual DOM diffing algorithm to make these updates. Svelte, on the other hand, compiles components to imperative code that updates the DOM directly. Angular uses a change detection mechanism based on Zones and observables.

Soon, it'll pretty much be React using vDOM and everyone else using some variety of signals.

Despite the different methods, the goal is the same: to efficiently update the UI in response to state changes, abstracting away the complex DOM manipulation and allowing developers to focus on the application logic.

Lifecycle Methods

React, Angular, Solid, and Svelte provide lifecycle methods or hooks, which are functions that get called at different stages in a component's life, such as when it's first created, when it's updated, and when it's about to be removed from the DOM. Developers can use these methods to run side effects, clean up resources, or make updates based on changes in props.

Ecosystem and Tooling

Each of these frameworks and libraries is supported by a rich ecosystem of tools, libraries, and resources. They all have support for modern JavaScript features and tooling, including ES6 syntax, modules, and build tools like Webpack and Babel. They also have excellent TypeScript support, allowing developers to write type-safe code and take advantage of TypeScript's powerful features.

Most of these technologies also come with or have available sophisticated developer tools that can aid in debugging and application profiling. React's and Angular's developer tools extensions for popular browsers are excellent examples of such tooling.

While React, Angular, Qwik, Solid, and Svelte have their unique strengths and philosophies, they share these common goals: providing a component-based architecture, enabling the creation of declarative UIs, offering reactivity to state changes, simplifying event handling, providing lifecycle methods or similar concepts, and supporting a rich ecosystem and modern JavaScript tooling. This shared set of features and concepts is a testament to the evolution of web development toward more modular, declarative, and reactive paradigms.

React Is Not Reactive

The term "reactive" has been used to describe many things in the world of programming, but it's often used to describe systems that automatically update in response to changes in data. The paradigm of reactive programming is fundamentally about building systems that respond to changes, and automatically propagating those changes through the system. This is why frameworks like Vue.js and Svelte are often described as being reactive. However, React does not follow the traditional model of reactivity, and its approach is distinctly different.

React was introduced as a library for building user interfaces in a declarative way—*declarative* meaning that those of us writing React merely describe *what* we want, and React deals with the *how*. It allows developers to describe the UI based on the current application state, and React takes care of updating the UI whenever the state changes. This description might sound like React is reactive, but when you delve deeper into the implementation details, it becomes apparent that React's model is quite distinct from the traditional reactive programming model.

To understand why React isn't reactive in the traditional sense, let's first look at what traditional reactivity looks like in a system. In a traditional reactive system, dependencies between computations are automatically tracked as your code runs. When a reactive dependency changes, all computations that depend on it are automatically rerun to reflect this change. This is typically done using techniques such as databinding, observables, or signals and slots.

Signals for example, are a reactive primitive that can be used to create reactive values: on read, the reader of the signal subscribes to it, and on write, all subscribers are notified. This is reactivity 101.

React uses a different approach to manage state and its updates. Instead of automatically tracking dependencies and propagating changes, React introduces a more explicit mechanism for updating the state—the `useState` hook. When state changes, instead of immediately rendering updates, React schedules a rerender, and during that rerender, the entire component function is run again with the new state.

What that means is in the case of this counter:

```
import React, { useState } from "react";

function Counter() {
  const [count, setCount] = useState(0);

  function increment() {
    setCount(count + 1);
  }

  return (
    <div>
      <p>{count}</p>
      <button onClick={increment}>Increment</button>
    </div>
  );
}

export default Counter;
```

When `setCount` is called, the `Counter` function is reinvoked, including the `useState` hook. This is different from the traditional reactive model, where instead of reinvoking the entire function, only the reactive portions of the UI would be updated, in this case, the `{count}` inside of `<p>`. This is called coarse-grained reactivity, and it is directly opposed to the fine-grained reactivity model of signals.

React is often identified with the following equation:

```
v = f(s)
```

That is, the view is equal to a function of its state. This equation itself describes React's nonreactive nature: the view is a function of the state, but it's not automatically updated when the state changes. Instead, the view is updated when the function is re-executed with the new state.

This is where React's virtual DOM diffing and reconciliation process comes in. When a component's state or props change, React rerenders the component, creating a new virtual DOM subtree. It then diffs this new subtree with the old one, computes the minimal set of actual DOM mutations needed, and applies those mutations to the DOM.

This model of explicitly setting state and rerendering, as opposed to automatic reactive propagation of changes, allows for more predictability: React, if anthropomorphized, would say, "Tell me your state expectations and I'll take care of it." It enables features like batching of state updates and makes it easier to reason about the state of the application at any point in time because the state update and the resulting UI update are linked in a single, atomic operation.

However, this also means that React components are less reactive in the traditional sense. They don't automatically react to changes in data. Instead, they explicitly describe what the UI should look like for a given state, and it's up to React to apply any necessary updates when the state changes through re-executing functions instead of the appropriate values just updating in place.

While React's approach is not reactive in the sense of automatically tracking and propagating changes, it still provides a highly effective mechanism for building dynamic, interactive user interfaces. The use of state and props to control rendering provides a clear and predictable model for understanding how changes propagate through the application, and the virtual DOM system efficiently manages updates to the actual DOM.

In the end, whether or not React's approach is considered reactive comes down to semantics. If you define reactivity as the automatic propagation of changes through a system, then no, React is not reactive. But if you define reactivity as the ability of a system to respond to changes in state in a predictable and controlled manner, then yes, React can certainly be considered reactive.

Looking at React and other frameworks/libraries, it's clear that there isn't a one-size-fits-all approach to managing state and reactivity in UI development. Each tool has its strengths and trade-offs and is suited to different use cases. Understanding these differences is crucial when choosing the right tool for the job and can also help in writing more effective and efficient code, regardless of the framework or library you're using.

React's model of handling state and updates provides an excellent balance between control and convenience. The explicit state update mechanism allows developers to reason about their application state more easily, while the reconciliation and diffing algorithm efficiently applies updates to the DOM. Despite not being traditionally "reactive," React's approach has proven to be incredibly effective for building complex user interfaces.

There's no denying that reactive programming models offer some compelling benefits, particularly when it comes to automatically managing dependencies and updates. But as we've seen, React's approach offers its own set of advantages, providing a high degree of control and predictability.

For completionists, we'll now look at how the same counter would look in Solid, a framework that uses a reactive model:

```
import { createSignal } from "solid";

function Counter() {
  const [count, setCount] = createSignal(0);

  function increment() {
    setCount(count + 1);
  }
```

```
  return (
    <div>
      <p>{count()}</p>
      <button onClick={increment()}>Increment</button>
    </div>
  );
}

export default Counter;
```

In this example, `count` is a reactive property of the component's data. When we first read `count` by calling `count()` in place inside our `<p>` elements, we implicitly subscribe that portion of our JSX to the reactive value of `count`.

Then, when we call `increment()` later, which then calls `setCount`, `setCount` updates the value and notifies all subscribers that the value changed, prompting them to update. This is a bit analogous to the pub/sub pattern, where a subscriber subscribes to a publisher, and the publisher notifies all subscribers.

The result is fine-grained reactivity: that is, the function component itself, `Counter`, is never called more than once, but the fine-grained, small reactive values are.

Example 2: Dependent Values

Consider a component that displays a list of items and the count of those items. In a reactive system like Svelte, the count would automatically update whenever the list changes:

```
<script>
  let items = ['Apple', 'Banana', 'Cherry'];
  $: count = items.length;
</script>

<p>{count} items:</p>
<ul>
  {#each items as item (item)}
    <li>{item}</li>
  {/each}
</ul>
```

Here, `$: count = items.length;` declares a reactive statement. Whenever `items` changes, the `count` is automatically recalculated.

In React, this looks a bit different:

```
import React, { useState } from "react";

function ItemList() {
  const [items, setItems] = useState(["Apple", "Banana", "Cherry"]);
  const count = items.length;
```

```
    // ... update items somewhere ...

    return (
      <div>
        <p>{count} items:</p>
        <ul>
          {items.map((item) => (
            <li key={item}>{item}</li>
          ))}
        </ul>
      </div>
    );
}

export default ItemList;
```

In this React component, `count` is not a reactive value that automatically updates when `items` changes. Instead, it's a value derived from the current state during the render phase. When `items` changes, we need to call `setItems` to update the state and cause a rerender, at which point `count` is recalculated not because `count` is reactive, but because the `ItemList` function component is reinvoked.

The Future of React

Given the widespread adoption of reactive primitives like signals across the entire frontend ecosystem, some would presume that React would eventually adopt a similar approach. However, the React team has expressed that they are "not excited" about signals and opt for an alternative approach to arrive at similar performance benefits that signals provide.

To understand this a little better, let's recap some of the things we've learned about React through an example. Consider this component:

```
import React, { useState } from "react";
import
{ ComponentWithExpensiveChildren } from "./ExpensiveComponent";

function Counter() {
  const [count, setCount] = useState(0);

  function increment() {
    setCount(count + 1);
  }

  return (
    <div>
      <p>{count}</p>
      <button onClick={increment}>Increment</button>
      <ComponentWithExpensiveChildren />
    </div>
```

```
    );
  }

  export default Counter;
```

In this very, very contrived example, we have a component that contains state called Counter with some children:

- A <p> element that displays the current count
- A <button> element that increments the count
- A <ComponentWithExpensiveChildren> component that renders some expensive children with a lot of computation

Now, let's say we click the button to increment the count. What happens? The Counter function is called/reinvoked/rerendered along with all its children. This is React's default behavior. This means that the <ComponentWithExpensiveChildren> component is rerendered even though it doesn't need to be: its props or state hasn't changed!

This coarse-grained reactivity makes React less performant than it could be. However, this is quite an easy fix: we just include memo at the right time and in the right place:

```
import React, { useState, memo } from "react";
import { ComponentWithExpensiveChildren } from "./ComponentWithExpensiveChildren";

function Counter() {
  const [count, setCount] = useState(0);

  function increment() {
    setCount(count + 1);
  }

  return (
    <div>
      <p>{count}</p>
      <button onClick={increment}>Increment</button>
      <MemoizedComponentWithExpensiveChildren />
    </div>
  );
}

const MemoizedComponentWithExpensiveChildren = memo(
  ComponentWithExpensiveChildren
);

export default Counter;
```

This works, as long as we remember to use `memo` everywhere we need to. Indeed, this provides the same fine-grained reactivity as signals. However, it's not as convenient as signals, because we have to remember to use `memo` everywhere we need to.

Many of us at this point may be thinking that signals could easily solve this problem, but the React team at Meta believes that signals, like `memo`, may be an implementation detail that everyday developers who use React ought not have to think about. They hearken back to the initial value proposition of React: "declaratively describe your UI, let React do the rest." The React team believes that the superior way is where developers don't concern ourselves with signals, `memo`, or any details, but that React should be able to figure out the optimal way to render the UI.

To this end, the team is working on a new piece of software to do just that: React Forget.

React Forget

Forget is a toolchain for React similar to a linter that has its `--fix` flag enabled: it enforces the rules of React and then automatically transforms React code to be optimal through intelligently memoizing values that will not change throughout the lifecycle of an application—like `ComponentWithExpensiveChildren`.

Because of the rules of React, the Forget compiler can predict these values and memoize them for us. This is a similar approach to what Svelte does, but instead of compiling to imperative code, Forget compiles to more performant React code.

What are these rules of React? Let's recap:

1. React components are expected to be pure functions.
2. Some hooks and custom event handlers are not required to be pure.
3. Forbidden actions within pure functions include:
   - Mutating variables/objects not newly created within the function
   - Reading properties that may change
4. Allowed actions include:
   - Reading props or state
   - Throwing errors
   - Mutating newly created objects/bindings
5. Lazy initialization is an exception allowing mutation for the purpose of initialization.
6. Objects or closures created during render should not be mutated after render completes, except mutable objects stored in state.

Because of these rules, the Forget compiler can predict which values will not change throughout the lifecycle of an application and memoize them for us. The result? Highly optimized, highly performant React code that rivals the performance of other libraries that use signals.

At the time of writing, Forget is in evaluation at Meta and exceeding expectations in use on Instagram and WhatsApp. It is not yet open source, but the React team is considering releasing it as open source software in the near future.

Forget versus signals

Because Forget isn't yet open source, it's somewhat challenging to comment on its trade-offs with any amount of authority. However, we can posit that if Forget indeed memoizes everything that doesn't change, fine-grained reactivity from signals may still be superior to coarse-grained reactivity with React Forget, because signals live in a parallel universe outside of the component hierarchy.

Thus, when an update happens, React will still have to walk the entire component tree and compare the new and old values of each component's props to determine which components need to be rerendered. This is not the case with signals, where only the reactive portions of the UI are updated without needing to walk a tree. This preliminary data does suggest that even with Forget, React may still be slower than libraries where signals are the default, but it is too early to tell.

Chapter Review

This chapter began with a recap of Chapter 9, where we covered the use of RSCs in detail. We then delved into the vast landscape of JavaScript frameworks beyond React, including Angular, Vue, Svelte, Solid, and Qwik, aiming to understand the differences and similarities among these libraries and frameworks.

We started with a look at Vue.js, and explored how it uses a declarative approach for building UIs and promotes a strong separation of concerns through its component-based architecture.

Next, we took a dive into Angular, Svelte, Solid, and Qwik, exploring their unique features and philosophies. We looked at how they use reactive primitives to automatically update the UI in response to changes in data, and how they differ from React in this regard.

After the individual examinations, we drew comparisons among these UI libraries, underlining their strengths, weaknesses, and overlaps. We looked at their reactivity models, architectural choices, development experience, and performance characteristics. Through code examples, we showed the unique qualities of each, helping us to understand their differences better.

We also examined the concept of reactivity and how it is implemented differently across various libraries. Interestingly, we discussed how React is not reactive in the traditional sense, as it follows a coarser approach where a change in state leads to a rerender, unlike the fine-grained reactivity model found in libraries like Vue or Svelte.

Finally, we looked at the future of React and how it might evolve in the coming years. We discussed the React team's approach to reactivity and how it differs from the traditional reactive programming model. We also looked at the Forget compiler, a toolchain for React that automatically optimizes React code by memoizing values that don't change throughout the lifecycle of an application.

Let's finally land the plane.

Review Questions

Here is a list of questions to help you track your understanding of the concepts covered in this chapter. If you can answer all of them confidently, great! That's a sign you're learning from this book. If you cannot, it might be worth rereading this chapter.

1. How does the reactivity model differ among React, Vue, Svelte, Solid, and Angular? What are the implications of these differences on the performance and development experience of these libraries/frameworks?

2. Discuss the unique approach of Qwik in maximizing performance. How does this differ from the approach of other UI libraries/frameworks we've discussed?

3. What are the core strengths and weaknesses of each UI library/framework discussed in this chapter? How might these strengths and weaknesses influence the choice of library/framework for a particular project?

4. React is not reactive in the traditional sense. Explain this statement in detail, comparing it with the "push-based" reactivity model found in libraries like Vue or Svelte.

5. What's React Forget? How does it work? How does it compare to signals?

Up Next

As we draw closer to the conclusion of this comprehensive journey through the world of React and its ecosystem, we're preparing to synthesize all that we've learned. In the next and final chapter, we'll be stepping back and reflecting on the whole landscape.

We'll be wrapping up this book and providing a holistic view of where we stand today and what we can anticipate tomorrow. In doing so, we'll be drawing on all the technical knowledge and insights that we've gathered throughout the course of this book.

From understanding the inner workings of React's reconciler and diving into asynchrony, to tackling server components and understanding various React frameworks, to comparing React with its peers—all this was done with a purpose. Now, we're ready to connect the dots, to see the bigger picture, and to chart the path forward.

So, are you ready to take a leap into the future of React and frontend development? Stay tuned for the grand finale!

CHAPTER 11

Conclusion

If you've made it this far, thank you for joining me on this journey through the React ecosystem. I hope you've enjoyed this adventure as much as I have. In our time together, we pursued a deeper understanding of React, exploring its core principles, inner workings, and broader ecosystem. Assuming we already know how to *use* React, we focused on understanding its mechanism: how it actually works—with the end goal being practical takeaways we can use in our engineering careers going forward.

Takeaways

Let's outline some of those takeaways now:

Rethink best practices.
> Sometimes, we need to rethink everything. React's introduction of JSX and the virtual DOM was a radical departure from the status quo. It challenged the established conventions and forced us to rethink how we build interfaces. This willingness to challenge the status quo and reimagine the way things are done is a hallmark of React's philosophy, and thus as engineers, we should always be willing to challenge the status quo and rethink the way things are done.

Fully understand how JSX works.
> If we're limited by a programming language—as in, if we can't have HTML-style syntax in JavaScript—we as engineers have the power to change that by creating a new language. This is what JSX is: a new language that compiles down to JavaScript. We can do this too now that we fully understand how JSX works and some compiler theory.

Constraints are not a bad thing.

Constraints are the mother of invention. React is fundamentally an innovation born out of the constraints of the web, where reading `innerWidth` of an element causes a reflow, and where different browsers have different APIs for events. The takeaway here is that constraints are not a bad thing. They force us to think outside the box and come up with creative solutions.

Declarative abstractions unlock powerful capabilities.

By decoupling the expression of JSX from the reconciler, React pioneered a "write once, run anywhere" approach to UI development, allowing us to use the same code to render to the DOM, the server, or even a native platform. This is a powerful capability that we can leverage in our own projects as we consider separating concerns and landing on the right level of abstraction.

Unlocking powerful capabilities allows us to build more flexible and maintainable applications.

We uncovered a number of patterns, from higher-order components to render props to hooks to context. These patterns are powerful tools that we can use to abstract logic, share behavior across components, and manage state more effectively. While these patterns introduce complexity, they also unlock powerful capabilities, allowing us to build more flexible and maintainable applications. Moreover, like HOCs, these patterns predate React. What patterns are we using today that will be the foundation of the next generation of UI frameworks? What patterns can we invent that will make our lives easier?

Powerful capabilities can be leveraged in our own projects.

We learned that when we go beyond the browser, through to the server, a slew of new possibilities open up. We can render our React components on the server, use the browser's native fetch API to load data, and we can use native HTML forms for user inputs. These are powerful capabilities that we can leverage in our own projects as we consider the trade-offs of server-side rendering and the benefits of leveraging the web's fundamentals.

The benefits of improving user experience.

We now are empowered to take full advantage of React's concurrent features, such as `useTransition`, to improve user experience by deferring work to be done "in an alternate universe" and then committing the changes to the DOM when they're ready. This is a powerful capability that we can leverage in our own projects as we consider the trade-offs of deferring work and the benefits of improving user experience.

All this is done in a language that we know and understand.

We explored the intricacies between Next.js and Remix through the lens of creating our own framework, ultimately recognizing that all of this is just JavaScript with some servers and things: we can build our own framework, too, given enough time and resources. While we're thankful for the work of the authors, we can also be empowered that all of this is done in a language that we know and understand.

Ship drastically less code to our users.

Similar to going beyond the browser to the server, we learned that going beyond the browser to the bundler unlocks an entire new world of possibilities, leveraging the bundler to split client components from server components and ship drastically less code to our users. What other cool compiler/bundler tricks can we use to improve our users' experience?

We can take inspiration from these other frameworks and apply them to our own projects.

We zoomed out and looked at how even outside React, everyone's sort of solving the same problem: how do we build user interfaces well, that are fast, responsive, reactive, and also come with great developer experience? We explored some ideas from Vue, Solid, Qwik, and more, and we learned that we can take inspiration from these other frameworks and apply them to our own projects.

As we draw the curtains on our exploration of React.js, it's essential to reflect on the journey we've taken and understand the transformative nature of this library. React's growth over the years stands as a testament to its adaptability, resilience, and the innovative spirit of its community. From introducing a more intuitive way of building interfaces with JSX, to reimagining how updates can be more efficient with the virtual DOM, React has undoubtedly left an indelible mark on the landscape of web development.

Our Timeline

The initial chapters of this book presented a gentle introduction to the core principles of React. At its heart, React's philosophy is about building components that make updates to web experiences more approachable, scalable, and maintainable. These self-contained units of work—components, fibers, elements—encapsulate both the logic and the UI, making it easier to reason about our applications as they scale.

With JSX, React offers a declarative approach to UI development. By making our interfaces a function of our application's state, we can easily understand and predict how changes in our data will affect our UI. The clear separation and the single source of truth concept have undoubtedly changed how developers approach UI construction.

As React gained traction, its influence inevitably rippled through the tech industry, inspiring many platforms and frameworks. One of the most noteworthy influenced platforms is Apple's SwiftUI, a framework for building user interfaces across all Apple devices.

Influenced by React and others, SwiftUI adopted a similar philosophy. Instead of the classic MVC (Model-View-Controller) design pattern often seen in iOS development, SwiftUI encourages developers to build UIs using smaller, component-like structures called views. Each view in SwiftUI is a self-contained unit, much like React components.

As UI frameworks continue to evolve, the cross-pollination of ideas will persist. Innovations from one platform can inspire improvements in another, leading to a richer, more cohesive development landscape. React's influence on SwiftUI and the broader ecosystem is a prime example of this symbiotic relationship, and it sets the stage for future collaborations and inspirations in the tech world.

The Mechanics Behind the Magic

The virtual DOM and the Fiber reconciler were some of the more technical topics we delved into. These concepts are the gears and pulleys behind React's efficient and performant updates. The virtual DOM acts as a mediator between our application's state and the actual DOM. By comparing differences and batching updates, React ensures that the least amount of work is done to keep the UI in sync with the state.

The reconciler, on the other hand, is the brain behind this operation. It decides when and how to update components, optimizing for performance and ensuring consistency. We explored the inner workings of the reconciler, learning about the different phases and the work that goes into each one. We also looked at how the reconciler prioritizes work, ensuring that the most important updates are processed first.

Advanced Adventures

Venturing into the advanced terrains, we looked at advanced patterns in React. These patterns, such as higher-order components, render props, hooks, and context, allow developers to abstract logic, share behavior across components, and manage state more effectively. While these patterns introduce complexity, they also unlock powerful capabilities, allowing us to build more flexible and maintainable applications.

Server-side React and concurrent React took us on a journey through the evolution of React applications. With the increasing need for fast initial loads and interactive experiences, leveraging the server and async operations has become vital. These techniques ensure our applications remain snappy, responsive, and user-centric.

We explored the server side of `react-dom`, including functions like `renderToString` and `renderToPipeableStream`, outlining the trade-offs of each. We also explored some of React's asynchronous capabilities, such as `useSyncExternalStore` and `useTransition`, and how they can be used to improve the user experience.

Finally, we dipped our toes into React Server Components, a more recent addition to the React ecosystem that represents the library's continued evolution. By enabling components to be rendered on the server only, we can create more efficient applications, optimizing for both performance and user experience.

In our final chapters, we explored the broader ecosystem surrounding React with the frameworks and the alternative libraries. React's success has spawned a plethora of tools, frameworks, and alternatives, each bringing its own set of advantages and trade-offs.

React has come a long way since its inception, and its journey is a reflection of the ever-evolving world of web development. As you've journeyed through this book, you've not only learned about a library but have also gained insight into the paradigms and principles that drive modern web development.

Staying Up-to-Date

Keeping up with the constantly evolving JavaScript ecosystem, including the many frameworks built around React, can feel like a daunting task. Every year, a number of new tools and libraries are introduced, each with its own set of features, benefits, and trade-offs. As a developer, making an informed decision about the right framework to use for a future project involves more than just a familiarity with the current state of the ecosystem. It also requires a forward-looking understanding of the trajectory of these tools and how they fit within the broader context of web development.

There are several strategies for staying up-to-date and continuously making informed decisions about choosing the right React framework for your future projects:

Follow trusted sources.
> The JavaScript ecosystem evolves at a rapid pace. It's essential to follow trustworthy sources that provide quality content and regular updates about the latest trends and tools. This could be blogs, YouTube channels, newsletters, podcasts, or online communities. For example, following the official blogs and Twitter accounts of Next.js and Remix could provide insights into their upcoming features, improvements, and overall roadmap.
>
> Some sources we recommend are:
>
> - The React docs at react.dev
> - React core members on 𝕏, formerly Twitter, including but not limited to:
>   — *@sophiebits*
>   — *@sebmarkbage*

- — @zmofei
- — @acdlite
- — @rickhanlonii
- — @dan_abramov2

- React community creators on X, including but not limited to:
  - — @kadikraman
  - — @kentcdodds
  - — @shaundai
  - — @Saurav_Varma
  - — @rachelnabors

Join relevant communities.

Online communities such as Reddit, Stack Overflow, GitHub, or various Discord and Slack groups are excellent places to keep an eye on emerging trends and tools. Community members often share their experiences with different frameworks, which can provide a useful perspective when deciding between different tools.

Some useful community resources are:

- The React subreddit
- The Reactiflux Discord server
- The bytes.dev newsletter
- The React Roundup podcast
- The "This Week in React" newsletter

Attend conferences and meetups.

Conferences and meetups are great for staying updated on the latest developments and best practices in the JavaScript and React ecosystem. Even if you can't attend in person, many of these events offer online streaming or record their talks for later viewing.

Some wonderful React conferences to attend are:

- React Brussels
- React Alicante
- React India
- React Day Verona

Experiment with different frameworks.

Nothing beats hands-on experience when it comes to understanding a tool. Allocating some time to build small projects or prototypes with different frameworks can provide invaluable insights. This can help you understand the strengths and weaknesses of each framework and how they fit with your development style and project requirements.

Build in public.

Popularized by Shawn Wang (*@swyx*), probably the best way to stay up-to-date is to build in public. This means sharing your work, thoughts, and ideas with the community. This can be as simple as posting on social media about your work, or as involved as writing a blog post or creating a YouTube video. By sharing your work, you can get feedback from the community, which can help you improve your skills and gain a deeper understanding of the tools you're using.

Writing a book has been a great way for me to learn React. I've learned so much from the community, and I've been able to share my knowledge with others. I highly recommend it!

As we conclude, remember that learning React isn't just about mastering a library; it's about embracing a mindset. A mindset of component-driven development, performance optimization, and continuously adapting to the ever-changing demands of the web.

The future of web development is bright, and React, along with its community, will undoubtedly play a significant role in shaping it. Whether you're a seasoned developer or someone just starting out, the skills and knowledge you've acquired from this book will serve you well as you continue your journey in the vast and exciting realm of web development.

Here's to building more intuitive, performant, and user-centric applications with React. Cheers to the future, and thank you for being a part of this adventure!

Index

microtasks, JavaScript event loop, 192-193

MobX library, 279

Model, MVC, 13

Model, MVVM, 19

Model-View-Controller (MVC) pattern, 13-16, 20-22

Model-View-ViewModel (MVVM) pattern, 18-21

modular architecture, AngularJS, 23

Mootools, 12

MPAs (multipage apps), 251

multipage apps (MPAs), 251

mutating data, 92, 234-236, 240-243, 272

MVC (Model-View-Controller) pattern, 13-16, 20-22

MVVM (Model-View-ViewModel) pattern, 18-21

N

native compilers, 46

native events, 65

navigation, and server rendering, 260-263

nesting views, 18

network waterfalls, 152, 154, 220

Next.js, 160, 179-182
   banning hooks in server components, 270
   in choosing framework, 245, 246-248
   frameworks, 237-244

Node objects, DOM, 53

Node.js, 47, 166, 167-168, 176-177

nonscalars, React.memo, 101-104

NormalPriority level, render lanes, 197

O

offsetWidth property, DOM versus virtual DOM, 54

onChange event, 65

optimizations (see performance)

owner property, React element, 70

P

parsing, 44-46

passive effects, in reconciliation, 94

performance
   AngularJS issues, 25
   challenge for web as it grew, 2
   CSR issues, 152-155, 157
   DOM pitfalls, 54, 58-64

frameworks for optimizing, 181, 227, 247

and immutability in React, 32

jQuery weight and load times issue, 12

lazy loading, 118-123

memoization as booster of, 98, 99, 101

Next.js's focus on, 245

React's improvements in, 31

Remix's priorities in, 246

renderToString disadvantage in, 165

rerender optimizations, 76

SSR versus CSR, 157

stack reconciler issue, 84

two-data binding issues, 27

unnecessary rerenders, 75-76

useMemo drawback with scalars, 111-117

pipe method, renderToPipeableStream, 169

piping data between streams, 168

placement effects, in reconciliation, 93

platform-agnostic, React as, 36

presentational/container components patterns, 129-130

primitive types (see scalars)

prioritizing updates, 84
   and declarative programming, 204
   Fiber reconciler's role in, 86
   render lanes' role in, 90, 194-198
   scheduling and deferring, 187-194
   synchronous rendering problem, 84

processing lanes, render lanes, 197

progressive enhancement, and SSR versus CSR, 153

prop collections pattern, 140-142

prop getters, 141

props property, React element, 70

propTypes, 42, 109

Q

Qwik, 286-288

qwikify utility, 288

R

React, 1-37
   component-based architecture, 26, 31
   and declarative programming, 28, 165, 167, 302
   development of, 26-36
   Flux architecture, 34-36
   future of, 294-297
   immutability in state management, 32

useTransition hook, 189, 198-201

V

view models, binding to element in browser, 21
View, MVC pattern, 13, 19
ViewModel, MVVM pattern, 19
views in Flux, 35
virtual DOM (vDOM), 28-31, 53-76
    diffing and reconciliation summary, 291
    efficient updates, 54, 58, 64, 74-76
    implementations similar to document fragments, 67
    lack of comparison for functions, 113
    React elements, 68-72
    React's use of, 14, 27
    versus real DOM, 54, 60, 72-74
    reconciliation process, 79-94

    unnecessary rerenders, 75-76
    Vue.js, 279
    workings of, 67-76
Vue Options API, 279
Vue.js, 42, 277-280

W

Walke, Jordan, 27
withAsync HOC factory, 132
work loop, in Fiber reconciliation, 87
Workers runtime, Cloudflare, 47
workInProgress, 90, 94, 109
writable streams, Node.js, 167

X

XSS (cross-site scripting), 2, 58

About the Author

Tejas Kumar has been writing React code since 2014 and has given multiple conference talks, workshops, and guest lectures on the topic. With his wealth of experience across the technical stack of multiple startups, Tejas has developed a deep understanding of React's core concepts and enjoys using it to encourage, equip, and empower others to write React apps fluently.

Colophon

The animal on the cover of *Fluent React* is a slender sheartail (*Doricha enicura*), a bee hummingbird found in the highland forests of El Salvador, Gautemala, Honduras, and Mexico. This hummingbird belongs to the Mellisugini (bee) tribe, one of three tribes in the Trochilidae family, which comprises all hummingbirds.

The slender sheartail is between 3 and 5 inches long and weighs less than one-tenth of an ounce, making it one of the smallest hummingbird species. They have green upperparts and a white underbelly. Males have an iridescent purple throat patch and a long forked tail. These hummingbirds primarily eat sugar-rich nectar and small arthropods. Males are highly territorial and will chase intruders from feeding sites.

Females build nests from plant fibers and spider silk. The female then lays 2 eggs, which she incubates alone for 15–19 days. Chicks fledge at around 25 days old.

The slender sheartail has a large range and a large mature population and is a species of least concern according to the IUCN. Many of the animals on O'Reilly covers are endangered; all of them are important to the world.

The cover illustration is by Karen Montgomery, based on an antique line engraving from *Shaw's Zoology*. The series design is by Edie Freedman, Ellie Volckhausen, and Karen Montgomery. The cover fonts are Gilroy Semibold and Guardian Sans. The text font is Adobe Minion Pro; the heading font is Adobe Myriad Condensed; and the code font is Dalton Maag's Ubuntu Mono.

O'REILLY®

Learn from experts.
Become one yourself.

Books | Live online courses
Instant answers | Virtual events
Videos | Interactive learning

Get started at oreilly.com.

Printed in the USA
CPSIA information can be obtained
at www.ICGtesting.com
JSHW051342150424
61202JS00013B/360

9 781098 138714